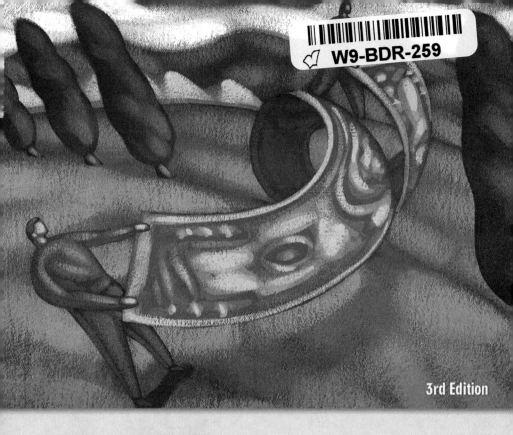

3rd Edition

THE
ANNUITY
HANDBOOK

A Guide to Nonqualified Annuities

By Darlene K. Chandler, J.D., CLU, ChFC

ISBN: 0-87218-618-0

3rd Edition

Copyright © 1994, 1998, 2002
The National Underwriter Company
P.O. Box 14367, Cincinnati, Ohio 45250-0367

To the memory of my mother, Mary L. Chandler,
to whom the pursuit of education and excellence
was always a high priority.

ACKNOWLEDGEMENTS

First Edition - 1994

Many people helped this publication become a reality by giving generously of both their time and expertise. My thanks to Debbie Miner for a superb editing job and to April Kestel, Robyn Lewis, and Lee Schweickart for their insight and information on numerous issues surrounding the use of annuities in today's marketplace. Also, my thanks to Connie Jump for her first-class work in producing this publication and to the Composition Department for making everything line up.

Finally, thanks to the other members of my department for their support during the time it has taken to create *The Annuity Handbook*.

Second Edition - 1998

Four years later, the second edition of *The Annuity Handbook* was possible thanks to the efforts of many talented individuals. Specifically, my thanks again to Debbie Miner for her editing expertise and to Connie Jump and Patti O'Leary for making all the pieces come together. For their insight into the equity-indexed annuity product, I am grateful to Brian Clark at AmerUs Life and Michele Olding at Great American Life. Finally, as always, thanks to my colleagues at National Underwriter for their support.

ABOUT THE AUTHOR

Darlene K. Chandler is Director of Advanced Markets Administration Support at Farm Bureau Financial Services in West Des Moines, Iowa where she works with annuities and qualified retirement plans in addition to other advanced markets concepts.

Prior to joining Farm Bureau, Darlene was an editor with the *National Underwriter Company* contributing to *Tax Facts 1*, the *Advanced Sales Reference Service*, and the *Taxline* newsletter. She has written several other books on life insurance and advanced market topics in addition to *The Annuity Handbook*. Additionally, for the past 15 years, Darlene has served as an associate editor for the *Journal of Financial Service Professionals*.

An honors graduate of Ball State University in Indiana where she majored in English, Darlene received her law degree from the University of Cincinnati. She holds the insurance industry designations of Chartered Life Underwriter (CLU) and Chartered Financial Consultant (ChFC) and maintains a registered principal license.

Darlene lives in West Des Moines, Iowa, with her husband, Bob Schneider, and their son, James.

TABLE OF CONTENTS

Dedication iii
Acknowledgements v
About the Author vii

CHAPTER 1: The Definition of an Annuity 1

    What Is An Annuity? 3
    What Is A "Nonqualified" Annuity? 3
    The Annuity's Unique Feature 5
    Who Purchases Annuities? 6
    The Time Line of an Annuity 9
        The Accumulation Phase 9
        The Annuitization Phase 10
    Other Types of Annuities 10

CHAPTER 2: The Parties to an Annuity 13

    The Owner 14
    The Annuitant 16
    The Beneficiary 18
    The Insurance Company 20

CHAPTER 3: Standard Annuity Contract Provisions 23

    Bailout Provisions and Rates 24
    Charges and Fees 25
        Fixed Annuities 25
        Variable Annuities 26
    Dollar Cost Averaging 28
    Interest Rates 28
        Fixed Annuities 28
        Variable Annuities 30
    Issue Ages 31
    Maximum Ages for Benefits to Begin 32
        Nonqualified Annuities 32
        Other Annuities 32
    Nursing Home Waiver 33
    Premium Payments 33
    Settlement Options 34
        Life Annuity 35
        Life With Period Certain Guarantee 35
        Refund Life Annuity 36

Joint and Survivor Life Annuity 37
Fixed Period Annuity.. 39
Fixed Amount Annuity 39
Interest Income 40
Surrender Charges 40
Withdrawals.. 43
Partial surrender 43
Full Surrender 44
10% Per Year Withdrawal... 44
Systematic Withdrawal Option...................................... 45
Loans 45

CHAPTER 4: The Various Types of Annuities 47

Single Premium Annuities 47
Flexible Premium Annuities 51
Fixed Annuities... 52
Equity-Indexed Annuities 54
Variable Annuities.. 54
Assumption of the Investment Risk 55
The Investment Options — The Variable Accounts 56
The Investment Options — The Guaranteed Acount 59
Transfers Among Investment Accounts 61
Automatic Rebalancing 63
Benefit Payments From Variable Annuities 64
Fixed Annuity Benefit Payout.. 64
Variable Annuity Benefit Payout.................................. 65
Variable Annuity Death Benefit 67
Immediate Annuities 68
Deferred Annuities 69
Charitable Gift Annuities... 71
Private Annuities.. 73

CHAPTER 5: The Newest Annuity — The Equity-Indexed
Annuity.. 77

Introduction — What is an Equity-Indexed Annuity?....... 78
Advantages and Disadvantages 78
How Does the Indexing Work? 81
Typical EIA Contract Features 85
Cap Rate 85
Death Benefit 86
Fees and Expenses.. 86
Indexing Methods 87

Maximum Issue Ages 87
Minimum Guaranteed Interest Rate 87
Minimum Premiums 88
Partial Withdrawal Provisions 88
Participation Rate 89
Policy Loans 90
Policy Term 90
Settlement Options 92
Surrender Charges 92
Surrender Provisions 93
Vesting Schedules 93
How is an EIA Used? 94
Who Can Sell EIAs? 96

CHAPTER 6: The Uses of Annuities 99

Retirement Planning 99
Other Retirement Planning Vehicles 101
Individual Retirement Arrangements 102
Qualified Retirement Plans 104
Tax Sheltered Annuities 105
Charitable Planning 106
Gift of an Annuity 106
Charitable Gift Annuity 108
Charitable Trusts 108
Charitable Remainder Trusts 108
Charitable Lead Trusts 110
Pooled Income Funds 110
College Funding 111
Business Planning 114
Retirement Planning 115
Nonqualified Deferred Compensation Plans 116
Sale of a Business 117
Bonus Plan 119
Alternatives to Annuities 119
Bank Savings Account 119
Certificates of Deposit 121
Mutual Funds 121

CHAPTER 7: Income Taxation of Annuities 125

Premiums 125
Cash Value Build-up 126
Natural Persons 126

Nonnatural Persons 126
Loans and Assignments 128
Partial Withdrawals 129
   Contract Surrender Charges 129
   10% Premature Distribution Penalty Tax 130
   Taxation of Withdrawals 132
   Multiple Annuity Contracts 135
   Effect of a Tax Free Exchange 135
Complete Surrender of the Annuity 136
Exchanges — Section 1035 136
Gift of an Annuity 139
Sale of an Annuity 141
   The Seller 141
   The Purchaser 142
Taxation of Annuity Benefit Payments 142
   The Basic Rule 142
   The Exclusion Ratio 143
   The Investment in the Contract 145
   The Expected Return 145
   The Annuity Tables 148
   Taxation of Variable Annuity Benefit Payments 148
Death of the Annuity Owner 150
Death of the Annuitant 152

CHAPTER 8: Estate Taxation of Annuities 157

What is the Estate Tax? 157
How is the Estate Tax Calculated? 157
Deductions From the Estate Tax 161
Annuity Contracts Owned at Death 162
   In the Accumulation Phase 162
   In the Annuitization Phase 164
Owner and Annuitant Are Not the Same Person 166
Annuity Contracts Purchased as Gifts 167
Private Annuities 167

CHAPTER 9: Gift Taxation of Annuities 169

What is the Gift Tax? 169
How is the Gift Tax Calculated? 169
The Annual Exclusion 173
The Unified Credit 174

Deductions From the Gift Tax 177
What Constitutes a Gift? 180
  Gift of an Annuity Contract 180
  Purchase of a Joint and Survivor Annuity 180
  Assignment of an Annuity Contract 181
  Payment of an Annuity Premium 181
  Naming an Irrevocable Beneficiary 182
How is the Gift of an Annuity Valued? 183

APPENDIX A: Actuarial Tables 185

  Table I 187
  Table II 187
  Table IIA 189
  Table III 191
  Table V 194
  Table VI 194
  Table VIA 196
  Table VII 198

APPENDIX B: Examples of Exclusion Ratio Calculations ... 201

  Single Life Annuity 201
  Refund or Period Certain Guarantee 201
  Joint and Survivor Annuity (Same Income to Survivor
    as to Both Annuitants Before Any Death) 204
  Joint and Survivor Annuity (Income to Survivor
    Differs from Income Before First Death) 205

APPENDIX C: Internal Revenue Code Sections 207

  Section 72 207
  Section 1035 224
  Section 2033 225
  Section 2039 225

APPENDIX D: Sample Annuity Applications 227

  Sample Fixed Annuity Application 227
  Sample Variable Annuity Application 229

INDEX 231

Chapter 1

THE DEFINITION OF AN ANNUITY

Before defining an annuity, it is important to understand why annuities are receiving so much attention and being purchased in large amounts by a large numbers of individuals. In 2001, the sales of annuities totaled more than $184 billion.[1] Nonqualified fixed annuities are annuity contracts that are not part of a qualified retirement plan, pay a fixed rate of interest and guarantee a fixed benefit payment amount. The close of 2000 saw almost 26 million individual fixed annuity contracts in force.[2] Further, annuity contracts in the benefit paying or annuitization phase paid out more than $68 billion in benefit payments in 2000.[3]

In 2001 variable annuity sales totaled nearly $113 billion, which was off from a record year in 2000, when sales were over $137 billion.[4] Life insurance industry figures show that over 19 million individuals were covered by variable annuity plans at the end of 2000.[5] By way of historical perspective, in 1985 variable annuity sales totaled a mere $4.5 billion. By 1990, that figure had increased to $12 billion and in 1993, total variable annuity sales amounted to $43.5 billion.[6] At the end of 2001 there were nearly $883 billion in total variable annuity assets, which was down from $956 billion at the end of 2000.[7]

In the last eight to ten years yet another new type of annuity has been developed—the equity-indexed annuity or EIA. Although this product is new, and reliable sales figures are difficult to find, it has been estimated that 2000 sales of EIAs totaled about $5.4 billion and that sales of EIAs for 2001 reached $6.4 billion.[8]

In the past several decades, annuity sales have made up an increasing portion of the total premiums received by life insurance companies. In 1976, annuity considerations made up only 21% of all premiums received by life insurance companies. In 2000, annuity considerations accounted for over 56% of the total premiums received by life insurance companies.[9]

In recent years those Americans born in the years following World War II, the "baby boomers," have begun reaching the age where retirement planning becomes a priority. Statistics show that in 1980 only 11.3% of the United States population was 65 years of age or older, but in the year 2000 that figure rose to 12.4%. By 2025 it is anticipated that 18.5% of the country's population, or nearly one person in five, will be at least 65 years of age.[10]

Many boomers are coming to realize that Social Security and their employer-provided retirement plans will not be sufficient to provide the type of retirement they desire. In fact, a recent survey found that retirement planning is the benefit that employees say that they want and need the most — even more than health care.[11] Nonqualified annuities are one of the best ways that individuals have to set aside money on a tax deferred basis. While the premiums paid into this type of annuity do not result in a current income tax deduction, the premiums and the interest earned on these funds accumulate on an income tax deferred basis. And, unlike employer-provided plans, anyone can purchase an annuity and contribute any amount of premium, (subject to certain maximum premium limitations imposed by some insurance companies).

In addition to their wide availability, nonqualified annuities offer those planning for retirement investment options that may keep pace, or even out pace, inflation. Variable annuities with their myriad of stock, bond, and other investment accounts are especially attractive for this reason. Additionally, the new equity-indexed annuity or EIA, which offers holders the ability to share in the stock market's gains without risking loss of principal, provides those looking toward retirement with another useful planning tool.

Although retirement planning is not the only use for nonqualified annuities, it is one of the most popular. Charitable planning and education funding are two other frequent uses for nonqualified annuities.

WHAT IS AN ANNUITY?

An annuity has one basic purpose—to provide a series of payments over a period of time. Usually, this period of time is an individual's lifetime. One highly-regarded insurance textbook offers this definition, "In its pure form, a whole life annuity may be defined as a contract whereby for a consideration (the premium), one party (the insurer) agrees to pay the other (the annuitant) a stipulated amount (the annuity) periodically throughout life."[12] Another textbook explains an annuity in these words, "... an annuity is a periodic payment to commence at a specified or contingent date and to continue throughout a fixed period or for the duration of a designated life or lives."[13]

Although textbook definitions are sometimes complex, what is clear is that for a purchase price or premium an annuity will pay an individual an income over a certain period of years, often over the individual's lifetime.

For example, assume Mr. Smith is age 50 and ready to begin planning for his retirement at age 65. As part of his financial plan, he purchases a nonqualified annuity and pays a monthly premium of $300 each month for 15 years. When he reaches age 65, Mr. Smith will have accumulated a sum of about $95,000, assuming an interest rate of 7%. If he chooses, he can ask the insurance company to pay his annuity to him for life. He will receive a check each month for approximately $635 for the remainder of his life, whether it is three years or thirty years. Figure 1.01 illustrates the premiums flowing into and the annuity benefits flowing out of Mr. Smith's annuity.

WHAT IS A "NONQUALIFIED" ANNUITY?

In the example concerning Mr. Smith's retirement planning, the annuity he purchased was referred to as a "nonqualified" annuity. To someone unfamiliar with the income taxation of retirement plans, purchasing something that is "not qualified"

Figure 1.01

THE "INS" AND "OUTS" OF MR. SMITH'S ANNUITY		
Age	Annual Premiums Paid In	Annual Benefits Paid Out
50	$3,600	$0
51	$3,600	$0
52	$3,600	$0
53	$3,600	$0
54	$3,600	$0
55	$3,600	$0
56	$3,600	$0
57	$3,600	$0
58	$3,600	$0
59	$3,600	$0
60	$3,600	$0
61	$3,600	$0
62	$3,600	$0
63	$3,600	$0
64	$3,600	$0
65	$0	$7,620
66	$0	$7,620
67	$0	$7,620
68	$0	$7,620
69	$0	$7,620
70	$0	$7,620
		And each year for remainder of Mr. Smith's life

may not sound like a very good idea. However, the use of the term "nonqualified" has nothing to do with the qualifications of either the annuity or the insurance company. Instead, it refers to whether the annuity is part of an employee benefit plan that has met certain requirements, or become "qualified," under the Internal Revenue Code. A "qualified" annuity is one used as part of or in connection with a qualified retirement plan. A "nonqualified" annuity is one that is not used as part of any qualified retirement plan. In very simplistic terms, a qualified retirement plan differs from a nonqualified arrangement in that the contributions made into a qualified plan are income tax deductible to the employer making the contributions and certain nondiscrimination requirements must be met. In other words, an employer must offer its qualified retirement plan to almost all of its employees. A nonqualified annuity may be purchased by any individual or entity and is not associated with an employer-provided plan.

THE ANNUITY'S UNIQUE FEATURE

As discussed throughout this book, annuities offer many useful features. One feature of the annuity is unique and not to be found in any other investment or accumulation vehicle. The unique feature of an annuity is that it provides a stream of income that the annuitant cannot outlive. If the annuity benefits are to be paid over the annuitant's lifetime, the monthly or annual benefit amount is guaranteed to come each and every month or year regardless of how long the annuitant lives.

It is often said that an annuity offers protection against living too long. At first impression, this may sound strange. How can a person live too long? In relation to an annuity, this statement about living too long refers only to the person's financial situation. It is possible, from an income viewpoint, to live beyond the point where all of an individual's savings, retirement plan benefits, and other financial means have been used up. An annuity paying benefits over the person's lifetime offers protection against this possibility.

To illustrate the annuity's unique feature, assume that Mr. Jones is now age 40 and wishes to retire at age 60. Toward this end, he can save about $300 per month in addition to the funds he is placing in the 401(k) plan offered by his employer. If he purchases a nonqualified annuity today and places the $300 each month into the contract, he will have accumulated approximately $123,000 in the annuity when he reaches age 60, assuming a 5% rate of return, as shown in Figure 1.02. At age 60, Mr. Jones' life expectancy is approximately 24 years or until he reaches age 84. If he begins taking benefit payments from the annuity at age 60, he will receive about $720 per month, or $8,640 annually. This amount will be paid to him, assuming he elects a life only settlement option, every year of his life whether he lives to age 70, to age 80, to age 90 or beyond.

On the other hand, if Mr. Jones had placed the same $300 per month for 20 years into another financial vehicle, such as a mutual fund, and received a comparable rate of return he could begin withdrawing the same monthly amount of $720 when he reached age 60. Assuming a 4% interest rate after he begins making withdrawals, if Mr. Jones lived to age 70, he would still have about $78,000 left in his mutual fund. If he lived to age 80, he would still have about $12,000 left in his mutual fund. However, at about the time that Mr. Jones turns 82, he will have completely depleted his mutual fund.

Of course like all of us, Mr. Jones does not know how long his life will be. However, should he survive to age 82 and beyond, Mr. Jones will probably have a much easier time paying his monthly bills if he had purchased the annuity as his retirement planning vehicle rather than the mutual fund. On the other hand, if Mr. Jones survived only to age 75, the life only annuity would offer no further payments to his beneficiaries while the mutual fund would still contain approximately $48,000. (However, most annuity contracts offer methods of receiving benefit payments with certain refund and guarantee features. See Chapter 3.)

WHO PURCHASES ANNUITIES?

Many think that annuities are purchased only by the wealthy— individuals who have already accumulated a large estate and can place thousands of dollars at one time into a single annuity

Figure 1.02

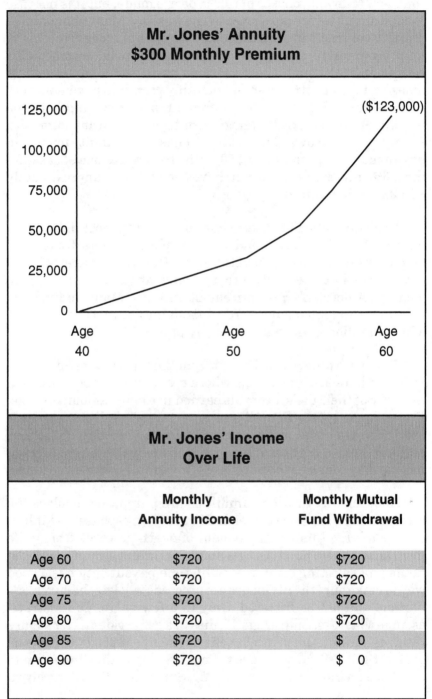

Mr. Jones' Income Over Life		
	Monthly Annuity Income	Monthly Mutual Fund Withdrawal
Age 60	$720	$720
Age 70	$720	$720
Age 75	$720	$720
Age 80	$720	$720
Age 85	$720	$ 0
Age 90	$720	$ 0

contract. Many purchases of this type are made, but it is not true that all annuities are purchased by the wealthy. Many nonqualified annuity contracts are purchased by persons of modest income to help accumulate an estate or provide financial income after retirement. Although the provisions vary from one annuity to another, many contracts accept monthly premium payments of as little as $50. Even this modest amount, over time and with the benefit of tax deferral, can grow into a significant sum. For example, if Ms. Edwards, age 35, purchases an annuity today and pays a monthly premium of $50 until she reaches age 65, assuming a 6% interest rate, she will have accumulated approximately $50,225 in her annuity.

In looking ahead to their retirement years, most individuals plan on Social Security and pension plan benefits from their employers to finance their retirement. But, many experts agree that these items usually provide only about one-half of the average American's pre-retirement income. Many individuals will want to supplement this retirement income and the purchase of nonqualified annuities is one way to do so.

There are others who benefit from the purchase of annuities. Included here are individuals whose occupation is one in which a majority of their life's income is earned in a short amount of time. Professional sports figures and entertainers fall into this category. Even a small business owner who lands a big contract or, perhaps, sells a portion of his business and has a large influx of income may consider the purchase of an annuity with those funds.

Another way in which annuities are purchased involves the receipt of life insurance proceeds. If a surviving spouse or children receive a large lump sum payment of death proceeds from a life insurance policy, purchasing a single premium annuity with the funds and selecting some type of lifetime payout option is a good way to make sure the life insurance proceeds will last the survivor's lifetime and not be frittered away in a few years. To illustrate, assume that Mrs. Smith, age 45, dies in a car accident. Her spouse receives a lump sum death benefit payment of $250,000 from one of Mrs. Smith's life insurance policies. By using this lump sum to purchase an immediate annuity, Mr. Smith, age 47, will receive a monthly income of approximately $1,380 for the remainder of his life, assuming an interest rate of about 5%. If he elects a life and ten year certain annuity (see Chapter 3) his monthly payment from the immediate annuity would be about $1,365.

THE TIME LINE OF AN ANNUITY

An annuity contract passes through two distinct phases during its existence, the accumulation phase and the annuitization phase. The single exception to this is the immediate annuity which does not actually pass through an accumulation phase but moves immediately after it is purchased into the annuitization phase.

The Accumulation Phase

The accumulation phase is that period of time from the purchase of the annuity until the annuity holder decides to begin receiving benefit payments from the annuity. It is during this period that the annuity builds up or accumulates the funds that will provide the annuity holder with future benefits. One important item that permits a significant build-up of funds within the annuity is that the interest credited to the annuity's premiums by the insurance company is not taxed each year to the holder of the annuity. Rather, payment of the tax on this income is delayed or deferred until the annuity holder begins drawing benefits from the contract.[14] This deferral of taxation allows interest to be credited on every dollar of interest previously credited, resulting in a much larger accumulation of funds than if a portion of the interest was withdrawn each year to pay the income tax due currently.

With a nonqualified annuity, the accumulation phase can last from a few years to many years. Take the case of Mr. Jones, age 60, who has just purchased an annuity. He plans to pay premiums for five years until he reaches age 65 and then receive benefit payments from the annuity for the remainder of his life. The accumulation phase of his annuity will be five years, a relatively short period of time. In contrast, take the case of Ms. Smith, now age 55, who owns an annuity that she purchased at age 25 with funds inherited from her grandparents. The accumulation phase of her annuity is currently 30 years.

The Annuitization Phase

The second phase that an annuity contract passes through is the annuitization phase which begins with payment of the first benefit amount from the annuity to the annuity holder. The annuitization phase is sometimes referred to as the payout period or the benefit period. As discussed later in this book, most nonqualified annuity contracts allow the annuity holder to elect to begin receiving benefit payments at any time, so the annuitization phase can start at age 20 or age 100, under some annuity contracts.

Continuing with the example of Mr. Jones, discussed above, the annuitization phase of his annuity will begin when he reaches age 65 and continue for the rest of his life. As the life expectancy of a 65-year-old male is about 20 years, Mr. Jones' annuity will have an accumulation phase of five years and an annuitization phase of about 20 years, on average. Ms. Smith's annuity, discussed above, has already been in the accumulation phase for 30 years and is just now passing into the annuitization phase. It is possible that this annuity will have had a longer accumulation phase than an annuitization phase. Figure 1.03 illustrates these two hypothetical annuity contracts.

OTHER TYPES OF ANNUITIES

Earlier in this chapter the definition of a nonqualified annuity was discussed and contrasted with that of a qualified annuity. This book confines itself to a discussion of nonqualified annuities and, therefore, does not address in detail annuities purchased as part of a qualified retirement plans, Individual Retirement Annuities (IRAs), or Tax Sheltered Annuities (TSAs). While there are some similarities between the nonqualified annuity and these other types, there are also many differences. It is not safe to assume that a particular aspect of a nonqualified annuity works in the same manner as an IRA or TSA. More often than not, there is a difference.

Figure 1.03

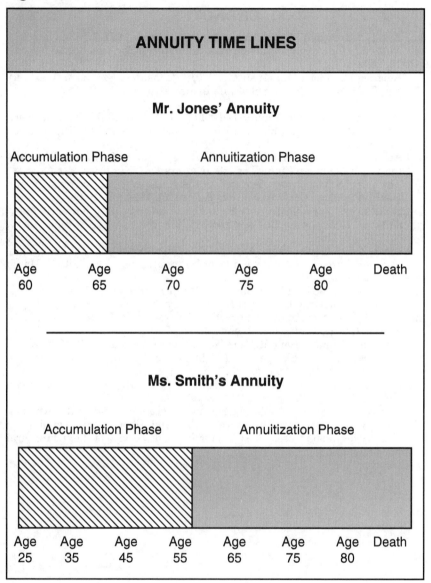

ANNUITY TIME LINES

Mr. Jones' Annuity

Accumulation Phase   Annuitization Phase

| Age | Age | Age | Age | Age | Death |
| 60 | 65 | 70 | 75 | 80 | |

Ms. Smith's Annuity

Accumulation Phase   Annuitization Phase

| Age | Age | Age | Age | Age | Age | Age | Death |
| 25 | 35 | 45 | 55 | 65 | 75 | 80 | |

ENDNOTES

1. Eric T. Sondergeld, "Fixed Annuity Sales Hit Record $71.5 Billion in 2001," *National Underwriter*, Life and Health/Financial Services Edition, March 18, 2002, p. 12.
2. American Council of Life Insurers, *2001 Life Insurers Fact Book* (Washington, D.C.: American Council of Life Insurers), p. 129.
3. Ibid., p. 68.
4. Rick Carey, "Variable Annuity Sales Fell 17.8% to $113 Billion Last Year," *National Underwriter*, Life and Health/Financial Services Edition, March 11, 2002, p. 16.
5. American Council of Life Insurers, *2001 Life Insurers Fact Book* (Washington, D.C.: American Council of Life Insurers), p. 129.
6. *The VARDS Report* as referenced in the *National Underwriter*, Life and Health/Financial Services Edition, August 15, 1994, pp. 1, 3.
7. Rick Carey, "Variable Annuity Sales Fell 17.8% to $113 Billion Last Year," *National Underwriter*, Life and Health/Financial Services Edition, March 11, 2002, p. 16.
8. Linda Koco, "Equity Index Annuity Sales Hit Another Record Last Year," *National Underwriter*, Life and Health/Financial Services Edition, March 18, 2002, p. 42.
9. American Council of Life Insurers, *2001 Life Insurers Fact Book* (Washington, D.C.: American Council of Life Insurers), pp. 59-60.
10. These figures come from the Statistical Abstract of the United States, 121st Edition (2001), Tables 11, 12, and 13.
11. "The Most Wanted Benefit," *The Washington Post*, March 22, 1998, p. H6.
12. K. Black, Jr. and H. Skipper, Jr., *Life Insurance*, 12th ed. (Englewood Cliffs, N.J.: Prentice Hall, 1994) p. 148.
13. E. Graves, ed., *McGill's Life Insurance* (Bryn Mawr, PA: The American College, 1994), p. 109.
14. The single exception to this general rule of income tax deferral is when an annuity is not owned by a natural person and, thus, is not treated as an annuity for tax purposes. See Chapter 7 for a discussion of the "nonnatural person" rule.

Chapter 2

THE PARTIES TO AN ANNUITY

As mentioned earlier, an annuity contract is just exactly that; a contract in which certain parties make certain promises and other parties have certain rights. It is important to understand who the parties are to the contract as well as to be familiar with the rights and obligations of each party.

Generally, there are four potential parties to a nonqualified annuity contract — the owner, the annuitant, the beneficiary, and the issuing insurance company. The rights and duties of each of these entities are discussed in this chapter. As a general overview, think of the owner as the person who purchases the annuity and the annuitant as the individual whose life is used in determining how payments under the contract are made. The beneficiary is the individual or entity that will receive any death benefits that become payable under the annuity contract and the issuing insurance company is the organization that accepts the owner's premium and promises to pay the benefits spelled out in the contract.

Although there are four potential parties to each annuity contract, the most common situation involves only three parties, because the owner and the annuitant are more often than not the same individual. Thus, the three parties are the owner-annuitant, a second individual or entity who is the beneficiary, and the insurance company. As an example of this commonly used arrangement, consider Mrs. Smith who has just attended the college graduation ceremony of her youngest child and now is turning her attention to seriously planning for her retirement years. One of the recommendations she receives is to purchase a nonqualified deferred annuity now and place $200 each month into the annuity. When she retires the contract will move from the accumulation phase to the pay-out phase and begin providing Mrs. Smith with a monthly benefit. In setting up the annuity, Mrs. Smith will be named as both the contract owner and the annuitant. She will name a beneficiary for any death benefits that are paid from the contract in the event she dies before she reaches retirement age. Most likely, Mrs. Smith will name one of her children as the beneficiary. The third party, the insurance company, will be the organization from which Mrs. Smith purchases the annuity.

THE OWNER

Every annuity contract must have an owner. Usually the owner is referred to as either the owner, the contract owner, or the annuity owner. Another name that is sometimes used is the annuity holder. With a nonqualified annuity contract the owner is usually a natural person, someone who has decided to purchase the annuity as part of a financial plan for retirement or some other purpose. However, there is no requirement that the owner be a natural person, as there is with the annuitant. Any entity can own an annuity contract, including trusts, corporations, or partnerships.[1]

In the most common instance where the owner and the annuitant are the same person, the owner pays money in the form of premiums into the annuity during the accumulation phase. At the end of this phase, the owner-annuitant begins to receive the annuity benefit payments from the insurance company. This is represented graphically in Figure 2.01.

As the term "owner" implies, the owner of the annuity contract holds a number of rights under the contract. It is the owner of the annuity who names the individual who will serve as the annuitant as well as the individual or entity who will be the beneficiary under the contract. Also, it is the owner who has the right to determine when the annuity contract will move from the accumulation phase into the payout (or annuitization) phase and begin paying benefits. For example, if Mr. Jones purchased a single premium annuity twenty years ago, as owner of the annuity contract, he can choose to begin receiving annuity payments today

Figure 2.01

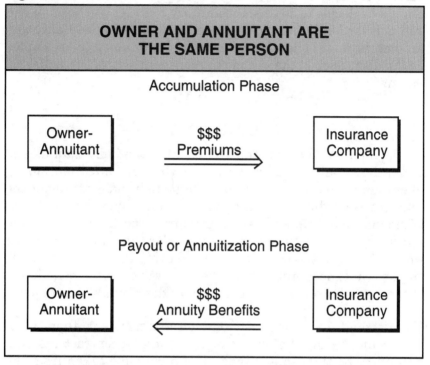

or to wait until some point in the future. (Most annuity contracts do specify a maximum age past which annuity payouts cannot be deferred, but in most contracts this age is well past the usual retirement age.)

Under a typical annuity contract, Mr. Jones also has the right to make a partial surrender and receive a portion of the funds accumulated inside the contract. Additionally, he can choose to end the contract completely by fully surrendering the contract. To illustrate Mr. Jones' options in this respect, assume that the contract value today is $50,000. As owner of the contract, Mr. Jones may make a partial surrender of an amount less than the full $50,000 value. If he chooses to receive $20,000 from the contract, the annuity contract will continue in force but with a reduced value of only $30,000. When Mr. Jones chooses to begin receiving the annuity benefit payments, he will be entitled to benefits calculated on the remaining $30,000 value in the contract. Mr. Jones, as owner of the contract, can also choose to fully surrender the contract, receiving the entire $50,000 value today. Should he decide to do this, the annuity contract will be at an end and neither Mr. Jones nor the insurance company will have any further rights or obligations relating to the annuity. (See Chapter 7 for a discussion of the income tax consequences of surrendering an annuity.)

THE ANNUITANT

As mentioned above, the annuitant is the individual named under the annuity contract whose life will serve as the measuring life for purposes of determining benefits to be paid out under the contract. According to the Internal Revenue Code, the annuitant is the individual whose life is of primary importance in affecting the timing or amount of the payout under the contract. In other words the annuitant's life is the measuring life.[2] Thus, it seems obvious that the annuitant, unlike the owner and the beneficiary of the annuity contract, must be a real flesh-and-blood person.

Although it is the most common arrangement, there is no requirement that the owner of the annuity contract and the annuitant be the same individual. An example taken from the Deficit Reduction Act of 1984 illustrates this. In discussing the distributions that are required to come from an annuity contract at the death of the owner, the *General Explanation* of this legislation gives an example in which a father, age 50, buys an annuity contract and is the owner. He names his son, age 25, as the annuitant, with annuity payments to begin when his son reaches age 45.

In the case where the owner and the annuitant are not the same individual, Figure 2.02 illustrates the relationship of the various parties to the annuity contract.

When the accumulation phase of the annuity draws to a close and the owner wishes to annuitize the contract and begin receiving annuity benefit payments, the life expectancy of the annuitant can come into play, depending upon which annuity payout or settlement option is elected. (See Chapter 3 for an explanation of the various settlement options.) For example, if Mr. Jones is both

Figure 2.02

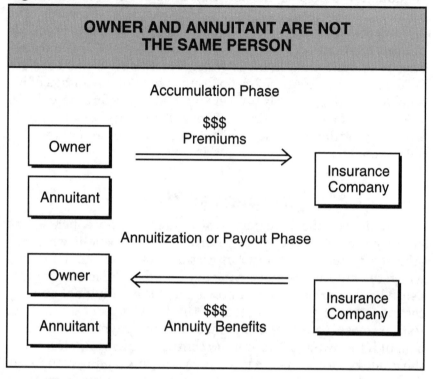

OWNER AND ANNUITANT ARE NOT
THE SAME PERSON

Accumulation Phase

$$$
Premiums

Owner

Annuitant

Insurance
Company

Annuitization or Payout Phase

Owner

Annuitant

$$$
Annuity Benefits

Insurance
Company

the owner and annuitant of an annuity that will begin paying benefits when he is age 65 and the payout option he elects is a life only option, the fact that Mr. Jones has a life expectancy of 20 years will be used in calculating the portion of the benefit payout that will be taxed to him. The 20 year life expectancy figure is taken, for income tax purposes, from the applicable annuity table issued by the Internal Revenue Service. (These tables are reproduced in Appendix A.)

In addition, a similar life expectancy figure will be used by the insurance company that sold the annuity to Mr. Jones in calculating the amount of his monthly annuity benefit. Thus, the annuitant's age (and therefore life expectancy) at the time the benefit payout begins will affect this monthly benefit amount. For example, assume that Mr. Smith is the owner-annuitant of a nonqualified annuity contract that currently has an accumulation value of $50,000. If Mr. Smith decides to begin receiving annuity benefits now at age 65, his benefit will be about $334 per month under a life only settlement option. However, if Mr. Edwards, who is currently 75 years old, begins to receive benefits from his annuity that has an accumulation value of $50,000, his monthly payout amount under a life only settlement option will be about $471 per month. If Mr. Johnson decides to take advantage of his employer's offer of early retirement and, therefore, is only 55 years old when he annuitizes his $50,000 annuity contract under a life only settlement option, his monthly benefit amount will be only $265.

THE BENEFICIARY

Similar to the beneficiary of a life insurance policy, the annuity contract beneficiary receives a death benefit when another party to the annuity contract dies prior to the date upon which the annuity begins paying out benefits. Payment of such a death benefit arises under a provision of the individual annuity contract and is not mandated by the laws of federal taxation. Rather, most insurance companies offer the payment of a death benefit if the owner of the annuity contract (or in some situations, the annuitant) dies before the contract begins paying benefits as a method by which the owner may recover his annuity premiums when death occurs earlier than anticipated. In effect, the payment of the death benefit allows an owner to recover his investment and pass it along to his beneficiary if he does not live long enough to begin receiving annuity contract benefits. The death benefit amount is equal generally to the value of the annuity contract at the time of death.

As an example, assume that Mrs. Smith purchased an annuity naming herself as both the owner and the annuitant. Mrs. Smith names her nephew, her only living relative, as the beneficiary of the annuity contract. Mrs. Smith purchased the deferred annuity contract when she was 50 years old and does not plan to begin receiving benefits (i.e., annuitize the contract) until she retires at age 65. If Mrs. Smith dies prior to retirement, the typical annuity contract will pay a death benefit to her nephew approximately equal to the premiums that Mrs. Smith paid into the annuity plus the interest earned on those premiums. The payment will be made to the nephew, as the annuity contract beneficiary, directly.

If, however, Mrs. Smith survives until she retires at age 65, begins receiving benefits from the annuity under a life only income option, and then dies at age 67, there will be no death benefit payable to the beneficiary or any other party. This will be true even though Mrs. Smith had not received in two years time benefit payments anywhere close to the amount of premiums she paid into the annuity. Although, if Mrs. Smith had elected a method of benefit payout that offered a refund or a guarantee instead of the life only income option some further benefit payments would be made to her nephew. Most annuity contracts offer a variety of benefit payout or settlement options. (See Chapter 3 for more information on settlement options.)

Payment of the death benefit at the death of an owner or annuitant is altered somewhat when there is a surviving spouse that has been named as the beneficiary under the contract. The Internal Revenue Code allows a surviving spouse to "step into the shoes" of the deceased spouse. In effect, the surviving spouse becomes the new owner of the annuity and is permitted to continue the annuity contract without change.[3] For example, assume that Mr. Jones purchased a single premium deferred annuity five years prior to his death, naming himself as owner and annuitant and his wife, Mrs. Jones, as the designated beneficiary. He had not yet started to receive payments from the annuity contract at his death. Mrs. Jones, as the designated beneficiary, would be treated as the annuity contact owner, and would be allowed to continue the annuity in its accumulation phase for the time being.

The beneficiary has no rights under the annuity contract, other than the right to receive payment of the death benefit. He cannot change the payout settlement option. He cannot alter the starting date for benefit payments. He cannot make any withdrawals or partial surrenders against the contract. Further, the owner has the right, under most nonqualified annuity contracts, to change the beneficiary designation at any time. However, some annuity contracts do permit a beneficiary designation to be made irrevocably. If this is the case, the irrevocable beneficiary does have certain rights under the contract.

Unlike the party named as the annuitant under an annuity contract, there is no requirement that the beneficiary be a flesh-and-blood individual. Often, a trust or other entity such as a charitable organization is named as the annuity contract beneficiary.

THE INSURANCE COMPANY

It is the insurance company who issues the annuity contract and, in doing so, assumes a number of financial obligations to the owner, the annuitant, and the beneficiary. While a detailed analysis of the provisions of a nonqualified annuity contract is beyond the scope of this book, a general discussion of the typical contract provisions appears in Chapter 3. It should be remembered, also, that the contract obligations undertaken by the issuing insurance company are different for other types of annuities such as Individual Retirement Annuities (IRAs), Tax Sheltered Annuities (TSAs), and annuities issued in connection with qualified retirement plans. It is important to remember these differences even though many insurance companies use a single annuity contract form for nonqualified as well as IRA and TSA purposes.

In a very general sense, the insurance company that issues an annuity contract promises to invest the owner's premium payments responsibly and credit interest to the funds placed in the annuity. How the premium payments are invested and how much, if any, control the owner retains over the investment decisions affecting his or her funds varies depending upon which type of nonqualified annuity is purchased. See Chapter 4 for information on fixed and variable annuities and Chapter 5 for a discussion of the equity-indexed annuity.

In addition to investing the owner's premium payments and crediting the funds with interest, the insurance company also promises to pay the contract death benefit in the event of the death of the owner prior to annuitization of the contract and to make

benefit payouts according to the contract settlement option selected by the contract owner. By fulfilling these contractual
obligations, the insurance company, through the annuity contract, helps the owner to avoid outliving his or her financial
means.

While it may seem at first glance that an annuity contract
issued by one company is just the same as a contract issued by any
other company, the truth is that annuity contracts do differ from
one company to the next. The Internal Revenue Code does require
that all annuities contain certain provisions in order to be eligible
for the tax benefits associated with the annuity contract, but there
remains considerable room for variation between companies.

Which annuity contract is right for a certain individual
depends upon the facts of the individual's situation. For example,
all companies have a maximum age past which they will not issue
an annuity contract. If an individual is 80 years old, he or she will
not be able to purchase an annuity contract from a company whose
maximum issue age is 75, even if all the other components of that
particular annuity are attractive. Annuity contract provisions
vary in many regards among issuing companies including surrender charges, interest rates credited, and settlement or payout
options available to name only a few. The best source of information on the specific provisions of an annuity contract is, of course,
the issuing insurance company itself. Many agents and financial
planners request a sample contract for each of the annuity
products they work with to maximize their understanding of each
annuity contract.

As mentioned above, one item that must be considered in
relationship to the insurance company is the various provisions
and strengths of the annuity contract itself. Of similar importance
is the financial strength and investment philosophy of the company that is issuing the contract. The purchaser of an annuity
contract should be knowledgeable about and comfortable with
this information.

To evaluate the company's financial strength, several "rating"
services are available and, indeed, are used extensively by agents,

financial planners, and consumers alike. These services include those from the A.M. Best Company, Moody's, Standard & Poor's, and Fitch.

The ratings services examine the items connected with the insurance company that are of importance in gauging how effectively, efficiently, and profitably the company is likely to perform in the future. Included in the list of information evaluated is the company's profitability, its capitalization, and its liquidity. In addition, ratings services generally examine the company's investment strategy and marketing philosophy, as well as the general stability of its business practices and history. The capability and competence of the company's management also comes under scrutiny during the rating process.[4]

ENDNOTES

1. It is important to remember that, under Section 72(u) of the Internal Revenue Code, annuities issued after February 28, 1986, that are not owned by natural persons lose certain income tax advantages associated with the annuity contract. See Chapter 6 for a more detailed discussion.
2. See IRC Sec. 72(s)(6).
3. IRC Sec. 72(s)(3).
4. A useful explanation and comparison of the various insurance company ratings systems can be found in the *Field Guide to Estate Planning, Business Planning, & Employee Benefits*, by Donald F. Cady, J.D., LL.M., CLU (published annually by The National Underwriter Company).

Chapter 3

STANDARD ANNUITY CONTRACT PROVISIONS

While all annuity contracts are not the same, there are certain standard provisions common to many. Some provisions, such as those that require distributions after the death of the owner to be made in a particular manner, are required by the Internal Revenue Code to be contained in the annuity contract. These provisions must be a part of the annuity contract if the insurance company wishes the contract to retain the income tax advantages associated with an annuity.

Other provisions may be unique to the annuities of one or a small number of companies, although once a company introduces a successful innovation it is often adopted by other insurance companies. This tendency has been illustrated by the rapid development of the equity-indexed annuity. Early in a product's development there tends to be greater variety among the products developed and issued by the various companies. Currently, this is true among the available equity-indexed annuities. As time passes, the equity-indexed annuities issued by different insurance companies will likely come to resemble each other more and more closely. (See Chapter 5 for more on equity-indexed annuities.)

This chapter contains a discussion of the typical provisions found in a nonqualified annuity contract. Not all annuities contain these provisions, but many do. Some contracts may contain generally the same provisions but differ as to the specific details. For example, Annuity A and Annuity B both may specify a maximum issue age for the annuity owner. However, the maximum age under Annuity A may be 75 while the maximum age under Annuity B is 80.

Many agents and financial planners have found that the best way to know precisely what a particular annuity contract provides is to request a sample copy of the annuity contract from the issuing company and study it carefully.

The following typical annuity contract provisions are addressed in this chapter:

1.   Bailout provisions and rates;

2.   Charges and fees;

3.   Dollar cost averaging;

4.   Interest rates;

5.   Issue ages;

6.   Maximum ages for benefits to begin;

7.   Nursing home waiver;

8.   Premium payments;

9.   Settlement options;

10. Surrender charges; and

11. Withdrawals.

BAILOUT PROVISIONS AND RATES

Generally, a bailout provision allows the contract holder to fully surrender the annuity contract without incurring any surrender charges imposed under the annuity contract if the current interest rate drops below a certain level. Another name for a bailout provision is an escape clause.

For example, an annuity might offer a bailout clause that allows the contract to be surrendered if the current interest rate drops to 1% below the interest rate of a previous period. Assume that the prior interest rate was 5.5%. If the current rate for the next period falls below 4.5% the annuity holder may surrender the annuity contract completely and not be subject to any contract surrender charges. (The 10% penalty tax on premature withdrawals may still apply to a surrender under the bailout provision. See Chapter 7 for more detail.)

While the existence of this "out" from low interest rates may ease the annuity holder's mind, as a practical matter it may not be of much value. If the issuing insurance company does not have sufficient investment returns to allow it to credit interest of more than 4.5%, other insurance companies and financial institutions are not likely to be able to do so either. Thus, even if the annuity holder retrieves his funds from the annuity, he may not have many investment alternatives that will pay a higher rate of return.

CHARGES AND FEES

Many, if not most, annuities assess charges of an administrative nature against the funds placed in the annuity contract. Often, an annuity will apply several different charges. Although the dollar amount of each charge may seem small, the cumulative effect can take its toll.

Fixed Annuities

Many annuities assess administration fees. For example, an annuity may charge a fee of $30 or $35 annually to cover the company's cost of preparing the annuity holder's statement, making ownership or beneficiary changes, etc. Typically, the fees associated with a fixed annuity are lower in amount and fewer in number than those applicable to a variable annuity. At first glance, it may seem that the variable annuity is more "expensive" than the fixed annuity. However, this is not necessarily true. With a fixed annuity the insurance company declares the current interest rate and thus can set the interest rate it promises to pay at a lower rate than the rate it expects to earn on its investments. This difference in rates, sometimes referred to as the "spread" or "haircut," allows the insurance company more leeway to recover its administrative costs than the insurance company has with a variable annuity where it does not set the interest rate itself but credits the rate earned on the funds in the underlying separate investment account.

Variable Annuities

Fees and charges levied under variable annuity contracts, while somewhat similar to those charged by fixed annuity contracts, are subject to a greater degree of regulation due to the fact that variable annuities are considered to be securities. In very general terms, this means that a variable annuity purchaser must always be given a prospectus, and an agent or planner must have a securities license in addition to a license to sell fixed annuities.

The annual fee mentioned above in relation to fixed annuities is also often applied to variable annuity contracts. With a variable annuity, charges of this nature are usually deducted proportionately from the various separate investment accounts in which the annuity holder has placed his funds. For example, if Mr. Smith has placed 50% of his funds in the bond account and 50% in an equity account, each account would be charged with 50% (or $15) of the $30 annual administration fee. Some variable annuity contracts waive the contract fee when the annuity's accumulation value exceeds a certain threshold, such as $50,000.

Also with a variable annuity, some companies assess a small charge against the balance in each variable investment account to cover the extra expense associated with such an investment alternative. Included in these fees might be a charge for investment advisory and management services and, possibly, for other expenses. In fact, some companies refer to this type of charge as an "investment advisory fee" or an "investment management fee." Thus, each variable account might be charged .20% annually. Some variable annuity contracts charge this type of fee at the fund level with each type of fund incurring a different percentage cost. For example, the investment advisory fee for a growth and income account might be .70% while the fee for a money market account would be only .30%.

Another type of expense is usually labeled as a mortality and expense risk charge. Sometimes referred to as an "M&E" charge, this charge typically is approximately 1% annually. The M&E charge is generally deducted proportionately from the variable accounts, as discussed above.

The following illustration brings these typical fees and charges together. A typical variable annuity contract might provide for the following fees:

1. An annual administration fee of $35;

2. An investment advisory fee equal to .15% of the average account value; and

3. An M&E charge equal to 1.25% of the average account value.

Of course, with a variable annuity, the costs and fees are disclosed in the annuity's prospectus.

Another fee that is charged under a few variable annuities is a fee for the transfer of funds between investment accounts. Typically, a variable annuity will allow the annuity holder to transfer funds from the guaranteed account to one or more of the variable accounts or from the variable accounts to the guaranteed account. Transfers between variable accounts are usually also permitted, although any transfer may be subject to restrictions concerning its timing or amount. (See Chapter 4 for more detail.) Today, most contracts permit these transfers without charge, although many reserve the right to levy such charges in the future. Some variable annuity contracts allow a certain number of transfers per year without charge and then assess a charge for transfers in excess of the permitted number. Typically, when a charge is assessed it amounts to $10 to $15 per transfer and is usually deducted from the account from which the transfer is made.

DOLLAR COST AVERAGING

Dollar cost averaging is, in very general terms, a system of buying securities such as mutual funds or stocks at regular intervals with a fixed amount of capital. In this long-term approach to investing, an individual purchases the same dollar amount of a fund or other type of investment each month, regardless of the current share price of the fund. By doing so, the individual buys more shares when the market price is low and fewer shares when the market price is high. The dollar cost averaging approach results in an average cost lower than the average price over a period of time.

Many variable annuity contracts facilitate dollar cost averaging by offering a type of transfer feature that allows the annuity holder to make transfers from one variable account to another on a systematic basis. A transfer is made each month or year from one account to another within the variable annuity for the purpose of purchasing whatever amount of the new fund can be purchased with the same amount of dollars each month. Many annuity contracts place limits on the amount that can be transferred, the amount that must remain in an account, and which accounts the transfers can go into or come out of.

For example, an annuity contract might allow dollar cost averaging and restrict transfers to a fixed dollar amount of at least $100 coming out of the general or guaranteed account and going to certain variable accounts. Some annuity contracts also allow an annuity holder to transfer the interest earned in the guaranteed or general account into another variable account for use in dollar cost averaging.

INTEREST RATES

Fixed Annuities

Typically, a fixed annuity contract will offer two interest rates: a guaranteed rate and a current rate. The guaranteed rate is the minimum rate that will be credited to funds in the annuity contract regardless of how low the current rate sinks or how poorly the issuing insurance company fares with its investment returns. Typically, the guaranteed rate is 3% to 4%.

The current interest rate varies with the insurance company's success or lack of success with its investment program. Some annuity contracts revise the current rate on a monthly basis, others change the current interest rate only one time each year.

Figure 3.01 below illustrates how the two interest rates work together. Assume that last year Mrs. Jones purchased a single premium deferred annuity on which the issuing insurance company was paying a current rate of 7%. The guaranteed rate for this fixed annuity is 4%. On the one-year anniversary of the purchase of her annuity, the company notifies Mrs. Jones that the new current rate will be 6.7%. Thus, for the first twelve months, Mrs. Jones' single premium amount was credited with interest at a rate of 7%. For the second twelve months, her original premium plus the first year's interest will be credited with a rate of 6.7%.

Figure 3.01

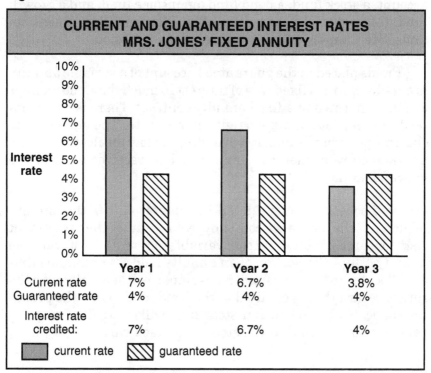

	Year 1	Year 2	Year 3
Current rate	7%	6.7%	3.8%
Guaranteed rate	4%	4%	4%
Interest rate credited:	7%	6.7%	4%

Although it is rather unlikely, if the insurance company decided that it could only credit 3.8% based upon its investment returns in Mrs. Jones' third contract year, the guaranteed interest rate provision would mandate that Mrs. Jones be paid at least 4% on the funds in her annuity.

Some annuities offer a current rate for a one year period, a three year period, and a five year period. Some contracts even offer seven and ten year periods for current interest rates. A typical provision of this type might offer a current interest rate of 5.3% for one year, 5.6% for three years, and 5.85% for a five year period.

Variable Annuities

Understanding how returns are credited on money invested within the framework of a variable annuity can be a bit more complicated than with a fixed annuity. With the variable annuity, the annuity holder may allocate his premium dollars among a number of investment choices including, usually, a guaranteed account, a stock fund, a bond fund, an income fund, and a growth fund. (Many variable annuities offer additional investment options. See Chapter 4 for a more detailed discussion.)

Funds placed in the guaranteed account of a variable annuity are credited with a fixed rate of interest in much the same manner as funds invested in a fixed annuity contract. There is a guaranteed interest rate and a current interest rate. The current rate changes periodically and, if it ever drops below the floor set by the guaranteed rate, then the annuity holder receives at least the guaranteed rate.

As discussed in more detail in Chapter 4, it is the annuity holder, not the insurance company, who assumes the investment risk for funds placed in the variable accounts of a variable annuity. Thus, the portion of an annuity holder's premiums that are allocated to the bond fund, for example, will generally earn the rate of return that is credited to the bond fund, while the premiums allocated to a particular stock fund will be credited with the same rate of return that the stock fund itself earns.

To illustrate further, assume that Mrs. Jones, mentioned above, purchased a variable annuity with her single premium. She allocated 50% of her $100,000 premium to the guaranteed account, 30% to a stock fund, and the remaining 20% to a bond fund. In the first contract year, $50,000 of her premium would be credited with the current rate for the guaranteed fund, $30,000 of her premium would earn the rate of return earned by the stock fund, and the remaining $20,000 would be credited with the rate of return earned by the bond fund. It is entirely possible that the rates of return on both the stock and bond funds will be less than the current interest rate credited on the funds placed in the guaranteed account.

ISSUE AGES

Regarding the oldest age at which an insurance company will sell an annuity to an individual, some companies set a maximum age and some do not. Some companies set a lower maximum issue age for the annuitant than for the owner of the annuity. Some companies set a maximum issue age only for annuities that will be paid out over the annuitant's life.

A typical maximum issue age is age 90 for both the owner and the annuitant. However, some companies set the maximum for the annuitant (i.e., the measuring life) a bit lower. Thus, the maximum issue age for the annuitant might be age 80 but the maximum issue age for the owner might be age 85.

Notice that the typical maximum issue age is well beyond the age at which most individuals retire. Thus, annuities may be used for retirement planning even after retirement has commenced. Single premium annuities and immediate annuities can be particularly useful in this regard. (See Chapter 6 for more about retirement planning and annuities.)

Joint and survivor annuities also have maximum issues ages. A typical provision states that the annuity will be issued for ages 35 to 85.

MAXIMUM AGES FOR BENEFITS TO BEGIN

Nonqualified Annuities

Under the Internal Revenue Code, there is no age at which distributions or benefit payments must begin for a nonqualified annuity contract. (This is not true for other types of annuities, such as Individual Retirement Annuities (IRAs), as discussed below.) However, most insurance companies specify a maximum age at which the annuity holder must begin receiving benefit payouts from the annuity in the nonqualified annuity contract itself. Like other annuity provisions, this maximum age varies, and indeed, in recent years, has generally been set at increasingly older ages. Many contracts currently require an annuity contract to begin paying benefits when the annuitant reaches age 80 or 85, although some allow the payment of benefits to be postponed to an even older age. Some annuities allow the payment of benefits to be delayed past age 100.

Other Annuities

As mentioned above, the Internal Revenue Code does set a minimum age for benefits to begin to be paid out of certain types of annuities. Generally, these are annuities into which the funds were placed either by an individual's employer, such as a qualified retirement plan, or by the individual on a tax-deductible basis, such as with some contributions to traditional IRAs. Rules for minimum distributions and the age at which they must begin are complex for these types of plans.

As a very general rule, traditional IRAs and Tax Sheltered Annuities (TSAs) must begin making distributions of at least a minimum amount in the year following the year in which the individual reaches age 70½.[1] Roth IRAs, however, are not subject to a minimum distribution requirement during the life of the owner.[2]

NURSING HOME WAIVER

Some annuity contracts offer a waiver of the annuity contract's surrender charges in the event that the annuitant is either hospitalized or confined to a nursing home for a certain period of time, such as 30 days. This provision allows the owner of the contract to extract funds from the annuity contract that might be needed to meet the expenses or lost income associated with the hospitalization or confinement. Other annuity contracts allow medically-related surrenders that are not subject to the contract's surrender charges. Generally, there is a requirement that the annuitant be confined in a medical care facility for a certain period of time or be diagnosed with a terminal illness.

Although not part of the annuity contract, the 10% premature distribution penalty tax may be applicable to a withdrawal made for this reason if the taxpayer is under age 59½. To avoid the imposition of this tax penalty, the taxpayer must be able to qualify as being "disabled" as that term is defined in the Internal Revenue Code.[3] The Code's definition may differ from the definition used in the annuity contract. In the Internal Revenue Code, for purposes of the 10% premature distribution penalty tax, "disabled" is defined as being "... unable to engage in any substantial gainful activity by reason of any medically determinable physical or mental impairment which can be expected to result in death or to be of long-continued and indefinite duration."[4]

PREMIUM PAYMENTS

Most annuity contracts require each premium payment to be at least a certain minimum amount. This is primarily to make the administration of the contract easier. The required minimum amount varies widely from one annuity to another. For example, one nonqualified deferred annuity might require a minimum monthly premium of only $50, while another nonqualified annuity might require a minimum initial single premium of $25,000 with subsequent payments subject to a minimum of $50. Yet another annuity might require an initial premium of $2,000 but state that subsequent premium payments must be at least $1,000. Often, a single insurance company will offer several versions of

one annuity contract with varying minimum premium requirements. Usually, the higher the required minimum premium, the
more likely the annuity is to offer a greater number of investment
options, free transfers among variable accounts, and certain
interest rate bonuses.

Because premium payments are continued at the election of
the annuity contract holder, he or she may choose to skip a
payment, to increase or decrease the amount of the premium, or
to discontinue premium payments altogether. Of course, any
decrease in or discontinuance of the planned premium will ad-
versely affect any accumulation amounts projected for future
planning purposes.

Usually, the buyer of an annuity can choose how often he or
she wishes to make premium payments. Most annuity contracts
will accept premiums annually, quarterly or monthly. Many
insurance companies will arrange for the funds to be transferred
directly out of the annuity owner's bank account. While this direct
transfer feature may be viewed as a convenience by some, it does
not appeal to all individuals.

SETTLEMENT OPTIONS

The settlement options in the annuity contract are the methods by which the annuity owner can select to receive payments of
benefits under the annuity contract. Other terms that are used to
refer to settlement options are payout options or benefit options.

Generally, it is the annuity owner who makes the settlement
option selection. It can be made when the contract is purchased or
delayed until the time that benefit payments are to commence.
Most annuity contracts allow the chosen settlement option to be
changed with proper notice to the insurance company. Although
not a complete list, the following settlement options are discussed
below:

1.   Life annuity;

2.   Life with period certain guarantee;

3.   Refund life annuity;

4.   Joint and survivor life annuity;

5.   Fixed period annuity; and

6.   Fixed amount annuity.

Life Annuity

If the life annuity settlement option is elected the annuitant will receive payments from the annuity until his or her death. This will be true whether the annuitant dies two years after payments begin or 25 years after payments begin. This settlement option is the purest form of insuring that the annuitant does not outlive his or her financial means.

To illustrate the life annuity with an example, assume that Mrs. Smith is age 50 and decides to begin receiving payments from her nonqualified annuity under the life annuity option. If her annuity has an accumulation value of about $200,000, her monthly payments will be $906. Mrs. Smith will receive the $906 each month until her death. If she lives only a few years, say to age 55, she will have received only $54,360 in annuity benefits. The difference of $145,640 ($200,000 less $54,360) will be lost to Mrs. Smith's family and heirs. On the other hand, if Mrs. Smith survives to age 90 receiving her $906 check each month, she will have collected a total of $434,880, an amount significantly in excess of the annuity's accumulation value of $200,000.

Life with Period Certain Guarantee

This settlement option is frequently selected because it provides a hedge against loss of much of the value in the annuity if the annuitant dies shortly after the contract is annuitized. Under this option, the insurance company agrees to pay the annuity benefit for the longer of the annuitant's lifetime or a certain period of years. Most annuity contracts offer a choice of the period certain. Often the choices include 5, 10, 15, or 20 years, although some insurance companies qualify this election by stating that the guarantee period may not exceed the annuitant's life expectancy. Thus, a 90-year-old annuitant probably would not be able to elect the life and 20 year certain settlement option.

If Mrs. Smith, age 50, decided to annuitize her nonqualified annuity contract with an accumulation value of $200,000, under a life and 5 year certain settlement option her monthly benefit payments would be about $904. Under a life and 10 year certain option, her monthly benefit would be $900. Electing the life and 15 year certain option would result in a benefit of $892 per month while choosing the life and 20 year certain option would bring a benefit of $880 per month. Thus, at Mrs. Smith's age, the difference between payments for life only and payments for at least a 20 year period is about $25 per month. To many, this lower monthly benefit is worth the security of the 20 year guarantee.

If Mrs. Smith had selected the life and 20 year certain settlement option at age 50 but only survived until age 65, her beneficiary would receive the monthly payment of $880 each month for the next five years. On the other hand, if Mrs. Brown lived 22 years, until age 72, the annuity payments would cease at her death and the beneficiary would not receive any payment from the annuity contract.

The life and period certain guarantee settlement option can be useful in financial planning situations where there is a set number of years until a particular benefit will begin. For example, if a married couple is in their late 50's and the sole income-earner decides to retire early, using a life and 10 year certain settlement option will insure that if the income-earner dies before reaching age 65, the annuity payments will continue to the survivor until he or she is eligible for retirement benefits at age 65.

Refund Life Annuity

Like the life and period certain guarantee option discussed above, this settlement option offers a hedge against the possibility of an early death. Under the refund life annuity settlement option, the insurance company will pay the monthly benefit for the life of the annuitant. At the annuitant's death, if the amount that was applied to the annuitization of the contract (i.e., the accumulation amount) is more than the total of installment payments received by the annuitant during his or her life, the difference is paid in a lump sum to the beneficiary. Thus, under this option, an amount equal to at least the amount in the annuity contract at the time of annuitization will be paid out either to the annuitant or to the annuitant and the beneficiary.

For example, assume that Mrs. Smith purchased a single premium nonqualified annuity for $200,000 when she was 50 years old. Her monthly annuity payments under the refund life annuity settlement option are $876. If Mrs. Smith lives for only 5 years to age 55, she will have received annuity payments totaling $52,560. Because she elected the refund life annuity option, Mrs. Smith's beneficiary would receive a lump sum payment from the insurance company equal to approximately $147,440, the difference between the accumulation value of $200,000 and the payments received by Mrs. Smith totaling $52,560. On the other hand, if Mrs. Smith lived to be 85 years old and collected annuity payments for 35 years, she would have received total payments of about $367,920. Because this total exceeds the accumulation value of $200,000, Mrs. Smith's beneficiary would not be entitled to any lump sum refund payment at her death.

Joint and Survivor Life Annuity

This settlement option involves two persons and their lifetimes. Under the joint and survivor life annuity the insurance company will pay benefits during the joint lifetimes of two individuals. Often the two persons are husband and wife, although there is no requirement that this be the case. (Each individual must be a real flesh-and-blood person, however. Trusts or corporations cannot serve this purpose because they do not have a life expectancy.)

Under the joint and survivor life annuity option, the insurance company pays the full benefit amount until the death of one of the annuitants. If the settlement option is a full joint and survivor annuity, the payments will continue in the full amount until the death of the surviving annuitant. Under a joint and one-half survivor annuity settlement option, payments are made in full until the death of one of the annuitants but then reduced to one-half the full amount until the death of the survivor. Many companies offer a joint and two-thirds survivor annuity, under which the payments to the surviving annuitant are equal to two-thirds the original full payment amount.

Some insurance companies offer this settlement option with a different twist. Here one annuitant is named as the primary annuitant. Payments are made in the full benefit amount until the death of one of the annuitants. If the primary annuitant dies first, the survivor receives payments of either one-half or two-thirds the original benefit amount. However, if the other annuitant is the first to die, the primary annuitant continues to receive benefit payments of the full amount.

To continue with our example from above, assume that Mr. Smith is age 55 and Mrs. Smith, age 50, has an accumulation value of $200,000 in her nonqualified annuity. Electing the full joint and survivor annuity settlement option would result in a monthly benefit of $854 paid to both Mr. and Mrs. Smith until the death of one of them. After the first death, this same amount of $854 would continue to be paid to the survivor until his or her death. If the Smiths elected a joint and one-half survivor settlement option, the amount paid to both of them would be $944 until the first death. Then, the survivor would receive one-half the benefit amount or $472 each month until his or her death. Electing the joint and two-thirds survivor settlement option would see a benefit of $912 until the first death, with the survivor receiving two-thirds or $608 of the benefit payment.

In some instances, the survivor of the two annuitants may see a reduction in living expenses and not need as much income to live as before the death of the other annuitant. However, some financial planners point out that, depending upon the remaining annuitant's other income, length of life, and the possibility of inflation, the remaining annuitant may not see a reduction in expenses over the long term.

Fixed Period Annuity

Probably the easiest of the settlement options to explain are the fixed period and fixed amount options. The fixed period settlement option allows the annuitant to receive the accumulation value in the annuity over a set number of years. For example, an owner-annuitant who is 60 years old may choose to annuitize his contract and elect to receive the benefits over a five year period which would end when he reaches age 65 and becomes eligible for Social Security and possibly benefits from retirement plans. Most companies offer the fixed period settlement option for any period from a few years to 25 or 30 years.

As an example, assume Mrs. Smith has an accumulation value in her nonqualified annuity of $200,000 and she decides to annuitize this amount. She elects the fixed period settlement option over a five year period so that her monthly benefit would be about $3,664. She would receive this benefit payment each month for 60 months or five years. At the end of this time, benefit payments to Mrs. Smith would cease. No further funds would remain in the annuity contract and no further benefits would be payable. If Mrs. Smith should die during the five year period, the benefit payments would continue to her beneficiary until the end of the five years.

Fixed Amount Annuity

Under this settlement option, the annuitant receives benefit payments of a set amount for as long as the annuity's accumulation value plus interest lasts. If Mrs. Smith has an accumulation value of $200,000, under this settlement option she could elect to receive a monthly benefit payment of $3,000 (or any other amount she preferred). The insurance company would send her a check each month for as long as the accumulation value and interest would support the benefit. After the funds in the annuity were exhausted, Mrs. Smith would not receive any further benefits from the annuity contract. In the event of Mrs. Smith's death before the funds in the annuity have been used up, the remainder is generally paid to her beneficiary.

Interest Income

Although it is not a "settlement" option strictly speaking, many annuity contracts offer the option of leaving the accumulation value of the annuity with the insurance company. While the funds remain with it, the insurance company credits the funds with a current rate of interest. The individual can either take receipt of the interest amounts or allow them to continue to accumulate.

SURRENDER CHARGES

Most annuity contracts levy a "charge" against partial and full surrenders from the contract for a period of years after the annuity is purchased. This charge, usually referred to as a "surrender charge" or a "deferred sales charge," is intended to make it less attractive for annuity owners to move funds in and out of the annuity and to allow the insurance company to recover its costs if the contract does not remain in force over the long run.

The surrender charge is usually applicable to surrenders made from the annuity for a certain number of years. Although this period varies from one annuity to another, it usually runs anywhere from 5 to 10 years. The surrender charge is usually a percentage that is applied to the funds received as a result of the surrender. Typically, the surrender charge percentage decreases with each passing year. For example, a nonqualified annuity contract might provide the following surrender charge schedule:

Contract Year	Surrender/Withdrawal Charges
1	8%
2	7%
3	6%
4	5%
5	4%
6	3%
7	2%
8	1%

Thus, any surrender made in the fourth contract year under this schedule will incur a surrender charge under the contract of 5%.

After the contract has been in force for 8 years, no surrender charge will apply.

If a Section 1035 exchange is being contemplated, it is important to keep in mind the fact that the contract surrender charge is no longer applicable to a specific annuity contract. Although, as explained in Chapter 7, Internal Revenue Code Section 1035 will prevent current income taxation on the exchange of one annuity for another, generally the newly-received annuity contract will be subject to contract surrender charges for several years after the exchange. However, if the Section 1035 exchange does not take place, the original annuity contract will still be in force and will not be subject to any contract surrender charges.

To illustrate in greater detail, assume that Mr. Smith makes a partial surrender of $10,000 from his annuity in a year in which the surrender charge is 5%. He will lose $500 (5% of $10,000) as a result of the surrender, effectively receiving only $9,500. Some insurance companies subtract the amount of the surrender charge from the amount actually paid to the contract holder, as illustrated with Mr. Smith. Other annuity contracts provide that, with a partial surrender, the surrender charge is applied against the values still remaining in the contract after the surrender. Thus, in this instance, Mr. Smith would receive a check for the full $10,000 partial surrender amount but a $500 charge would be levied against the funds remaining in his annuity. In the event of a full surrender, of course, the check sent to Mr. Smith would be reduced by the amount of the surrender charge.

As illustrated above, some companies apply the surrender charge percentage against the full amount surrendered and, after a specified number of years have passed, no surrender charge is applicable regardless of when premiums have been paid into the annuity. However, other companies use a method of applying the surrender charge percentage that is a bit more complicated. The provision in an annuity contract in this instance might provide that the percentage will be applied only against premiums paid in. Premiums are considered to be taken out of the annuity on the basis that the first premiums paid in are the first taken out. Thus, if a contract had been in force for five years with a premium payment made each year when the contract holder decided to fully surrender the contract, an amount of the surrender equal to the premium paid in the first year would be subject to the surrender charge applicable in the fifth contract year, an amount equal to the second year's premium would be subject to the fourth contract year's percentage charge, and so on. Any premium that remains in the contract for five years before a surrender takes place is not subject to any surrender charge.

Many annuity contracts provide that no surrender charge will be levied if the annuitant dies or becomes disabled.

Having looked at how surrender charges are assessed under the annuity contract, it bears restating that this surrender charge is one that originates in the annuity contract itself. This "contract" surrender charge should not be confused with the 10% penalty tax that is applicable to premature withdrawals from annuities under the Internal Revenue Code.[5] These two "penalties" or "charges" are often confused. This confusion is easy to understand because it is possible for a surrender from an annuity to be subject to both or only one of the contract surrender charge and the 10% penalty tax. It is also possible that a surrender of funds from an annuity will not be subject to either of these items as the penalty tax generally applies to distributions received prior to age 59½ and the contract surrender charges apply during the first few years after the annuity is purchased.

To illustrate, assume that Mr. Smith, age 65, purchased a deferred annuity two years ago. If he surrenders the contract this year, he will incur the third year contract surrender charge of 6% but he will not be subject to the Internal Revenue Code 10% penalty tax because he is older than age 59½ at the time of the surrender. However, if Ms. Jones, age 44, surrenders a deferred annuity contract purchased 20 years ago, it is not likely that any contract surrender charges will still be applicable, but the Internal Revenue Code's 10% penalty will still apply because Ms. Jones is younger than age 59½.

WITHDRAWALS

Partial Surrender

Almost all nonqualified annuity contracts permit the contract holder to make a surrender of a portion of the values accumulated in the annuity prior to the time that the annuity begins paying benefits. Some contracts limit the frequency with which partial surrenders may be made and some require that a minimum amount remain in the annuity after any surrender is made. For example, an annuity might allow only one partial surrender each contract year and might require that at least $5,000 remain after such a surrender. Some annuities require that the amount of the partial surrender be at least a certain minimum amount such as $100 or $500.

A myriad of tax legislation over the past 20 years has complicated the taxation of a partial surrender from a nonqualified annuity. This is discussed in detail in Chapter 7. For now, it is sufficient to say that if the annuity was issued after August 13, 1982, a partial surrender will be taxed as income first and return of basis second. To illustrate this method of taxation assume that Mrs. Jones purchased an annuity for a single premium payment of $50,000. The value of the annuity today is $80,000, resulting in interest earned in the contract of $30,000 ($80,000 surrender value minus the $50,000 single premium). Mrs. Jones decides to make a partial surrender of $20,000. Under the interest first rule, Mrs. Jones will pay income tax on the full $20,000 received as a result of the partial surrender. This is true because amounts coming out of the annuity first are deemed to be interest, so until the partial surrender amount exceeds the interest in the annuity of $30,000, any partial surrender amount will be fully taxable.

Some annuity contracts will waive the contract surrender charge for a certain number of partial surrenders from the contract. A common number here is one per contract year. Even though the insurance company does not assess a surrender charge under the annuity contract, the 10% premature distribution penalty tax assessed under the Internal Revenue Code may still be applicable.[6] See Chapter 7 for a more detailed discussion.

Full Surrender

An annuity can be surrendered in full at any time prior to the time it is annuitized and begins to make benefit payments. In addition to the income tax ramifications, contract surrender charges and income tax penalty taxes may be applicable. The taxation of such a complete surrender is treated in Chapter 7.

After a full surrender, the annuity contract is no longer in existence and, of course, will not pay any benefits to the annuitant, owner, or beneficiary.

10% Per Year Withdrawal

Many annuities allow the contract holder to withdraw or make a partial surrender of an amount equal to 10% of the accumulation value each contract year without the contract surrender charges being applied. Usually this feature is not available until the second contract year. With some annuity contracts, this 10% is cumulative or, in other words, can be carried over from one contract year and added to the next year's 10% amount. For example, if an annuity holder makes a 10% surrender in the second year of the contract and then does not make any surrender in the third contract year, in the fourth contract year the annuity holder would be able to surrender as much as 20% of the annuity's accumulation value without paying the contract surrender charges. Usually, there is a maximum amount, such as 50%, that may be accumulated.

The amount subject to withdrawal without the contract surrender charge being assessed is not 10% in all annuities. Some annuity contracts offer a choice of 10% or the earnings on the funds placed in the annuity. Others apply this free surrender provision to 10% of the contributions to the annuity in the past five or seven years. Still others apply the free surrender provision to something along the lines of the lesser of the accumulation value less premiums or 10% of the accumulation value.

It is good advice to read the details of an annuity contract's free withdrawal provision before making such a surrender. The requirements vary from contract to contract and some companies credit a potentially lower rate of interest on funds that are surrendered out of the contract than they would credit if the funds remained in the contract.

Whatever the specifics of the free withdrawal provision, it does not release the contract holder from the income tax consequences, including the 10% premature distribution penalty tax. See Chapter 7 for a full explanation.

Systematic Withdrawal Option

Many annuity contracts offer the contract holder a systematic withdrawal option as a way to take money out of the annuity contract during the accumulation phase. The annuity holder can elect to withdraw a set amount each month or each year without any contract fee or surrender charge assessed. Usually, the contract holder can terminate or alter the systematic withdrawal option at any time. Under some annuity contracts, the annuity holder can make lump sum withdrawals from the annuity in addition to the withdrawals made under the systematic withdrawal option.

Usually, there must be a minimum amount in the annuity before the systematic withdrawal option can be put into effect. Also, there is generally a limit on the amount that may be taken out of the annuity contract under the systematic withdrawal option each year. A typical provision limits the yearly withdrawals to 10% of the purchase payments.

As mentioned above, the fact that the insurance contract waives fees and surrender charges under the annuity contract does not alter the income tax consequences, including the 10% premature distribution penalty tax. See Chapter 6 for a full explanation.

Loans

Most nonqualified annuity contracts do not offer the option of taking a loan against the annuity values. This is probably due largely to the fact that any amount received as a loan under a contract entered into after August 13, 1982 is taxable to the extent that the cash value of the contract immediately before the loan exceeds the investment in the contract.[7] The taxation of loans, as well as assignments, made under annuity contracts is discussed in Chapter 7.

ENDNOTES

1.   See IRC Secs. 403(b)(10), 408(a)(6), 408(b)(3), 401(a)(9).
2.   See IRC Sec. 408A(c)(5).
3.   IRC Sec. 72(q)(2)(C).
4.   IRC Sec. 72(m)(7).
5.   IRC Sec. 72(q).
6.   Ibid.
7.   IRC Sec. 72(e).

Chapter 4

THE VARIOUS TYPES OF ANNUITIES

As anyone exposed to annuities quickly surmises, annuities come in many different shapes and sizes. They may be classified according to how and when the premiums are paid (i.e., single or flexible premium annuities), according to the investment options they offer (i.e., fixed, equity-indexed, or variable annuities), or according to when the benefits are paid out (i.e., immediate or deferred annuities). (See Figure 4.01.) And, to make matters even more complicated, a single annuity can embody a number of these different characteristics. For example, one annuity can be a single premium fixed immediate annuity. Another might be a flexible premium variable deferred annuity.

This chapter discusses the basic types of annuities according to how the premiums are paid, the investment options that are available, and when the benefit payments are made. It concludes with a short treatment of charitable gift annuities and private annuities, two complex arrangements that are not really annuities in the usual sense of the word.

SINGLE PREMIUM ANNUITIES

A single premium annuity is basically just what the name implies; an annuity that is purchased with only one premium, as illustrated in Figure 4.02. Usually, this lone premium is fairly large. Many insurance companies have annuities designed to accept only the single premium payment and then begin paying benefits when the annuity holder elects to do so. However, there is another way that a single premium annuity can be purchased. An individual might purchase an annuity contract that is designed by the insurance company to accept multiple premiums over a period of years. Either by design or as a result of a change

Figure 4.01

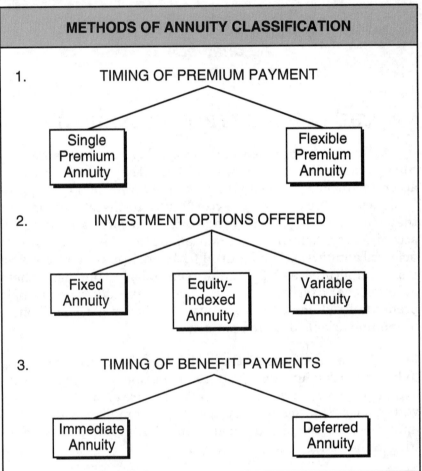

METHODS OF ANNUITY CLASSIFICATION

1.   TIMING OF PREMIUM PAYMENT

Single Premium Annuity   Flexible Premium Annuity

2.   INVESTMENT OPTIONS OFFERED

Fixed Annuity   Equity-Indexed Annuity   Variable Annuity

3.   TIMING OF BENEFIT PAYMENTS

Immediate Annuity   Deferred Annuity

in circumstance, the individual pays only one premium. Because most annuity contracts do not require the payment of any set number of premium payments or dollar amount other than the initial premium, any contract can probably be used in this manner. Of course, if the individual's plan is to pay only the single premium from the start, the best type of annuity to purchase will be the one that offers the best combination of rate of return, desired investment options, financial stability of the issuing company, and so forth.

Figure 4.02

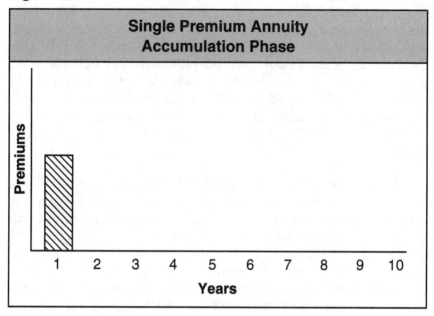

As discussed earlier in this book, many assume that annuities, and especially single premium annuities, are financial options designed only for the wealthy. This is not true. Many individuals who purchase a single premium annuities are not wealthy, but rather have received a large lump sum of money at one time. Because it is likely that these funds will be needed in the future to meet basic living expenses, the purchase of a single premium annuity often makes good financial sense.

Take the example of Mr. Smith, age 62, who recently lost his wife. He has elected to receive the death proceeds of Mrs. Smith's group life insurance in a lump sum of $75,000. Mr. Smith, who is self-employed and does not have any retirement plan for himself, plans to work for several more years. He does not need these funds for current expenses, but he does want to use them to supplement his income after he retires. If Mr. Smith purchases a single premium annuity with the $75,000, he can elect to begin receiving benefits at his retirement age and, by electing a life income settlement option, he will have an income to supplement his Social Security benefits and Mrs. Smith's pension plan benefits that will continue throughout his lifetime.

Another type of individual who may benefit from the purchase of a single premium annuity is someone who works in a field where his or her income is sporadically received. Artists, actors, authors, and others in the field of performing arts can fall into this category. For a successful actor, the purchase of a single premium annuity with the income from a project that was financially successful can offer freedom from future financial concerns, allowing the actor to pursue his craft without the need to consider whether a particular project will generate a certain level of income.

Another person who can benefit from the purchase of a single premium annuity is a professional sports figure whose playing career will last for only a few years of his working life but will generate large amounts of income in this short time span. The single premium annuity that begins paying benefits when the sports career ends can provide financial security for the person's activities after his competitive years are finished. Yet another individual who might benefit from the purchase of a single premium annuity is a business owner who has just sold a portion or perhaps all of his company. Often, these sales are made due to the owner's desire to retire, and an annuity can provide a retirement income. This can be especially important to a business owner or self-employed person who has not been able to set up a qualified retirement plan during the years spent building his business.

Once a single premium annuity has been purchased, the annuity holder can choose when to begin receiving the benefit payouts from the annuity. If the annuity is an immediate annuity, benefit payments will usually begin within one year of the annuity's purchase. However, if the annuity is a deferred annuity, the annuity holder may delay the receipt of benefits for years or even decades. The length of time for which the receipt of benefits can be delayed will be influenced by the maximum age for benefits to begin, which is contained in the annuity contract itself. See Chapter 3 for a more complete discussion.

A single premium annuity may also be a fixed annuity, an equity-indexed annuity, or a variable annuity. The differences between the fixed and variable annuities are discussed later in this chapter while the "new-kid-on-the-block" equity-indexed annuity is addressed in Chapter 5. For now it is sufficient to say that a fixed annuity pays a set or "fixed" rate of interest over the life of the annuity and also pays a set benefit payout amount once the annuity has passed through its accumulation phase. In contrast, a variable annuity pays a rate of interest that varies based upon the investment results of the underlying investment accounts and also pays a benefit payout amount that can vary from month to month. Falling midway between the fixed annuity and the variable annuity is the equity-indexed annuity which offers a rate of return that is linked to some type of market index.

FLEXIBLE PREMIUM ANNUITIES

In contrast to the single premium annuity discussed above, the flexible premium annuity allows premium payments to be made at varying intervals and in varying amounts, as shown in Figure 4.03. This type of annuity is very useful as a tool for accumulating a sum of money that will provide benefits at some point in the future.

Figure 4.03

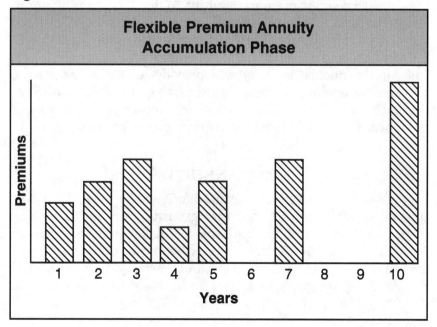

For example, a flexible premium annuity contract might be purchased by Mrs. Jones to plan for her grandson's college education. Since Mrs. Jones wishes to keep control over the funds she will be placing in the annuity, she names herself as the owner and the annuitant of the contract. Over the next fifteen years, she will make a monthly deposit of a set amount into the annuity. Should she choose to do so, the annuity contract offers her the flexibility to make a larger monthly payment every so often. At the end of fifteen years when her grandson is ready to begin college, Mrs. Jones can draw the funds out of the annuity in one of several ways. She could simply surrender the annuity contract completely and pay the college expenses out of the proceeds. (The amount received from the surrender would be partially taxable to Mrs. Jones but would not be subject to the 10% penalty tax on premature distributions because Mrs. Jones would be older than 59½. See Chapter 7.) Alternatively, she could annuitize the contract over a five year period and use the income received each year to meet the college expenses. Should Mrs. Jones' grandson decide not to attend college or be awarded a scholarship, Mrs. Jones can elect to annuitize the contract over her lifetime and use the funds to supplement her retirement income.

As with a single premium annuity, a flexible premium annuity can be a fixed, equity-indexed, or variable annuity. The fixed annuity pays a set rate of interest during the annuity's accumulation phase and a fixed amount of benefits after it is annuitized. The equity-indexed annuity will provide a return based on a market index, while the variable annuity's rate of return will vary depending on the performance of the underlying investment accounts. The benefit payout amounts may vary also.

FIXED ANNUITIES

As mentioned above, the term "fixed" when used to describe a type of annuity refers to the interest rate paid by the issuing insurance company on the funds placed in the annuity. When an individual purchases a fixed annuity he knows what the current and guaranteed interest rates are and, barring the insolvency of the insurance company, he knows that these rates of interest will be credited to the funds in his annuity.

For example, if Ms. Smith purchases a flexible premium fixed deferred annuity that is paying a current interest rate of 7%, Ms. Smith knows, without assuming any of the investment risk herself, that the insurance company will credit interest at a rate of 7% on the funds in her annuity until the date at which the current rate is altered. This will be true whether or not the insurance company earns a sufficient rate of return on its own investments to support the current rate of 7%.

Fixed annuities offer security in that the rate of return is certain. The fixed aspect of the annuity also offers security in that the annuity holder does not take on responsibility for making any decisions about where or in what amount the funds in his annuity should be invested. This is in contrast to the variable annuity, discussed below, in which the annuity holder does take on this type of responsibility.

Another aspect of the fixed annuity that is "fixed" is the amount of the benefit that will be paid out when the contract is annuitized. When Ms. Smith, mentioned above, decides to receive benefit payments from her annuity contract and selects the settlement option she wishes, the amount of the check that she receives from the insurance company will be the same in each month during the annuitization phase. If she chooses a settlement option based on her life expectancy, the same amount will come to her each month for the rest of her life without any investment decisions or risk on her part.

The down side of the fixed aspect is that, over time, such an approach may fall behind the cumulative effects of inflation. The variable annuity, discussed below, offers one possible alternative to this outcome. Another way to guard against the possibility of falling behind inflation is offered by a fairly new type of annuity called the equity-indexed annuity. As its name implies, the equity-indexed annuity, while generally believed not to be a security (unlike the variable annuity, which is a security) provides the holder with a rate of return that is linked to some type of market index. (See Chapter 5 for more information on the equity-indexed annuity.)

EQUITY-INDEXED ANNUITIES

An equity-indexed annuity (EIA) is generally believed to be a fixed deferred annuity that credits earnings based on the movement in an equity index, but guarantees a certain minimum return. In other words, an EIA allows the holder to participate in market index increases without completely giving up the guarantee of principal and a minimum interest rate offered by the more traditional fixed annuity. In very general terms, the EIA allows the holder to participate in stock market gains without assuming the risk of losing money when the market declines. In a financial environment where interest rates on fixed annuities and other financial products such as certificates of deposit are relatively low this ability to share in stock market gains with some limits on potential loss is understandably appealing to prospective annuity buyers.

One of the disadvantages of the EIA is that because of its link to the equity index it is considerably more complex than the "plain vanilla" fixed annuity. Life insurance companies do not all calculate the rate payable on their EIAs in the same manner. In fact, there is quite a bit of difference on this point with various crediting methods that are used such as the high water mark method, the point-to-point method, and the annual reset (or ratchet) method. The methods of crediting market index gains and other features of the EIA are addressed in greater detail in Chapter 5.

VARIABLE ANNUITIES

With a variable annuity the annuity holder receives varying rates of interest on the funds that he places inside the annuity and, depending upon his choice of investment options at the time of annuitization, can receive benefit payments from the annuity that vary in amount from month to month or year to year. In addition, the holder of a variable annuity assumes the risk that is associated with investment decisions that do not turn out as well as the investor hoped that they would.

One major difference between the fixed annuity and the variable annuity is that a variable annuity is considered to be a "security" under federal law and is therefore subject to a greater degree of regulation. Anyone selling a variable annuity must have the required securities licenses. Any potential buyer of a variable annuity must be provided with a prospectus, a detailed document that provides information on the variable annuity and the investment options available. A shorter summary-style document called a profile prospectus has been approved for use with variable annuities. This document, which does not replace the more detailed prospectus, provides summary descriptions of the key features of the variable annuity. Further, with any sale of a variable annuity, the person making the sale must ascertain that the variable annuity is a suitable choice for the individual purchaser.

The following discussion addresses those attributes unique to the variable annuity. However, there are many other attributes that are common to fixed, equity-indexed, and variable annuities. Included in this list of shared characteristics are typical annuity contract charges and fees, methods of interest rate crediting, issue ages, minimum premium payments, settlement options, surrender charges, and annuity contract withdrawals. These common characteristics are covered in Chapter 3.

Assumption of the Investment Risk

This assumption of risk by the holder of the annuity is a key element of the variable annuity; it is the product's most distinguishing characteristic. By way of explanation, consider the risk assumed by Mr. Smith who has just purchased a fixed annuity. The insurance company from which the purchase was made has promised to credit the funds in Mr. Smith's annuity with a current interest rate of 6.5% for the next contract year. After that, the funds will be credited with the new current rate declared by the insurance company unless the current rate is less than the annuity's guaranteed rate of 4.5%. In any event, Mr. Smith will receive at least the guaranteed rate on his funds regardless of how well or how poor the insurance company's investments perform during that time period. In other words, if the investments pay a return that is less than predicted, with a fixed annuity it is the insurance company who must still meet its obligations on the interest rates it has declared on its annuity contracts. It is the insurance company who has assumed the risk that investment returns will be less than expected.

In contrast, with a variable annuity, it is the annuity holder who assumes this risk. To illustrate, assume that Mr. Smith, mentioned above, was concerned that the return on his annuity premium dollars not be out paced by inflation. To combat this possibility, Mr. Smith decided to purchase a variable annuity which offered investment choices of a guaranteed account, a stock fund emphasizing growth potential, a stock fund emphasizing income potential, a money market fund, and a bond fund. With inflation in mind, Mr. Smith allocated 75% of his premiums to the stock fund that emphasizes growth potential and the remaining 25% to the variable annuity's guaranteed fund. On the funds in the guaranteed account, which functions similarly to a fixed annuity, Mr. Smith will receive the current interest rate of 6.5%. On the funds in the stock fund, however, Mr. Smith has no guarantee from the insurance company or any other party that he will receive a certain rate of return. In fact, he has no guarantee from any party that he will not lose part of the premium dollars that he has allocated to the variable investment account.

The Investment Options — The Variable Accounts

A variable annuity typically offers an annuity holder several different variable accounts in which to invest all or a portion of the premiums paid into the annuity. Typically, a variable annuity offers between seven and ten variable accounts. Other names that are sometimes used to describe these variable investment accounts are variable subaccounts, flexible accounts, and flexible subaccounts. While these terms do not share the same precise meaning, they are often used interchangeably.

When an annuity holder purchases a variable annuity he determines which portion of his premium payments, usually on a percentage basis, will be allocated to (or paid into) the different variable accounts. Once this percentage is determined, it remains in effect until the annuity holder notifies the insurance company that he wishes to alter his allocation arrangement. In addition to changing the amount of premium going into a certain variable investment account, most variable annuities allow an annuity holder to transfer funds between accounts, subject to certain dollar amount and timing limitations. Many variable annuities offer an option called "dollar cost averaging" which provides a method for the systematic transfer of dollars from one fund to another inside the variable annuity. (See Chapter 3 for a more complete discussion.) Also, some companies offer "automatic rebalancing" which is another way in which funds are moved between accounts and is discussed later in this chapter.

As illustrated in Figure 4.04, a typical variable annuity might offer the following investment options:

1.   Money Market Fund;

2.   Government Securities Fund;

3.   Bond Fund;

4.   Total Return (or Balanced) Fund;

5.   Growth (or Common Stock) Fund;

6.   Growth with Income (Stock) Fund; and

7.   Guaranteed Account.

Theoretically, an annuity purchaser could choose to allocate one-seventh of his premium dollars to each of these accounts, although, in reality this investment strategy would not be a likely one. Take Mr. Smith, discussed above, who wants to invest his annuity premiums in such a way as to minimize the bite that inflation will take out of his financial capability over a period of years. Mr. Smith would probably be wise to invest a sizable portion of his premium dollars in the Growth Fund with smaller portions going into the Total Return Fund and, perhaps, the Guaranteed Fund. What the actual percentage allocations should be will vary with Mr. Smith's age and tolerance for risk.

Figure 4.04

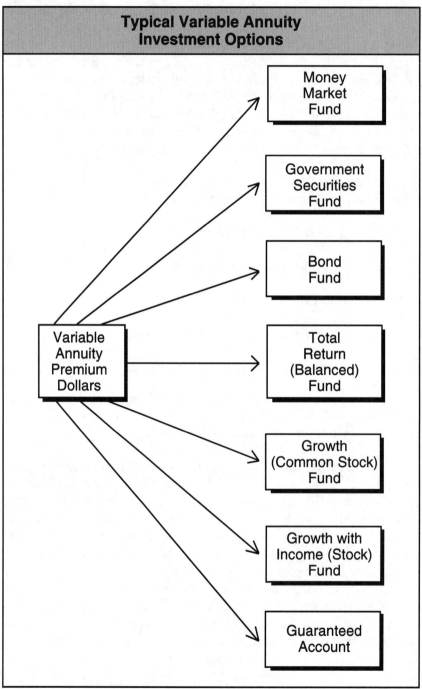

Typical Variable Annuity Investment Options

- Money Market Fund
- Government Securities Fund
- Bond Fund
- Total Return (Balanced) Fund
- Growth (Common Stock) Fund
- Growth with Income (Stock) Fund
- Guaranteed Account

Variable Annuity Premium Dollars

In contrast to Mr. Smith, take the example of Mr. and Mrs. Jones, who will retire in about five years. They have accumulated a sizable amount in a variable annuity that they have owned for a decade. At this point in their lives, preserving the capital they have accumulated is probably of greater importance to them than taking any large degree of risk. Repositioning their funds in the Guaranteed Fund and the Money Market Fund would provide an investment approach that Mr. and Mrs. Jones would feel comfortable with. The variable annuity's ability to offer varying mixes of investment options that are appropriate at different points in the annuity holder's life is one of its most attractive features.

The Investment Options — The Guaranteed Account

As mentioned earlier, most variable annuity contracts offer a guaranteed account as an investment option. Another term often used for the guaranteed account is a fixed account. The account takes its name, whichever one is used, from the fact that the interest rate paid on any funds placed in this type of account by the annuity holder receive a fixed or guaranteed rate of interest. For example, if Mr. Jones places $5,000 in the guaranteed account of his variable annuity when the current interest rate is 7%, Mr. Jones knows that he will be paid 7% on the funds in this account for the current interest rate period.

Although at first the guaranteed account may seem the simplest of the typical variable annuity investment options, it is important to look carefully at the manner in which the guaranteed or fixed interest rate is credited. While all guaranteed accounts pay a fixed rate of interest, not all companies calculate the fixed rate payable in exactly the same manner.

Generally, there are two methods used to determine how the fixed interest rate is paid on a variable annuity's guaranteed account: the portfolio interest rate method and the new money interest rate method. The portfolio rate method pays the same rate of interest on all premiums in the guaranteed account regardless of when the premiums were contributed. When the interest rate changes, all investors with funds in the guaranteed account earn the same rate of interest on all premiums.

In contrast, the new money rate method pays a set interest rate for the same period of time on each premium paid into the guaranteed account. This method is sometimes referred to as the "rate banded" or "guaranteed rate" method. To illustrate, assume that Mr. Edwards pays a monthly premium of $500 into the guaranteed account of his variable annuity. The annuity declares a new current interest rate on the guaranteed account each month and the rate is applicable for a one year period. As shown in Figure 4.05, under the new money rate method, the $500 premium that Mr. Edwards pays on January 1 will earn the 7% current rate of interest from January 1 until December 31 while the $500 premium that he pays on February 1 will earn the 6% rate in effect on February 1 until the following January 31. In other words, under the new money method each "pot" of new money that comes into the guaranteed account will earn the current interest rate for the next year. In theory, after paying monthly premiums for one year, Mr. Edwards could be earning interest at twelve different interest rates at any one time.

In contrast, if Mr. Edwards' variable annuity used the portfolio rate, all premiums in Mr. Edwards' "portfolio" of the guaranteed account would earn the same interest rate at the same time. To continue with the example in Figure 4.05, the $500 premium that Mr. Edwards pays on January 1 would earn interest at the current rate of 7% until the rate changes. If the rate changed to 6% on February 1, the premium paid on February 1 and the premium paid on January 1 would earn the same rate of 6% until the next interest rate change. If the current interest rate changed to 5% on March 1, all $1,500 that Mr. Edwards has in the guaranteed account would earn 5% until the next time the rate was changed.

In looking at Figure 4.05, it becomes obvious that the amount of interest earned under the two methods will vary depending upon the direction in which interest rates move. Generally speaking, the new money or guaranteed interest rate method is more sensitive to the ups and downs of the market overall than is the portfolio method. When interest rates are rising, insurance companies may be willing to credit a higher rate more quickly on only incoming money than on entire portfolios. On the other hand, when interest rates are dropping, insurance companies may be

Figure 4.05

Guaranteed Account Interest Rate New Money Method vs. Portfolio Method				
MONTH	CURRENT INTEREST RATE	PREMIUM PAID	NEW MONEY METHOD	PORTFOLIO METHOD
Jan	7%	$500	$500 @ 7%	$500 @ 7%
Feb	6%	$500	$500 @ 7% $500 @ 6%	$1,000 @ 6%
Mar	5%	$500	$500 @ 7% $500 @ 6% $500 @ 5%	$1,500 @ 5%
Apr	5.5%	$500	$500 @ 7% $500 @ 6% $500 @ 5% $500 @ 5.5%	$2,000 @ 5.5%

more aggressive in lowering rates on new money if they must continue to pay higher rates on money that was recently paid into the annuity. This heightened sensitivity can be a plus when rates are moving up but, of course, tends to be less attractive when rates are falling.

Transfers Among Investment Accounts

As mentioned above, a variable annuity will allow the annuity holder to transfer funds from one investment account to another. This flexibility to reposition investments under the umbrella of the variable annuity offers the annuity holder the opportunity to change his investment focus in response to changes in the market generally or to changes in a specific industry in which he may have invested heavily. It also allows an annuity holder to change the level of risk that he is willing to accept as his tolerance or desire for risk increases or decreases.

For example, an annuity holder who purchases a variable annuity at a young age, say 35, and plans to use the funds for retirement will usually be willing, and financially able, to assume a fair degree of risk and volatility in his rate of return as a trade-off for the potential of significant growth in the value of his annuity. This same annuity holder at age 60 will not be as likely to assume such a high degree of risk, preferring instead a lower risk level and more income-oriented, rather than growth-oriented, investments. The ability to transfer funds from one investment account to another allows this annuity holder to reposition his premium dollars over the years in a manner consistent with his changing investment outlook.

Most variable annuities place some limits on either the number of transfers between accounts or the amount that may be transferred out of or that must remain in a particular account. To illustrate the effect of these restrictions, assume that Mrs. Smith has a variable annuity that currently has $5,000 in the money market account, $3,000 in the stock growth fund and $2,000 in the guaranteed fund. The variable annuity's transfer features might provide Mrs. Smith with the ability to transfer funds at any time during the accumulation phase of the annuity without a fee subject to the requirement that the amount transferred be at least $100. An additional restriction might be that the total amount of all transfers in or out of the guaranteed account during the contract year is limited to the greater of 15% of the guaranteed account balance or $1,000. Thus, if Mrs. Smith wanted to transfer $500 out of the guaranteed account into the stock fund early in the contract year she could do so, as shown in Figure 4.06. However, if she wished to move $1,200 out of the guaranteed account later in the same year, she would not be able to make such a transfer. Under the contract's transfer provision, she would be limited to further transfers out of the guaranteed account of $500 for the remainder of the contract year.

Many times the limits on transfers between investment accounts are different for transfers made during the accumulation phase of the annuity than they are for transfers made while benefits are paid out during the annuitization phase. After benefit payments begin, transfers may not be permitted in or out of the guaranteed account and may only be permitted between the variable investment accounts on certain dates during the year.

Figure 4.06

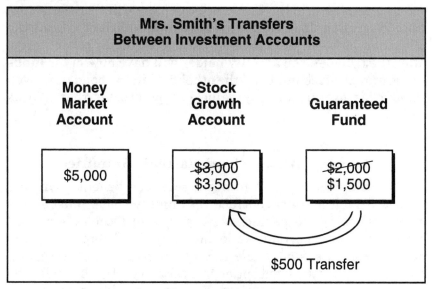

**Mrs. Smith's Transfers
Between Investment Accounts**

Money Market Account	Stock Growth Account	Guaranteed Fund
$5,000	~~$3,000~~ $3,500	~~$2,000~~ $1,500

$500 Transfer

Automatic Rebalancing

Automatic rebalancing is one way that a variable annuity holder can maintain the same distribution of his funds among the various investment options he has selected. Some annuity holders find this feature useful because the allocation of funds in the various investment choices remains the same, on a percentage basis, without any action on their part. The same outcome can be accomplished simply by transferring funds between accounts, as discussed above, but this method requires action on the part of the annuity holder. Under a contract that offers automatic rebalancing the insurance company takes responsibility for transferring funds among accounts so that each account always has the same percentage of the annuity funds invested in it at any time.

For example, assume that an annuity holder allocates 50% of his premiums to a bond fund and 50% to a growth stock fund. If the growth stock fund outperforms the bond fund, after some time has passed, the allocation of funds in the two accounts will no longer be 50/50. It may, for example, have changed from 50/50 to 53/47. The percentages will have changed simply because the funds in the growth stock fund have earned a higher return than the funds in the bond fund. If the annuity holder has selected the automatic rebalancing feature, the insurance company will transfer a sum from the growth stock fund to the bond fund sufficient to bring the allocation between the accounts back to 50/50. In other words, after the transfer, the annuity holder will have 50% of his funds in the growth stock fund and the other 50% in the bond fund even though his overall annuity value is now greater than it was earlier.

Benefit Payments from Variable Annuities

When the time comes to begin receiving benefit payments from a variable annuity contract, the annuity holder must decide what portion of the payments he wishes to receive as a fixed annuity and what portion as a variable annuity. There are usually no requirements, under the annuity contract, that a certain portion be under the fixed option or a certain portion be under the variable option. If he so desires, the annuity holder may receive the full amount of his annuity benefit payout on a fixed basis, on a variable basis, or under some combination of the two options.

Fixed Annuity Benefit Payout

Under the fixed annuity option, the benefits will be calculated and paid to the annuity holder in a manner similar to that used with a fixed annuity. At the time benefit payouts are to commence, all funds in the variable annuity are transferred into the general account of the insurance company and the insurance company agrees to pay an annuity which will not vary in amount from one payment to the next. In other words, if the entire benefit amount will be paid under the fixed annuity option, each check that the annuity holder receives will be for the same amount. If Mr. Jones chooses the fixed annuity option under a life annuity settlement option and his first monthly check is for $467.89, each monthly check that he receives for the remainder of his life will be for $467.89. This will be true whether the insurance company's investment returns are better, or worse, than the company predicts they will be at the time it promises to pay Mr. Jones an annuity of this amount.

Variable Annuity Benefit Payout

In contrast to the fixed annuity option discussed above, an annuity holder who elects to receive all or part of his benefit payouts under the variable option will not receive a check for the same amount each month. Figure 4.07 shows how the annuity payments made to an annuity holder might vary under the variable payment option and how the benefit amount would remain constant under the fixed payment option.

Figure 4.07

DIFFERENT BENEFIT PAYOUTS	
Fixed Annuity Payments	
Month	**Payment Amount**
January	$1,000
February	$1,000
March	$1,000
April	$1,000
May	$1,000
June	$1,000
	$6,000
Variable Annuity Payments	
Month	**Payment Amount**
January	$1,000
February	$ 995
March	$ 982
April	$ 997
May	$1,017
June	$1,024
	$6,015

To understand why and how the benefit payment amount will vary under the variable payout option, it is necessary to understand the concept of "annuity units." An annuity unit is a unit of measure used to determine the value of each income payment made under the variable annuity option. How the value of one unit is calculated is a fairly complex process involving certain assumptions about investment returns. It is probably sufficient to understand that the amount of each month's variable annuity benefit payment is equal to the number of annuity units owned by the annuity holder in each investment account multiplied by the value of one annuity unit for that investment account.

Thus, if Mr. Smith was entitled to a monthly benefit payment based on 100 annuity units each month, the amount of his payment would differ from month to month according to the investment results of the investment account. More specifically, if the dollar value of an annuity unit was $12.10 in the first month, Mr. Smith's benefit payment would equal $1,210 (100 annuity units multiplied by the annuity unit value of $12.10). If the value of one unit rose during the next month to $12.50, Mr. Smith's payment would also increase to $1,250 (100 units multiplied by $12.50). If the next month's investment returns dropped and the annuity unit value was $11.89, Mr. Smith would receive a benefit check for $1,189 (100 units multiplied by $11.89).

Using the variable accounts during the annuitization phase of a variable annuity offers the annuity holder the opportunity for his benefit payment amounts to increase sufficiently so that they keep up with the inflation rate. However, not all annuity holders are comfortable with the variable aspect of their monthly or yearly income from the annuity. To "split the difference" between these approaches, most annuity contracts allow the annuity holder to place a portion of the accumulation value in the guaranteed general account and thus receive a fixed amount benefit payment from these funds and place the remainder of the accumulation value into a separate investment account and receive a variable benefit amount from these funds.

To illustrate, let's take Mr. Jones, age 65, and assume that when he is ready to annuitize his variable annuity contract his total accumulation value is $500,000. He decides that he wants one-half of this amount to provide a fixed annuity. Thus, $250,000 is transferred into the insurance company's general account and, as a result, Mr. Jones will receive a monthly benefit amount of $1,670. Assuming that Mr. Jones elects a life annuity settlement option, this benefit amount will come to him each month for the rest of his life, regardless of the investment returns that the insurance company receives.

The other $250,000 Mr. Jones decides to place in a variable investment account. If at the time of annuitization, the value of one annuity unit in this variable account is $4.75, Mr. Jones will own 352 units (250 multiplied by the per thousand annuity purchase rate in the contract of $6.68 divided by $4.75). His first benefit payment will equal about $1,670. This figure is arrived at by multiplying the annuity unit value of $4.75 by 352, the number of annuity units owned. If the value of the annuity unit changes to $4.82 the next month, Mr. Jones' benefit payment from the variable portion of his annuity will be $1,697 ($4.82 annuity unit value multiplied by 352 annuity units.)

Overall, Mr. Jones' first monthly payment will be $3,340, which is made up of the $1,670 fixed annuity payment plus the $1,670 variable annuity payment. His total monthly benefit for the second month will be $3,367 consisting of the fixed amount of $1,670 and the variable amount of $1,697. If the value of an annuity unit increased again to $4.90, Mr. Jones' monthly variable annuity payment would be $1,724 (352 units multiplied by the annuity unit value of $4.90). His total payments for the third month would be the $1,670 fixed amount plus the $1,724 variable amount for a total of $3,394.

Variable Annuity Death Benefit

Most nonqualified annuity contracts, including variable annuities, provide that if the annuitant dies before the contract has started paying out benefits, a death benefit will be paid to the beneficiary named in the annuity contract. This is not a true "death benefit" as is paid from a life insurance policy at the death of the insured, but it does offer the annuity holder a guarantee that he will not lose all of the funds he has paid into the annuity if he should die before he begins to receive annuity benefit payments.

The exact manner in which the amount of the death benefit is calculated varies from one contract to the next, particularly among variable annuity contracts. One garden-variety method makes the death benefit equal to either the amount of premiums paid or the annuity's account value. (Generally, any surrenders made against the contract are subtracted from this amount when arriving at the death benefit figure.) Another method used to determine the death benefit amount uses three values with the death benefit being equal to the largest value. The three values are the contract value, the premiums paid into the annuity credited with a certain (usually fairly modest) interest rate, and value of the annuity contract on the most recent policy anniversary plus any premiums paid since this date. Many variable annuity contracts use some variation of this method to arrive at a death benefit figure.

With variable annuities, the differences in the calculation of the death benefit amount can be attributed to the insurance companies' attempt to pay the greatest amount feasible even if the annuity holder has lost money as a result of some of his investment option selections. The fact is that the contract value of a variable annuity can actually be less on a given day than the amount of premiums paid into the contract. This is in contrast to the situation with a fixed annuity where the death benefit that will be paid generally will never be less than the amount of premiums (less any surrenders) the annuity holder has paid into the fixed annuity contract. A variable annuity holder may derive some peace of mind from knowing that his beneficiary will receive a death benefit payment that is not calculated solely on the current annuity value of the contract upon the day of his death.

IMMEDIATE ANNUITIES

An immediate annuity begins paying benefits very quickly, usually within one year of the time it is purchased. By its nature, an immediate annuity is almost always purchased with a single premium.

The immediate annuity can be useful for an individual who has received a large sum of money and must count on these funds to pay expenses over a period of time. Examples of this situation include life insurance proceeds and the funds received from the sale of a business or the completion of a large project. Consider the situation of Mrs. Smith, age 62, who has just sold her consulting business for a lump sum payment of $75,000 plus a yearly percentage of the company's income for the next three years. Mrs. Smith was divorced many years ago and will receive a small payment from her ex-husband's pension plan. This payment, in addition to her Social Security benefits, will be her only retirement income because she did not have a retirement plan within her consulting company. Purchasing a single premium immediate annuity with the $75,000 would provide Mrs. Smith with a monthly income that she could not outlive, assuming she elected a settlement option based upon her life expectancy.

DEFERRED ANNUITIES

A deferred annuity is one under which the annuity holder defers or delays the receipt of the benefit payouts until a later date. Most deferred annuity contracts provide a great deal of flexibility concerning the timing of premium payments and benefit payouts.

As mentioned in Chapter 1, a deferred annuity's existence can generally be divided into two parts: the accumulation phase and the annuitization phase. During the accumulation phase the annuity holder makes premium payments into the annuity upon which the issuing insurance company credits some rate of interest. This accumulation phase may last only a few years or it may continue for many years.

When the annuity holder decides to stop paying premiums into the annuity and begin drawing benefit payments out, the annuity moves into the annuitization phase. Depending upon the method of benefit payment selected, this phase could last only a few years (in the case of a short fixed period settlement option) or even beyond the annuitant's lifetime (in the case of an annuitant who dies before the end of the settlement option's guarantee period.) (See Chapter 3 for more on settlement options.)

For example, Mr. Jones might purchase a deferred annuity at the age of 40 with the purpose of accumulating an amount of money over the next 25 years that will be used to supplement his retirement income. As illustrated in Figure 4.08, this plan works well with Mr. Jones making monthly premium payments for five years. At age 45, he decides to start his own consulting service and, in view of his start-up costs and reduced income, makes no premium payments for the next five years. At age 50 Mr. Jones inherits a substantial sum of money from his favorite uncle and decides to add several large premium payments to his existing annuity. At age 55, he decides to annuitize the contract and begin receiving benefits over his lifetime. Although Mr. Jones does not consider himself to be officially retired at age 55, he wants the financial freedom to work fewer hours and have more time to fish.

The annuity that Mr. Jones purchased at age 40 with the original plan of making regular monthly payments for 25 years and then receiving benefits at age 65 was flexible enough to allow premium payments to stop altogether, to resume in a larger amount for a few months, and then to begin paying benefits ten years earlier than planned. Although, the benefit amounts would

Figure 4.08

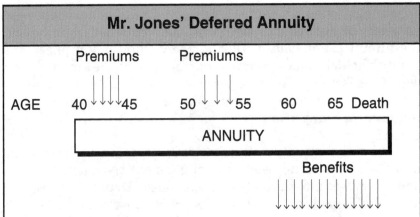

not be the same as projected under Mr. Jones' original plan, the annuity contract provided him with a great deal of flexibility as his plans and lifestyle changed.

CHARITABLE GIFT ANNUITIES

Thus far in this chapter, the types of annuities under discussion have been commercial annuity contracts issued by insurance companies. While these are, by far, the most common types of annuities, there are several other annuity arrangements that function in a similar manner but are used for a specific purpose. One such annuity is the charitable gift annuity. Another annuity of this type is the private annuity, discussed later in this chapter.

In general terms, a charitable gift annuity is an agreement entered into by a charitable institution and an individual who wishes to make a contribution of money or property to the charity. For example, if Mrs. Smith wishes to donate a piece of land to the Childrens Hospital under a charitable gift annuity, she will receive an annuity from the hospital for the remainder of her lifetime in return for her gift of property.

More specifically, a charitable gift annuity agreement is a contractual obligation undertaken by a charity to pay an annuity to an individual in return for an amount of cash or property transferred by the individual. It is possible that the total amount paid by the charity to the individual will exceed the value of the donated property. With this type of annuity, no annuity contract is issued. Rather, the contractual obligation is backed by the charity's assets. For tax reasons, the property that is given to the charity is often property that has appreciated in value during the time it was owned by the individual making the gift.

The tax consequences of a charitable gift annuity are complex. They involve an immediate income tax deduction for the person making the gift. The amount of this deduction may be limited.[1] Also, there is income tax due on a portion of the annuity payments received by the individual. In addition, part of the annuity payments is treated as a recovery of principal which may consist of part taxable gain and part excludable adjusted basis.[2]

A charitable contribution is made in the amount by which the cash or the fair market value of the property transferred to the charity exceeds the value of the annuity that will be paid to the individual making the gift. A uniform annuity rate is applied to the transfer and determines the amount of the annuity to be paid each year. There are certain groups, such as the Committee on Gift Annuities, that make recommendations concerning these uniform annuity rates.

When an individual such as Mrs. Smith receives the annuity payments, a portion of each payment is considered to be a return of principal. This is determined by arriving at an "exclusion ratio" as discussed in Chapter 7. Generally, the exclusion ratio is determined by dividing the investment in the contract by the expected return. The investment in the contract in the charitable annuity situation is the lesser of the present value of the annuity or the fair market value of the property transferred to the charity. In general, the expected return is the annual annuity amount multiplied by the number of years in the life expectancy of the person making the gift at the time the gift is made. (See the Annuity Tables in Appendix A). The portion of each payment in excess of the return of principal element is ordinary income.[3]

It should be noted, however, that if appreciated property has been transferred to the charity, the tax consequences of the charitable gift annuity are even more complex. In that case, the return of principal portion will consist of part taxable gain and part excludable adjusted basis.

For example, assume that Mr. Jones, age 70, owns securities with an adjusted basis of $6,000 and a fair market value of $10,000. On January 1st, he transfers the securities to the Childrens Hospital in exchange for a life annuity. The annuity, according to the uniform annuity rates mentioned above is 7.2% or $720 per year. Thus, in exchange for his gift of securities valued currently at $10,000, Mr. Jones will receive an annuity payment from the hospital of $720 each year for the rest of his life.

Without looking into the complex calculations needed to arrive at this figure, let's assume that the present value of Mr.

Jones' annuity is approximately $6,387. The difference between the $10,000 fair market value of the property and the $6,387 value of the annuity, or $3,613, is the charitable contribution portion of the transfer.

Of each $720 annuity payment, a portion will be considered a return of principal, a portion will be considered a capital gain, and the balance will be considered ordinary income.

PRIVATE ANNUITIES

Unlike the commercial annuity contracts sold by insurance companies, a "private" annuity is an arrangement between two individuals that does not involve the purchase of an annuity from an insurance company or any other institution. Rather, one individual transfers property to another individual in return for a promise that the person receiving the property will pay an annuity for life to the person making the transfer.

Often, the private annuity is used by members of the same family to transfer a full or partial interest in a business or piece of real estate. For example, Mr. Smith, a widower, owns the family farm estimated to be worth $2,000,000. He wishes for his daughter and son-in-law to own the farm because he has no other children and they are already managing the farm for him. He does not want to wait until his death to make the transfer, largely because of certain estate tax considerations. He would be willing to sell the farm to his daughter but, as both she and her husband work on the farm and have no significant savings, they could not pay the purchase price without taking on a significant mortgage. Mr. Smith could simply make a gift of the farm but this presents two problems. First, a sizable gift tax will be due and, second, because the farm is Mr. Smith's only asset and he has no retirement plan income (other than Social Security), he would be left without any assets or sufficient income to support himself if he gives the farm away.

By entering into a private annuity, Mr. Smith could transfer the farm prior to his death and receive an income for life in return. Ownership of the farm would be transferred to his daughter and son-in-law. In return for the transfer of the farm, Mr. Smith's daughter and son-in-law would agree to pay Mr. Smith an annuity of a certain amount for the remainder of his lifetime. This promise to pay is not and, indeed cannot, be secured by the farm or any other asset for tax reasons.

The basic rules for taxing the payments received by Mr. Smith, the annuitant, under a private annuity state that the payments must be divided into three elements. The first is a "recovery of basis" element. The second is a "gain element" which is eligible for capital gain treatment for the annuitant's life expectancy, but taxable as ordinary income afterwards. The third is an "annuity element" which is taxable as ordinary income.[4]

The portion of each payment that is to be excluded from gross income as a recovery of basis (the first element above) is determined by applying an exclusion ratio which is calculated by dividing the investment in the contract by the expected return under the contract. With a private annuity the investment in the contract is generally equal to the adjusted basis of the property transferred.[5]

From the tax perspective of Mr. Smith's daughter and son-in-law, the annuity payments made by them are treated as capital expenditures for the purchase of the property. No interest deduction is allowed with respect to the payments.[6] However, depreciation deductions may be taken if the property transferred is depreciable.[7]

From an estate tax viewpoint, in the usual private annuity transaction the annuitant's transfer of the property given in exchange for the annuity is complete and absolute. Since the annuity payments cease at the death of the person receiving them there is nothing to be taxed in the estate. Under such circumstances, no part of the transferred property is includable in the annuitant's estate for estate tax purposes.[8]

From a gift tax perspective there is no gift if the purchase of the private annuity is a bona fide ordinary business transaction.[9] However, where closely related parties are involved, a gift may be considered to have been made in certain circumstances.[10] But even in a transaction involving family members, if generally equal values are exchanged and there is no intent to make a gift, there will be no gift.[11]

ENDNOTES

1. IRC Sec. 170.
2. Treas. Reg. §1.1011-2(c), Ex.8.
3. IRC Sec. 72(b)(2).
4. Rev. Rul. 69-74, 1969-1 CB 43.
5. *LaFargue v. Comm.*, 86-2 USTC ¶9715 (9th Cir. 1986), *aff'g* TC Memo 1985-90; *Benson v. Comm.*, 80 TC 789 (1983).
6. *Garvey, Inc. v. U.S.*, 83-1 USTC ¶9163 (U.S. Cl. Ct. 1983), *aff'd* 84-1 USTC ¶9214 (Fed Cir. 1984), *cert. den.* 469 U.S. 823 (1984); *Bell v. Comm.*, 76 TC 232 (1981).
7. Rev. Rul. 55-119, 1955-1 CB 352.
8. See, generally, IRC Section 2033.
9. Rev. Rul. 69-74, 1969-1 CB 43; Treas. Regs. §§25.2511-1(g)(1), 25.2512-8.
10. *Est. of Bell v. Comm.*, 60 TC 469 (1973); *Fehrs v. U.S.*, 79-2 USTC ¶13,324 (Ct. Cl. 1979); *LaFargue v. Comm.*, 86-2 USTC ¶9715 (9th Cir. 1986), *aff'g* TC Memo 1985-90.
11. *Ellis Sarasota Bank & Trust Co. v. U.S.*, 77-2 USTC ¶13,204 (M.D. Fla. 1977). See also Rev. Rul. 76-491, 1976-2 CB 301.

Chapter 5

THE NEWEST ANNUITY –
THE EQUITY-INDEXED ANNUITY

A new type of nonqualified annuity has been developed by several life insurance companies and made available for sale to the public. This new kid on the block is generally referred to as an "equity-indexed annuity," or "EIA" although, as with other products, each company generally has its own specific name for its contract. One survey of insurance companies showed that at the end of 2001, 37 insurance companies were selling EIAs.[1]

This annuity is called "equity-indexed" because the amount of interest that a holder earns on an equity-indexed annuity is linked to changes in some type of stock index. There is no requirement that a life insurance company designate any specific index but a commonly used index seems to be the Standard & Poor's 500 (S&P 500). In addition to the index linking, most EIAs offer some minimum interest rate guarantees to the annuity holder. Thus, it is generally said that an EIA provides the ability to participate in stock market gains without completely giving up the guarantee of principal and a minimum interest rate similar to that offered by the more traditional fixed annuity.

In a financial environment where interest rates on fixed annuities and other financial products such as certificates of deposit are relatively low, this ability to share in stock market gains with some limits on potential loss is understandably appealing to prospective annuity buyers. Despite the fact that EIAs have been available for only a few years, it has been estimated that 2000 EIA sales totaled about $5.4 billion and that sales of EIAs for 2001 reached $6.4 billion.[2]

INTRODUCTION — WHAT IS AN
EQUITY-INDEXED ANNUITY?

An equity-indexed annuity or EIA, as mentioned above, generally offers the ability to participate in the gains associated with a rising stock market while, at the same time, offers some minimum guarantees that essentially keep the EIA holder from losing money when the stock market declines. In other words, an EIA guarantees a certain level of interest earnings but credits excess earnings based on movement in a particular equity index. An EIA resembles a variable annuity in that the EIA allows a holder to take advantage of stock market gains but it also is somewhat similar to a traditional fixed annuity in that an EIA offers a minimum interest rate guarantee.

The fact that the EIA combines features of the variable annuity and the traditional fixed annuity has led some in the industry to describe the EIA as a "blended" or "in between" type of annuity product. In other words, in terms of the amount of investment risk taken and the guarantees provided, the EIA falls somewhere between the variable annuity, in which the purchaser assumes the full investment risk and is given no guarantee on his investment, and the traditional fixed annuity, in which the purchaser receives a guaranteed rate of return on his funds and does not assume any investment risk. See Figure 5.01.

Although there is some disagreement within the industry on this point, an EIA is generally believed to be a fixed deferred annuity as opposed to some type of securities product. As discussed later in this chapter, this distinction is important because it affects the types of sales materials and licenses required to sell the product.

ADVANTAGES AND DISADVANTAGES

As mentioned earlier, the EIA is a relatively new product. The idea of linking an annuity to the performance of a stock market index was just being considered and talked about as recently as 1994 when the first edition of this book was published. And, as with any new idea, there are those very much in favor of the

Figure 5.01

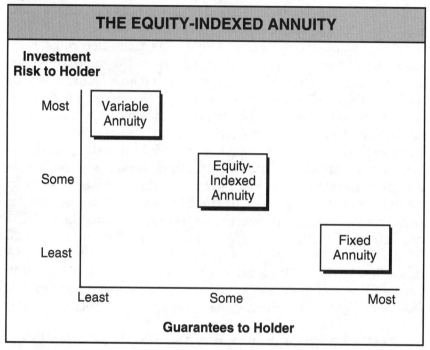

THE EQUITY-INDEXED ANNUITY

Investment
Risk to Holder

Most — Variable Annuity

Some — Equity-Indexed Annuity

Least — Fixed Annuity

Least   Some   Most

Guarantees to Holder

product and there are others who point out several disadvantages of the EIA.

One of the primary advantages of the EIA is that it allows a purchaser to participate in stock market index increases without completely giving up the principal and minimum interest rate guarantees available with the traditional fixed annuities. In very general terms, this means that an EIA holder will make money when the market rises but will not lose money when the market falls. To individuals planning for retirement the EIA offers the ability to earn a return that will keep pace with inflation without the necessity of risking the loss of the funds they have already saved. In an economic landscape where fixed annuities and certificates of deposit are paying fairly low interest rates, the ability to share in stock market gains with some limits on potential losses offered by the EIA looks attractive to many.

However, the EIA is not a product for everyone. Many in the industry agree that the primary disadvantage of the EIA is its complexity. An individual contemplating the purchase of EIA must become familiar with a number of concepts that do not come into play with a traditional fixed rate annuity. Included in this list of "EIA-specific" concepts are indexing, participation rates, vesting schedules, policy terms, and certain types of surrender charges. This means, of course, that an agent selling an EIA must also be well-versed in these concepts and be able to explain what can be fairly involved concepts to potential purchasers. This necessity of explaining the concept of market indexing has led to some controversy in the industry over whether an individual selling an EIA is actually selling a fixed annuity and, thus, needs only the license for fixed annuity products or whether, in fact, the EIA is actually a type of securities product. If the EIA is considered a security, then many other requirements must be met including the fact that an individual selling an EIA would be subject to additional licensing requirements. In fact, concern over whether the EIA more closely resembles a security product than a fixed annuity product has prompted some state insurance departments to look closely at the product during the state approval process.

Another possible drawback to the EIA, in addition to the product's complexity, is the difficulty in comparing one EIA to another. While it is fairly easy to make a simple comparison of one traditional fixed annuity to another by looking at the interest rates of the two contracts, (although this basic approach does not always give the full picture), it is much harder to compare one EIA to another. Simply comparing one number from each contract, such as the participation rate, will not give an accurate picture of the two contracts involved. Thus, if the two contracts each use a different indexing method comparing the participation rate will not provide any useful information because, in all likelihood, the participation rate is being applied to a different amount under one contract than under the other. For example, an EIA using the high water mark indexing method and offering a 75% participation rate may, at first glance, appear less attractive than an EIA using a point-to-point indexing method with a 100% participation rate. In actuality, which EIA will provide a better return depends on many variables. It is entirely possible that, over a given period of time, the EIA with the 75% participation rate will provide greater gains than the contract with the 100% participation rate.

Another potential disadvantage to an EIA may come to light if a purchaser finds that he or she needs to surrender the contract before the end of the contract term. In this case, depending on the provisions of the specific EIA, it may be both difficult and costly to take funds out of the EIA due to the potential application of vesting schedule percentages, company surrender charges, and the premature distribution penalty tax. However, many EIAs offer "free" withdrawal type provisions which allow a contract holder to withdraw some funds from the contract without these charges. (See the discussion of these topics under the heading of Typical EIA Contract Features, below.)

Finally, unlike a variable annuity which is segregated into an account separate from the insurance company's general assets, EIAs are typically considered to be obligations of the insurance company's general account. This may cause concern for some.

HOW DOES THE INDEXING WORK?

Before explaining what indexing is, it is important to take note of what indexing is not. An individual who purchases an equity-indexed annuity is not investing directly in the stocks that make up the index applicable to the annuity, nor is this individual purchaser investing in the index itself. The individual is investing in the annuity, the return on which is linked to the growth in the applicable index.

As mentioned earlier, the index most commonly used with equity-indexed annuities seems to be the Standard & Poor's 500, generally referred to as the S&P 500. The S&P 500 index is a stock market index that is generally recognized as the index that most closely mirrors the stock market's performance. In other words, the S&P 500 measures the changes in the stock market. Thus, it functions as a measuring device for the equity-indexed annuity, giving the issuing insurance company a way in which to calculate what the market has done. Most equity-indexed products that make use of the S&P 500 index use the version of this index that does not include dividends.

Although the S&P 500 seems to be the index most often used, there is no particular requirement that an insurance company use this index, or any other index, with its equity-indexed products. If fact, some of the new equity-indexed products are beginning to offer the purchaser a choice among several indexes. Along the same lines, although most products seem to use an equity index there are a few products linked to some other type of index. One product, for example, has tied its returns to an interest index rather than an equity index.

The insurance company issuing an EIA invests the premiums received from these contracts in a slightly different manner than it does for the traditional fixed annuity. Basically, the insurance company invests most of the premium paid into the EIA in long-term bonds and other fairly conservative investments in much the same manner that traditional fixed annuity premiums are invested. However, with an EIA the insurance company keeps a small portion of the premium out of the usual bond investment and uses this amount to purchase call options on the index to which the EIA is linked. Thus, if the market goes down over the EIA's policy term the insurance company's call options will not be of much value but the company has the bond investments from which it has earned sufficient income to credit the EIA with the guaranteed minimum interest rate. If the market goes up over the EIA's policy term the insurance company sells the call options and credits the growth to the EIA.

There are several different indexing methods that insurance companies use with equity-indexed annuities. This means, generally, that even if two equity-indexed annuities are linked to the same index, the returns on the two annuities will not necessarily be the same. As mentioned earlier in this chapter, this variety of indexing methods and the complexity of at least some of the methods is one of the potential drawbacks to the equity-indexed annuity product.

There are a number of indexing methods, some with unique names, used by insurance companies. Included in this list are the high water mark method, the point-to-point method, the annual reset (or ratchet) method, the Asian-end call method, the European method, the Asian method, the cliquet method, and the capped cliquet method.[3] Some of these methods are similar to others while some vary significantly. This chapter will discuss three of these methods in an effort to give an overview of the possible ways in which indexing methods work. It is extremely important for an individual who is selling or considering purchasing an EIA to understand how the indexing method in the specific annuity operates.

The high water mark method, which is sometimes referred to as the high water look back method, uses a fixed starting point for calculating the value of the index. It does not, as some of the other indexing methods do, reset the starting point of the index calculation each year or several times during the contract term. Thus, the EIA holder with a product using this indexing method will only receive positive interest appreciation when the index level is above the level of the index at the starting point. In other words, an EIA using the high water mark indexing method should perform well when the stock market is in a period where returns are moving continuously upward.

In very general terms, an EIA using the high water mark method sets an index figure as a starting point when the annuity is purchased. At subsequent check points, the current index figure is noted. At these points, the insurance company "looks back" over the contract term and credits interest to the EIA if the index figures have resulted in a new high water mark being reached. In effect, the company is selecting the index figure reached by the EIA at either a single (or numerous, depending on the EIA's design) "high water mark" during that contract term. The company then credits the EIA with a rate based on the difference between the EIA's starting index figure and its high water mark figure. If the starting point index figure is never exceeded during the contract term, the EIA's minimum guaranteed interest rate comes into play.

To illustrate, consider the following example. Assume that Mrs. Smith purchases a single premium EIA with an index starting value of 400 and a participation rate of 95%. The index figures during the five year contract term are:

YEAR 1	YEAR 2	YEAR 3	YEAR 4	YEAR 5
425	415	475	465	495

At the end of the first year a new high water mark of 425 is encountered. It is a new high water mark because the 425 index figure is greater than the starting point index figure of 400. Thus, at the end of year one, the EIA is credited with interest equal to the participation rate of 95% multiplied by the increase in the index. Since an increase of 400 to 425 is a 6.25% increase (425 minus 400 divided by 400), the 6.25% increase is multiplied by 95% and the resulting rate of 5.94% is credited to the EIA.

At the end of the second year, the current index figure is 415. Since this figure is not higher than the current high water mark of 425, no interest is credited to Mrs. Smith's EIA at the end of the second year. However, at the end of the third year, a new high water mark of 475 is reached. Thus, the rate credited at this point is equal to the participation rate of 95% multiplied by the increase in the index of 11.76% (475 minus 425 divided by 425) to reach a result of 11.17%.

As was the case at the end of the second year, at the end of the fourth year the index figure of 465 is lower than the EIA's current high water mark figure of 475. Therefore, at the end of year four no interest is credited. At the end of the fifth year, Mrs. Smith's EIA reaches a new high water mark of 495. The interest credited at this point is 4.00% which is equal to the participation rate of 95% multiplied by the 4.21% increase in the index (495 minus 475 divided by 475).

A second type of indexing method is the annual point-to-point method which calculates the interest return every contract year and then, ultimately, combines these returns to arrive at the total return for the contract term. In other words, this method resets the starting point for the calculation each year on the contract anniversary and thus permits an owner to take advantage of a market recovery after a year of market loss or correction.

From a liquidity viewpoint this method may not be the best choice because under at least some contracts if a withdrawal is made during the policy term the amount is deducted from the principal and then is completely excluded from the crediting of any gain. Unlike the high water mark method discussed above, the annual point-to-point method should perform well in a market which is both rising and falling during the contract term.

Yet another indexing method, sometimes referred to as the daily average method, takes the average of the daily closing market levels for the entire contract year to determine the index level at the end of the contract term. In other words, this method "resets" the starting point for the calculation each year on the contract anniversary. One advantage of this averaging type of method is that it should provide a more consistent return throughout the year as it is not so heavily dependent upon the index figure on a contract anniversary date. It is true that if the market finishes strong near a contract anniversary, the anniversary day closing level will most likely be higher than the daily average level for the year. However, if the market declines or has a correction near a contract anniversary, the daily average level for the year may, in fact, be higher than the closing market level on the anniversary day.

As mentioned earlier, there are other indexing methods used by companies that are, essentially, variations on these general themes. For example, one type of indexing method takes the average value of the index as compared to the initial value[4] while another variation measures index growth from the first day to the last day of the period. Yet another method measures growth from the first day to an average of the final three to six months.[5]

TYPICAL EIA CONTRACT FEATURES

Cap Rate

Along with the participation rate and vesting schedules, the cap rate operates to limit the amount of growth in the applicable market index that will be credited to an EIA. Some, but not all, EIA contracts impose an upper limit or "cap" on the amount of growth that can be passed on to the EIA holder. The cap rate is generally expressed as a percentage. For example, an EIA with a participation rate of 100% (see the discussion of participation rate below) might provide that only 12% of the gain in the index will be passed on to the EIA holder. Thus, the cap rate operates to limit the contract holder's return.

Another example of the use of a cap rate is an EIA that provides that the contract will be credited with 75% of the S&P 500 index each year as measured on the policy anniversary but not to exceed 12%. Since the contract holder is entitled to "participate" in the market gains up to 75% of the increase in the index, the 75% figure is the participation rate. However, the 12% cap rate operates to limit the amount of the index gain credited to the EIA.

Death Benefit

Like other nonqualified annuities, most EIAs pay a death benefit to the beneficiary named in the contract if the contract owner dies before the contract enters the benefit paying phase. See Chapter 4 for more on annuity death benefits.

How the exact amount of the death benefit payment is arrived at differs from one contract to the next, although with the EIA the calculation is apt to be more complex than with a traditional fixed annuity. A typical method of arriving at the death benefit payable under an EIA is for the death benefit to be equal to the greater of the guaranteed minimum surrender value or the indexed account value.

Fees and Expenses

Some EIAs do not impose separate fees. Rather, the life insurance company issuing the contract sets the participation rate and other policy provisions at such a level that the company earns a sufficient return from the "spread" between what it earns on its investments and what it credits to the EIA contracts to pay the company's administrative and other costs. This approach is similar to the one used with traditional fixed annuities. See Chapter 3.

However, some EIAs do assess specific fees such as an annual fee charge charged against the account value. This charge usually does not exceed 1% and is more likely to be about 0.5%. This method of imposing specific fees more closely resembles the approach typically used with variable annuities. See Chapter 3.

Indexing Methods

As discussed earlier in this chapter there are different methods of calculating the amount of interest to be credited based on the change in the applicable index. Some of the more commonly used methods are the Asian method, the high water mark method, the point-to-point method, and the annual reset or ratchet method.

Which indexing method a particular EIA uses can make a significant difference in the overall return that the contract holder will earn. Some methods give better results in rising markets while others produce a more attractive return when the market moves up and down.

Maximum Issue Ages

Life insurance companies typically decline to issue an annuity contract for individuals who have lived past a certain, or maximum, age. For EIAs a common maximum issue age is 75, although some companies will issue an EIA to individuals older than this. See Chapter 3.

Minimum Guaranteed Interest Rate

Almost all EIA contracts provide a minimum guaranteed interest rate typically equal to 3% per year credited to a minimum of 90% of the initial premium. This minimum guaranteed rate is paid, generally, when the applicable market index does not increase over the measurement period. Although, it should be noted that when and how the minimum guaranteed interest is paid varies depending upon the type of indexing method used by an EIA.

The fact that this minimum guaranteed interest rate exists is what allows the EIA to be considered, at least by many in the industry, to be a fixed annuity as opposed to a security product. It is also the contract provision that allows the EIA holder to not be exposed to the potential of losing principal if the market does not perform as anticipated.

Minimum Premiums

The first EIAs to come on the market tended to be single premium products. Now, many companies offer EIAs that accept continuous premiums. Like most nonqualified annuity contracts, the EIA typically requires an initial premium of at least a certain amount. With the EIA, a $5,000 minimum initial premium requirement seems to be common although some companies require an even higher minimum amount. See Chapter 3 for more on typical annuity contract premium requirements. Some companies set a maximum limit on single premiums. While the company may ultimately decide to accept a single premium above this limit, it generally requires some type of additional approval.

Partial Withdrawal Provisions

Withdrawing funds from an EIA, other than at the end of a contract term, can be a fairly complicated and costly undertaking. Many companies permit a withdrawal "window" of between 30 to 45 days after one term ends but before a new term begins. During this window, withdrawals can be made from the EIA without being subject to the contract's surrender charge.

Another provision found in many EIAs allows the contract holder to withdraw up to a certain amount each year without surrender charges applying. The amount available is usually stated as a percentage of the contract's value. (Exactly which value—such as a guaranteed minimum value, an indexed value, or a premium value—varies from one contract to the next.) A fairly typical provision of this type would allow a contract holder to withdraw up to 10% of the contract's accumulated value each year without paying surrender charges. Often, there are limits as to the overall amount that can be surrendered in this manner. For example, a contract may allow 10% to be surrendered each year but subject to a limit of 50% of all premium payments during the policy's first contract term. Also, a minimum amount, such as $500, may be required for any partial surrender.

Withdrawals in excess of the amounts allowed by these types of withdrawal windows and "free withdrawal" percentage provisions are generally subject to a surrender charge imposed by the company as part of the EIA contract. See the discussion under Surrender Charges below. Further, any withdrawals made prematurely from an annuity contract that do not qualify under one of several exceptions may be subject to a 10% penalty tax imposed by the Internal Revenue Code.[6] See Chapter 7 for more on this penalty tax.

It should be noted that there are some EIAs that do not provide any type of surrender-charge-free or penalty-free liquidity feature. These contracts often trade off this lack of liquidity in the design of the product against a higher rate of return or lack of caps on the participation rate. While this type of product design might work well for some, any potential buyer of this type of EIA should definitely be aware of this feature before making a purchase.

Participation Rate

The participation rate in an EIA is the amount or percentage of the growth or gain in the market index that will be paid on the funds placed in the EIA. It is set by the insurance company and stated in the EIA contract. Generally speaking, participation rates range from 60% to 110%. The newer product designs show a reluctance to use a participation rate of less than 100% largely because of a perception on the part of consumers that there is no good reason why they should not be credited with all of the gain in the market index.

It is important to note the relationship between a contract's participation rate and its cap rate, as discussed earlier in this section. Some EIA contracts offer a 100% participation rate but then impose a cap or upper limit on the amount of gain that will be passed on to the contract owner. For example, a contract may state that only 12% of the gain in the applicable market index will be passed on to the contract holder even if the index gain exceeds this amount. If there is such a cap in a contract, the fact that the participation rate is 100% or even 110% simply will not be a factor if the market does well.

Some EIA contracts offer the holder a choice of the term of years (as discussed below) with a different participation rate for each term of years. For example, if the contract holder selects a six year term, the participation rate might be 75% but if the contract holder selects a ten year term the participation rate might be 85%.

It is important to note that while most EIA contracts seem to guarantee the initial participation rate for the full length of the first contract term, many reserve the right to set a new participation rate for subsequent terms should the contract holder elect to enter into a second or later contract term. Other companies do guarantee the participation rate but for a shorter period than the full contract term. A contract of this type might offer a 100% participation rate but guarantee that this rate will be in effect for only a one year period. Of course, at the end of the year the company may set the new participation rate at 100% also, but, then again, it may not.

Policy Loans

Like other nonqualified annuities, most EIAs do not permit a contract holder to take a loan against the value of the contract. One of the major reasons for this is that the income tax consequences of taking a loan are not particularly attractive. Generally, any amount received as a loan or the value of any part of an annuity contract pledged or assigned under an annuity contract is taxable.[7] Annuity contracts, EIA and otherwise, used as part of a qualified retirement plan, an IRA, or a TSA, are generally subject to a different set of rules regarding loans.

Policy Term

The policy term is the period of time over which the growth in the applicable market index is measured. It is also called the "contract term," the "annuity term," or the "term of years." Early

EIA products offered policy terms from five to seven years but later contracts offer longer periods such as ten years. Many EIAs allow the purchaser to select the policy term for the EIA.

The policy term is an important concept for any potential purchaser of an EIA to understand because once the term is selected and the EIA entered into, it may be difficult and costly for the purchaser to access these funds during the policy term. (See the discussion under the headings of Partial Withdrawal Provisions and Surrender Provisions in this chapter.) With some contracts if the contract owner surrenders the contract before the end of the full policy term he will not receive the benefit of any market gain that has occurred since the EIA was purchased. Further, with a surrender of the contract before the end of the policy term there are various surrender charges, vesting schedule percentages, and income tax penalties that may apply. It is extremely important for anyone selling an EIA to review how this feature works for each contract and advise his or her clients of what will happen if they need to get out of the contract before the policy term is at an end.

At the end of the policy term the EIA owner usually has several options open to him. First, he can choose to renew the EIA for another term of either the same number of years as the previous term or, possibly, for a term of a different length. Second, the EIA owner can typically elect to exchange the EIA for another type of annuity such as a traditional fixed annuity or a variable annuity. Such an exchange is generally accomplished under Section 1035 of the Internal Revenue Code and results in no current income taxation to the contract holder.[8]

Of course, the contract owner can elect to surrender the contract completely with the attendant income tax consequences (see Chapter 7) or he can elect to annuitize the contract and begin receiving benefit payments under one of the available settlement options (see Chapter 3).

Most EIA contracts provide for an automatic or default type election if the contract holder does not notify the company of his or her decision within a certain number of days after the end of the policy term. Typically, the company will renew the EIA for another term of the same number of years in this situation.

Settlement Options

EIAs offer the contract holder settlement options much like those offered under other nonqualified annuity contracts. Settlement options are the methods by which the annuity owner can select to receive payments of benefits under the annuity contract. They are sometimes called payout options or benefit options. See Chapter 3 for more information.

Surrender Charges

Like most other types of annuity contracts, a typical EIA contract imposes a "charge" against partial and full surrenders from the contract for a certain period of years. This surrender charge is intended to make it less attractive for annuity owners to move funds in and out of the annuity and to allow the insurance company to recover its costs if the contract does not remain in force over the long run.

Surrender charges in EIA contracts may be a set percent for each year during the policy term or they may be imposed according to a decreasing schedule that more closely resembles the traditional fixed annuity. For example, an EIA with a seven year term may impose an 8% surrender charge during each year of the seven year term and, often, if the contract holder renews for a second term the 8% surrender charge will be applicable to any surrenders made during the second (and subsequent) terms also. Another EIA might impose a surrender charge equal to 8% in the first year of the contract term, 7% in the second year, 6% in third year and so on until the end of the term. This decreasing type of surrender charge often begins all over again if the contract holder renews for another term.

It is important to consider several provisions in connection with surrender charges that apply to EIAs but do not necessarily come into play with other types of annuities. First, surrenders over a certain amount from an EIA may be subject to vesting schedule percentages that will decrease the amount of the surrender that is ultimately available to the contract holder (see the discussion under the head of Vesting Schedules in this section). Second, because the surrender charge schedule often begins anew with a second (and subsequent) term, the contract holder may never reach a point where there is no surrender charge applicable on the contract as is usually possible with traditional and variable types of contracts. Finally, the surrender charge on an EIA may apply even upon annuitization if the contract holder makes the election to begin receiving benefit payments during a policy term.

Surrender Provisions

The early surrender, or the surrender of the EIA before the policy term is up, is treated differently under the various EIA contracts. Some EIAs return only the guaranteed minimum, not allowing the contract holder to participate in any equity or market index increases until the end of the policy term. Other EIAs use a gradual scale which allows a contract holder to move to a higher level of equity participation over time. Still other EIAs allow the policyholder to participate in the market index growth up to the date of surrender. However, it should be noted that, apparently, there are some EIA contracts that do not permit a complete contract surrender until the end of the policy period, although such EIAs may allow less-than-complete surrenders to be made during the policy term.

Vesting Schedules

Some EIAs have a vesting schedule which, in very general terms, sets forth the amount of the annuity value in which the policyholder is vested for purposes of making withdrawals from the contract. Typically, the schedule starts at 0% during the first year and then increases each year until it approaches 100% at the end of the policy term. Although called by the same name, this type of vesting schedule used in an EIA is not the same kind of a vesting schedule associated with a qualified retirement plan.

To illustrate, assume that under an EIA vesting schedule a contract holder is 70% vested in the fifth year of a seven year term.

If the contract holder wishes to make a gross withdrawal from the policy in the fifth year of $10,000 the company divides the $10,000 by the vesting percentage of 70% to get $14,286. Thus, the contract holder's account balance is actually reduced by $14,286 but the contract holder receives only $10,000. Although this example greatly oversimplifies the application of a vesting schedule to amounts withdrawn from an EIA, it serves to illustrate the point that getting funds out of an EIA at any time other than at the end of the contract term can be difficult and costly.

Any individual contemplating the purchase of an EIA should be as sure as possible that the funds will not be needed during the EIA's contract term. On the other hand, many EIAs do have provisions that allow withdrawals up to a certain amount each year to be made without application of the vesting schedule or surrender charges. (See the discussion under the heading of Partial Withdrawal Provisions in this section.)

HOW IS AN EIA USED?

As mentioned earlier, a typical EIA buyer is someone who does not want to put money in a product where there is a risk of loss yet wants to find a way to take advantage of the potential gains to be made in the stock market. An individual who is new to the ways of the stock market will likely be interested in an EIA. And, the EIA may look quite attractive to the growing group of individuals who have concluded that it is necessary for them to take personal responsibility for their retirement planning. It seems that the EIA is particularly well-suited to individuals who have started planning for retirement but will not be ready to retire for some years. Individuals in their late 40s, 50s and early 60s fall into this category.

EIA contracts that accept on-going premium payments may be more useful for retirement planning than the single premium variety first introduced to the market. However, even the single premium contracts have their retirement-oriented uses. An individual may choose to move funds from a certificate of deposit (CD) into an EIA when the CD matures in hopes of benefiting from future market increases without taking the risk of losing principal. Or, any other time an individual comes into a lump sum of money, placing the funds in an EIA for retirement planning purposes could be considered. For example, a business owner who sells his business and then chooses to go to work for the new owner might place all or a portion of the business sales price in an EIA to be used when he or she decides to retire. As a second example, consider the parents who find that a sum of money originally saved for college expenses has been freed up for their retirement use when one of their children attends college on a scholarship. An EIA might be an attractive product for individuals in these situations.

It seems important to note that when using an EIA for retirement planning there is at least one product feature that will require some additional attention on the part of the annuity holder. The EIA holder will want to make sure than he or she does not miss the window period at the end of policy term. It is at this point that a decision to annuitize the contract or to exchange the EIA for another type of annuity must be made. If this window period is allowed to expire before a decision is made, the EIA holder may find that, under the terms of the EIA contract, the EIA has been automatically renewed for another term. This renewal, in turn, could result in the individual's funds becoming locked into another contact term for five to ten years with access to the funds being fairly limited without paying surrender charges or encountering vesting schedule percentages. An individual coming to the end of an EIA contract term who plans to retire relatively soon can usually exchange the EIA for either a traditional fixed annuity or a variable annuity. Since these two types of annuities do not have a contract term, they may offer greater flexibility to an individual about to retire.

In considering the retirement planning uses of the EIA it should be remembered than many EIA contracts can be used as Individual Retirement Arrangements (IRAs) and Tax Sheltered Annuities (TSAs), although these types of retirement plans have completely different rules concerning many provisions including contribution limits, loans, and distribution requirements. See Chapter 6.

Generally, an EIA can be used for many of the same purposes for which traditional fixed annuities and variable annuities are suited. Included in this list are college funding, charitable giving, and other purposes for which funds accumulated on a tax deferred basis are useful (see Chapter 6). However, the complexity of the EIA, its relative lack of liquidity during a policy term and the necessity to make renewal decisions at the end of a policy term lead to the conclusion that retirement planning is probably the best use of the EIA.

WHO CAN SELL EIAs?

Currently, the opinion of many in the insurance industry is that an EIA is a traditional fixed annuity and not a security that must be registered with the Securities and Exchange Commission (SEC). The distinction is an important one that significantly affects not only who can sell the product but the manner in which it may be sold. While it seems that most EIAs available currently are sold as fixed annuities, there are several companies who have registered their EIA products.

If the EIA is considered a traditional fixed annuity, the only license required to sell the EIA is the state license needed to sell annuities. If, however, the EIA is labeled as a registered product it will be treated more like a variable annuity and an individual selling the EIA will need to be licensed by the appropriate securities authorities as well as hold the state license. Further, if the EIA is labeled a registered product it will be subject to other requirements including those which mandate that a product prospectus be prepared and given to each individual who is considering the purchase of an EIA. Obviously, if all EIAs come to be considered registered products, there will be fewer agents holding the proper licenses to sell EIAs and there will be much greater demands on the companies developing these products during the approval process.

The reasons that many industry experts feel the EIA is properly considered a fixed annuity are fairly technical. An in-depth analysis is beyond the scope of this discussion.[9] In very general terms, the SEC has provided some safe harbor rules that exclude from the securities registration process any annuity contract issued by a corporation subject to supervision by the appropriate state insurance regulatory authority. These rules, generally, provide that a contract will fall within the safe harbor exclusion from registration if three requirements are met. First, the contract must be issued by a corporation, subject to the supervision of a state insurance commissioner. Second, the insurer must assume a prescribed investment risk under the contract and third, the contract must not be marketed primarily as an investment.[10]

The aspect of the EIA that troubles some industry experts is the fact that the purchaser of an EIA does not know the final rate of return that he or she will earn on the EIA until the end of the contract term. (Although, it is true that with almost all EIAs the purchaser does know the minimum guaranteed interest rate at the beginning of the contract term.) This aspect causes the EIA to more closely resemble a mutual fund or some other type of security than it does a traditional fixed annuity, in the opinion of some. With the traditional fixed annuity the rate of return is set when the annuity is purchased and the purchaser knows what the return will be at the beginning of the crediting period. Whether the stock market goes up or down during this period is of no consequence to the return that will be earned on the fixed annuity. However, with the EIA whether the stock market rises or falls, and to what extent, does affect the final rate of return.

ENDNOTES

1. Linda Koco, "Equity Index Annuity Sales Hit Another Record Last Year," *National Underwriter*, Life and Health/Financial Services Edition, March 18, 2002, p. 42.
2. Ibid.
3. James B. Smith, Jr., "Survey Shows Strong Interest in Offering EIAs," *National Underwriter*, Life and Health/Financial Services Edition, January 20, 1997, pp. 14-15; Thomas F. Streiff, "Three Basic Ways of Achieving Equity Indexing," *National Underwriter*, Life and Health/Financial Services Edition, November 4, 1996, p. 18; Edward J. Horwitz, "Learn Which Equity Indexing Method Fits the Need," *National Underwriter*, Life and Health/Financial Services Edition, October 14, 1996, p. 34.
4. See Thomas F. Streiff, "Three Basic Ways of Achieving Equity Indexing," *National Underwriter*, Life and Health/Financial Services Edition, November 4, 1996, p. 18.

5. James B. Smith, Jr., "Survey Shows Strong Interest in Offering EIAs," *National Underwriter*, Life and Health/Financial Services Edition, January 20, 1997, pp. 14-15.

6. See IRC Sec. 72(q).

7. IRC Sec. 72(e)(4)(A). This is true for annuity contracts entered into after August 13, 1982.

8. IRC Sec. 1035. See Chapter 7 for more information.

9. See Christopher M. Gregory and Jeffrey S. Pruetz, "Should Equity Index Annuities be Registered?," *National Underwriter*, Life and Health/Financial Services Edition, January 20, 1997, p. 22.

10. See Sec. 3(a)(8) of the Securities Act of 1933 (15 USC 77c(a)(8)); 17 CFR 230.151.

Chapter 6

THE USES OF ANNUITIES

RETIREMENT PLANNING

Although the nonqualified annuity can be used for many purposes, probably its best and most frequent use is retirement planning. Retirement has been the focus of much attention in recent years. Since people are generally living longer than at any time in history, there are more retirement years to be planned for and, particularly, to be paid for. Another reason for the focus on retirement planning is, of course, the baby boomer generation. Born between 1945 and 1964, those on the older edge of the boomers are now entering their late 50's and beginning to plan seriously for their retirement years. The recent down-sizing of major American corporations also has called attention to the fact that employers cannot be counted on to finance the full cost of an employee's retirement years.

The result of these factors, and others, has been an increased interest in, and focus on, the financial aspects of retirement. Most Americans expect to receive Social Security benefits at retirement and many are fortunate enough to be participants in qualified retirement plans provided by their employers, although many who are self-employed do not have retirement plans. However, experts warn that if the baby boomer generation is to afford the retirement lifestyle it seems to want, these two sources of retirement income will not be sufficient. Personal savings must make up the difference.

One of the best vehicles to accumulate funds to supplement retirement income from Social Security and qualified retirement plans is a nonqualified annuity. The use of the labels "qualified" and "nonqualified" have nothing to do with the qualification of the annuity or the insurance company issuing it. Instead, these terms refer to whether the annuity is being used as part of a retirement plan that is "qualified" under certain sections of the Internal Revenue Code.[1] A "qualified" annuity is one which is used as part of, or in connection with, a qualified retirement plan. A "nonqualified" annuity is one that is not used as part of any qualified retirement plan. If the annuity is labeled as nonqualified, this simply means that it may be purchased by any individual or entity and is not associated with an employer-provided plan.

As with many financial planning strategies, earlier is better than later when deciding to start saving for retirement. Figure 6.01 illustrates the difference in the benefits available at retirement depending upon when an annuity holder first begins to pay a regular monthly premium into a nonqualified annuity. If the annuity holder, Mrs. Smith, begins saving for retirement at age 40, she will have accumulated $138,598 at age 65 by saving $200 each month. The same monthly amount started at age 50 would result in a retirement sum of $58,164. Waiting until age 60, with retirement only five years away, severely cuts down on the available funds, resulting in a sum of only $13,954. If Mrs. Smith elected a life income settlement option under the annuity started at age 40, her monthly benefit payment would be $812. Under the annuity started at age 50, the benefit would be $341 while under an annuity started at age 60, she would receive only $82 each month.

Figure 6.01

Mrs. Smith's Retirement Income $200 Monthly Premium		
Age When Premium Payments Begin	**Amount Accumulated at Age 65***	**Amount of Monthly Annuity For Life**
40	$138,598	$812
50	$ 58,164	$341
60	$ 13,954	$ 82
*Assumes a 6% interest rate.		

The usefulness of starting early can be illustrated another way. Assume that Mrs. Smith, with the help of her financial planner, determines that she needs $500 per month at retirement to supplement her retirement income from other sources. If Mrs. Smith begins paying premiums into the annuity at age 40, she will need to pay a monthly premium of $123 in order to accumulate the sum of $85,320 which will pay her a life income annuity of about $500 each month when she reaches age 65. This is illustrated in Figure 6.02. If Mrs. Smith delays starting the premium payments until she reaches age 50, she will need to pay a premium of $293 each month in order to accumulate funds sufficient to provide the $500 monthly benefit. Waiting until age 60 to begin saving money in the annuity will result in a required monthly premium of $1,223. Clearly, starting early is the best course of action for this type of retirement planning.

Figure 6.02

Monthly Premiums Needed to Pay Mrs. Smith $500 per Month at Age 65			
Monthly Annuity at Age 65	Accumulation Amount Needed at Age 65	Age When Premium Payments Begin	Amount of Monthly Premium Payments Required*
$500	$85,320	40	$ 123
$500	$85,320	50	$ 293
$500	$85,320	60	$1,223
*Assumes a 6% interest rate.			

Other Retirement Planning Vehicles

To make the best use of the nonqualified annuity in retirement planning, it is essential to have a basic understanding of the other retirement planning techniques available and how these other options fit together with nonqualified annuities. A short discussion of the more commonly-encountered types of retirement plans follows.

Individual Retirement Arrangements

An Individual Retirement Arrangement (IRA) offers several advantages. First, with a traditional IRA, depending upon income levels and participation in other employer-provided retirement plans, an IRA contribution may result in an income tax deduction in the year the contribution is made. Second, interest earned on the funds placed in a traditional IRA is taxed on a deferred basis. That is, interest earned on IRA funds is generally not taxed until funds are withdrawn from the IRA. In addition, another form of IRA, the Roth IRA, is available. While contributions made to a Roth IRA are not deductible, funds distributed from a Roth IRA may be received completely free of any income tax, provided certain conditions are satisfied.[2]

A traditional IRA and a Roth IRA can be either an annuity (an Individual Retirement Annuity) or an account (an Individual Retirement Account). The term "Individual Retirement Arrangement" is often used to refer to both types of IRAs. Typically, annuities are offered by insurance companies and accounts are offered by banks and other financial institutions, but this is not always the case.

With the traditional IRA, an individual can contribute up to $3,000 to an IRA in his own name for 2002 through 2004, assuming that the individual has at least this much earned income for such year. This amount is increased by $500 for individuals who have attained age 50 before the close of the tax year. Further, the individual may contribute up to same amount to a traditional IRA for a nonworking spouse, assuming that certain conditions are met.[3] Generally, the amounts of any contributions made to Roth IRAs must be subtracted from this amount.[4]

This contribution to a traditional IRA may or may not be deductible for income tax purposes, depending upon the individual's income level and participation in other retirement plans. If the individual is an active participant in certain types of employer-provided retirement plans, the amount of his traditional IRA contribution that is deductible may be limited. Generally, for 2002, if a single person has adjusted gross income over $44,000 or a married couple has adjusted gross income over $64,000, no portion of an IRA contribution will be deductible. For 2003, these amounts jump to $50,000 and $70,000, respectively. For incomes less than these amounts, a portion or all of the contribution will be deductible.[5] For individuals who do not participate in other employer-provided plans, the full contribution may be deducted.

Contributions to a Roth IRA, as mentioned above, are not deductible. An individual may contribute the lesser of $3,000 or 100% of his compensation to a Roth IRA for 2002 through 2004. This amount is also increased by $500 for individuals who have attained age 50 before the close of the tax year. However, the maximum annual limit must be reduced by the amount of any contributions made to a traditional IRA in the same year. Further, an individual may contribute up to the same amounts to a Roth IRA for a nonworking spouse. This amount must also be reduced by the amount of any contributions made to a traditional IRA on behalf of the nonworking spouse in the same year. Lastly, it should be noted that the amount that can be contributed to a Roth IRA is lessened and even eliminated for high income taxpayers. Generally, single taxpayers with adjusted gross incomes of at least $110,000 and married taxpayers with adjusted gross incomes beginning at $160,000 cannot make contributions to Roth IRAs.[6]

However, for those taxpayers who are eligible to make contributions to Roth IRAs, there are significant tax advantages. Generally, if a distribution from a Roth IRA meets certain requirements and is, therefore, considered to be a "qualified distribution" no portion of the distribution will be includable in the taxpayer's income.[7] Generally, the requirements are that the distribution is not made for at least five years after the Roth IRA is started and it is made either after the individual reaches age 59½, upon the individual's death or disability or the distribution is a qualified first-time homebuyer distribution.[8]

Like a nonqualified annuity, the interest earned on a traditional IRA is tax deferred. Thus, a traditional IRA holder does not pay income tax on the earnings in his IRA until he begins to withdraw benefits. In contrast, the interest earned on a Roth IRA may never be taxed if received as part of a qualified distribution.

Also like a nonqualified annuity, there are certain penalties for early IRA withdrawals. Generally, to the extent includable in income, distributions from both traditional and Roth IRAs received before the IRA holder reaches age 59½ are subject to a 10% penalty tax.[9] Benefits which are paid out from a traditional IRA after this age has been reached are fully taxable, if all contributions to the IRA were made on a tax-deductible basis. If some contributions to a traditional IRA were deductible when made but others were not, a portion of each benefit payment will be taxable and a portion will not.[10] Unlike nonqualified annuities, traditional IRAs require that the holder begin receiving distributions of at least a minimum amount at about age 70½.[11] In contrast, a Roth IRA is subject to minimum distribution requirements only upon the death of the owner.[12]

From a financial planning perspective, it is important to note that for high income taxpayers who, because of their income levels, cannot take advantage of IRAs, the use of a nonqualified annuity to accumulate funds for retirement purposes can be attractive. While it is true that premiums paid into a nonqualified annuity are not income tax deductible and benefit payments from such an annuity will be partially taxable, there is no limit on the amount of funds that may be placed in a nonqualified annuity. And, of course, the interest earned on the funds inside the annuity is tax deferred. (See Chapter 7 for more on income taxation of nonqualified annuities.)

Qualified Retirement Plans

Generally, a qualified retirement plan is an employee benefit arrangement offered by an employer to its employees that meets certain requirements set forth in the Internal Revenue Code. There are several different types of qualified plans including defined benefit plans and defined contribution plans, such as profit-sharing plans, 401(k) plans, and employer stock ownership plans. A detailed explanation of these plans is beyond the scope of this book. However, it is important to understand that while these plans are designed to provide an employee with some type of benefit at retirement, most employees have little control over the type of plan offered by their employer or the manner in which the funds inside the plan are invested (with the exception of 401(k) plans). The nonqualified annuity offers a method of supplementing the employee's retirement income over which the employee retains a much greater degree of control.

Contributions made to a qualified retirement plan are income tax deductible to the employer making the contributions provided certain requirements are met. For example, in order to be qualified, a plan must meet certain nondiscrimination requirements; in other words, an employer generally must offer its qualified retirement plan to almost all employees. The employee does not pay any current income tax on the qualified plan contributions made on his behalf. The contributions are subject to income tax only when the employee begins receiving retirement benefits from the plan.

Most large corporations provide their employees with some type of qualified retirement plan. A few provide more than one plan. However, many small companies and self-employed individuals do not have sufficient income to make contributions to such a plan. Contributions to a nonqualified annuity by these individuals may provide their only source of retirement income, other than government benefits such as Social Security.

Tax Sheltered Annuities

A Tax Sheltered Annuity (TSA) is a special type of annuity that is available only to individuals employed in public schools and nonprofit organizations that are operated exclusively for religious, literary, charitable, scientific, or educational purposes.[13] Included here are churches, synagogues, hospitals, and colleges.

A TSA is usually issued by an insurance company. It may be either a fixed or a variable annuity contract.[14] Some companies are offering an equity-indexed annuity for use as a TSA. (See Chapter 5 for more on equity-indexed annuities.) In certain instances, a limited amount of life insurance may be offered as part of the TSA arrangement.[15]

To eligible individuals a TSA can provide a good retirement benefit and is usually something that the individual will want to take full advantage of. Contributions to a TSA are made by the employer on either a salary reduction or additional compensation basis. In other words, the employer can pay the TSA premiums by simply giving the employee that much additional compensation or the employer can require that the TSA premium come out of the salary already being paid to the employee.[16] An employee may exclude from income TSA contributions that are made on his behalf, subject to certain limitations.[17] Usually, the employee owns the TSA personally.

Similar to qualified retirement plans, TSAs generally must meet certain requirements as to minimum participation and nondiscrimination.[18]

There is a penalty tax equal to 10% of the taxable amount of the distribution that applies generally to TSA distributions received before the annuity holder reaches age 59½.[19] An individual generally must begin receiving benefits from a TSA at about age 70½.[20] The benefit amount from a TSA is generally fully taxable at the time it is received.[21]

CHARITABLE PLANNING

Gift of an Annuity

There are occasions when an individual who has purchased an annuity finds that he would like to make a gift of either the contract itself or the funds held in the contract. There is no reason that an individual cannot make a gift of a nonqualified annuity contract, if that is his wish. However, there may be some unanticipated tax results.

If the annuity holder decides to surrender the annuity fully and make a gift of the funds, he will pay income tax on the amount received from the insurance company less his basis in the contract. Barring previous partial surrenders, his basis will likely be equal to the amount of premiums he has paid into the annuity. If the annuity holder is not at least age 59½ at the time of the surrender, he may encounter the 10% penalty tax on premature distributions, which is discussed fully in Chapter 7. After surrendering the annuity and paying the necessary taxes, the individual can make a gift of the cash he receives from the surrender. Generally, a gift of up to $10,000 as indexed ($11,000 in 2002) per person can be made before any gift tax will be due.[22] In addition, an unlimited deduction from gift tax is generally available for gifts to charity.[23]

If the annuity holder chooses, he can simply make a gift of the annuity contract itself. Doing so has the advantage of providing the person who receives the gift of the annuity contract with the advantage of the income tax deferral on the interest earned inside the annuity. However, if the gift is of an annuity contract issued after April 22, 1987, the person making the gift is treated as having received an amount equal to the cash surrender value of the contract at the time of the gift minus the annuity holder's investment in the annuity.[24]

Of course, once the gift of the annuity is completed, the new owner may choose to surrender the contract and obtain the cash immediately. Another option after the gift is made is for the new owner to annuitize the contract right away and begin receiving benefit payments. If the recipient of the gift selects this option, the benefit payments from the annuity are taxed under the general annuity rules, which call for the application of an exclusion ratio resulting in the taxation of a portion of each annuity payment. See Chapter 7 for a more detailed analysis.

One situation where the gift of an annuity becomes a possibility concerns a parent or grandparent who purchased an annuity as a means to accumulate funds needed for a child's or grandchild's college education. If the child either does not attend college or obtains the funds to pay the cost from another source, the annuity holder may wish to make a gift of the funds earmarked for college expenses. Another instance concerns a parent who purchased an annuity for retirement income, but at retirement finds that he does not need the income from the annuity and, perhaps for estate planning purposes, decides to make a gift of the contract.

Charitable Gift Annuity

As opposed to making a gift of an annuity, as discussed above, an individual can enter into a charitable gift annuity arrangement. There is no previously-purchased annuity contract in this instance. Generally, a charitable gift annuity is an agreement between a charitable institution such as a church or college and an individual who wishes to make a contribution to the charity. If an individual donates property to the charity under a charitable gift annuity, he receives an annuity from the charity for the remainder of his life. There is no transfer of an annuity contract, rather the annuity payments are made directly from the charity to the individual and are backed by the charity's assets and good name. The tax consequences of a charitable gift annuity can be complicated as discussed in Chapter 4. There is usually an immediate income tax deduction for the person making the gift although the amount of this deduction may be limited.

Charitable Trusts

The field of charitable planning often involves intricate arrangements because large amounts of money and property are changing hands. There are several complex trust arrangements specific to the area of charitable planning. While an annuity is not usually a part of these types of trust arrangements, a planner or agent may find a very general understanding of these arrangements to be useful. A brief description of the charitable remainder trust, the charitable lead trust, and the pooled income fund follow.

Charitable Remainder Trusts

A charitable remainder trust, or CRT, is a trust arrangement involving an irrevocable gift to a charity and payments for life or a term of years to an individual who is not a charity. At the beneficiary's death (or other termination of the trust) the property "remaining" in the trust becomes the property of the charity. Hence the name charitable *remainder* trust. The amount that must be paid out of the trust each year is at least 5% and not more than 50% of the net market value of the trust assets as mandated by the Internal Revenue Code; however the Code allows for some flexibility in design as described below. The requirements in the Internal Revenue Code for setting up and maintaining the CRT are detailed.[25]

If certain requirements are met, the gift of property to the trust will result in an immediate charitable income tax deduction for the person making the gift.[26]

There are two basic types of charitable remainder trusts: the charitable remainder unitrust (CRUT) and the charitable remainder annuity trust (CRAT).

A charitable remainder unitrust provides payment of a variable amount to a beneficiary who is not a charity with an irrevocable remainder interest to be paid to or held for the benefit of a charity. The payout must be a fixed percentage of not less than 5% and not more than 50% of the net fair market value of the trust assets and generally must be paid at least annually to the noncharitable beneficiary or beneficiaries. The remainder interest must equal at least 10% of the net fair market value of each contribution on the date it is contributed to the trust.[27] However, a charitable remainder unitrust may be designed to pay out only its net income. It may (but does not have to) provide for payments not made in earlier years to be made up in later years. Since the trust is valued annually, the donor may make additional contributions to the trust.

In contrast, a charitable remainder annuity trust provides for payment of a fixed amount of at least 5% and not more than 50% of the initial fair market value of the assets at the time placed in the trust to the beneficiary that is not a charity. The remainder interest must equal at least 10% of the initial fair market value of the trust assets. Additional gifts are not permitted into the charitable remainder annuity trust since it is not subject to annual valuation.[28]

In recent years, CRTs have been combined with several other arrangements. One of the more popular of these combinations is the CRT and the wealth replacement trust, a form of irrevocable life insurance trust. Typically such a plan calls for an individual to give appreciated capital gain property in trust to a charity, retaining the right to payment out of the value of the property for his life. Since the trust owns the property, it either holds onto it or sells it and reinvests the sale proceeds. The wealth replacement trust (so called since its purpose is to replace the wealth "lost" to the charity) owns a life insurance policy on the life of the person making the gift. The life insurance trust pays the premiums on the policy, finding these dollars, in theory, through the tax benefit of the charitable deduction to the donor from the gift of the property to the CRT. As mentioned above, at the termination of the trust the property remaining in the trust goes to the charity and the life insurance proceeds are paid to the beneficiaries of the life insurance trust. Typically, these beneficiaries are the family members of the person who arranged the CRT.

Charitable Lead Trusts

A charitable lead trust essentially reverses who receives the income interest and who receives the remainder interest with the charitable remainder trust. Here, it is the charity that receives the income or "lead" interest (hence the name charitable *lead* trust). The person setting up the trust (the donor) grants a right to payment to the charity, with the remainder interest in the property coming back to the donor or to beneficiaries he has named. The value of a gift of such an interest in property is deductible if certain requirements are met.[29]

To meet these requirements, a charitable lead trust must be in the form of either a guaranteed annuity interest or a unitrust interest. A guaranteed annuity interest is the right to payment of a fixed amount, whereas a unitrust interest is the right to receive payment of a fixed percentage of the value of the property placed in the trust. In either case, payments may be made to the charity for a period of time or over the life of an individual who is living when the trust is arranged.[30]

Pooled Income Funds

A "pooled income fund" operates in the charitable marketplace in much the same manner as a mutual fund. A "pool" is formed, into which individuals (donors) may make an irrevocable gift of property that they wish to give to charity. Each donor then names a beneficiary to receive income from the fund, often for the beneficiary's lifetime. The amount of income is generally determined by the rate of return earned by the trust. The charity receives the remainder interest in the trust property.[31] The donor receives an immediate charitable contribution income tax deduction in an amount equal to the present value of the remainder interest, subject to certain limitations.[32]

As with the charitable trust arrangements discussed above, a pooled income fund must comply with a number of requirements. One such requirement mandates that neither a donor nor a trust beneficiary may act as a fund trustee.[33] There are also rules dealing with what types of investments a fund may own and particular rules regarding depreciable property.[34]

COLLEGE FUNDING

Even before planning for their own retirement, the expense of providing their children with a college education is a primary concern for parents. Not all children go to college and, of course, some who do attend are fortunate enough to be awarded scholarships. However, no parent wants to think that his or her child might not be able to go to college solely because of a lack of funds. The cost of a college education has increased rapidly in the last few years. Currently, the cost to attend four years at a private college can run as high as $120,000 while the cost of four years at a state university runs about $40,000.

Over recent years, as annuity sales have increased rapidly, there has been much discussion over the use of nonqualified annuities as a vehicle to assist parents in accumulating funds to meet college expenses. In some instances, the annuity can be a useful tool. However, it is not always the best answer to the college funding dilemma.

The major advantage in using an annuity for this purpose is that the funds placed in the contract accumulate on a tax-deferred basis, as discussed in Chapter 7. In other words, the annuity holder does not pay income tax on the interest earned on the annuity funds until the funds are withdrawn from the contract. Since all the interest stays in the contract to accumulate even more interest, the tax-deferred annuity provides a greater rate of return, generally, than a financial vehicle that is not taxed on a deferred basis.

The primary drawback to using the annuity for college funding appears when it is time to take the funds out of the contract. As discussed in Chapter 7, there are several ways that an annuity holder can withdraw funds from an annuity including a full surrender, a partial surrender, or annuitization of the contract. If the annuity holder decides on some type of surrender, either full or partial, to withdraw the college funds, he will incur the 10% premature distribution penalty tax unless he is at least age 59½.[35] By the time that the parent pays the regular income tax due on the surrender and then the penalty tax, the advantage gained by using the tax-deferred funding vehicle often is eliminated.

To illustrate, take the example of Mr. Jones and his daughter, Sarah, who will be a freshman next fall. When Sarah was ten years old her father inherited a sizable amount of money from his uncle. He purchased a single premium deferred annuity with a premium of $20,000, naming himself as both the owner and annuitant. Today, Mr. Jones is age 52 and the value of the annuity is $31,877 assuming an interest rate of 6%. Since Mr. Jones is younger than age 59½, the 10% penalty tax will be applicable to any amounts surrendered out of the annuity. If he completely surrenders the contract, he will pay income tax on $11,877 which is calculated by subtracting his basis of $20,000 from the current annuity value of $31,877. In addition to the income tax, Mr. Jones will also owe a penalty tax equal to 10% of the taxable amount of the surrender. In this case, 10% of $11,877 is $1,188.

For the most part, the only way that Mr. Jones can take funds out of the annuity contract before he reaches age 59½ is to annuitize the contract over his life expectancy. Using the figures in the example above, doing so would result in a monthly payment to Mr. Jones of approximately $160 or $1,920 annually. This amount would assist with college expenses, but in the four years that his daughter will incur the majority of her educational costs, this amount will probably not be sufficient.

If a parent is slightly older than Mr. Jones and will be age 59½ during the child's college years, the nonqualified annuity makes a viable choice for accumulating the college funds. In this instance, the annuity contract could be surrendered completely or a partial surrender in each of the years that the child is in school could be made. The income tax will be due, of course, but the penalty tax would be avoided. Some quick subtraction shows that this course of action works well for a parent who is at least 42 years old when the child is born.

Of course, there is no requirement that the parent be the owner and annuitant of the annuity contract. One logical alternative that eliminates the age 59½ problem is for a grandparent to be the owner and annuitant of the contract that will be used for funding a grandchild's college education. If the grandparents purchase an annuity contract when a grandchild is born and then make regular premium payments over eighteen years, there will likely be a significant sum accumulated to finance the education. Figure 6.03 shows the monthly premium needed to accumulate $100,000 depending upon the age of the child when premium payments begin. An aspect of this approach that is typically appealing to the grandparents is that they retain control over the funds right up until the time that the grandchild begins college. There is no opportunity for the funds given to the parents to pay for a college education to be used for other purposes. Also, the funds will not be dissipated if the grandchild's parents divorce before the grandchild is college age.

If it is the grandparents or other family members that pay the college expenses, (whether an annuity is involved or not) there may be gift tax implications. In other words, the payment of the expenses by the grandparent will likely be considered a gift from the grandparent to the grandchild. Current tax law provides that up to $10,000 may be given to one individual by another each year without any gift tax being due. (This $10,000 figure ($11,000 in 2002) is the annual exclusion amount from the federal gift tax and will be adjusted for inflation after 1998.) Thus, at least the annual

Figure 6.03

Accumulations Needed for College Funding*			
Amount of Monthly Premium Payment	Number of Years to College Age	Age of Child When Premium Payments Begin	Amount Desired at Age 18
$ 283	17	1	$100,000
$ 425	13	5	$100,000
$ 814	8	10	$100,000
$2,542	3	15	$100,000
*Assumes a 6% interest rate.			

gift tax exclusion amount could go to the grandchild each year without the grandparent incurring any gift tax. If both grandparents join in the gift, this would allow $20,000 (or twice the current gift tax annual exclusion amount) to be given to the grandchild without gift tax being due. If the amount needed for one year exceeds this, the grandparent might make an additional gift to the grandchild's parents (who would each be able to receive the annual gift tax exclusion amount per year) and avoid gift tax in this manner. Also, payments made directly to certain educational institutions on behalf of another person for that person's education are excluded from gift tax, so parents and grandparents can avoid the gift tax by making payments directly to the educational institution for a child's or grandchild's expenses.[36]

BUSINESS PLANNING

There are several uses of annuities within the context of a business. The first is discussed above generally under the heading of retirement planning and more specifically below.

Retirement Planning

For a self-employed individual, the use of a nonqualified annuity may provide the only source of retirement income, other than government benefits such as Social Security. Many small business owners spend the early years of their careers struggling to get the business started and do not have the income to contribute to a retirement plan. In the later years of the business, the business owner may decide against putting in a qualified retirement plan because he would have to provide benefits for most, if not all, of the company's employees. Thus, it is not unusual for a 60 or 65 year-old owner of a successful business to approach retirement age without the prospect of income coming from any source other than the continued existence of his business. If the business owner had purchased an annuity at the point where his income level from his business could support even a modest monthly premium payment, his retirement income would be enhanced. Many agents and financial planners find that a business owner who has just purchased an individual disability income policy is also interested in beginning his retirement planning.

To illustrate the difference in retirement income that this use of an annuity might make, take Mr. Smith, the sole owner of a dry cleaning business which he started 30 years ago at the age of 20. From a single store, Mr. Smith's business has grown to 20 locations spread through three cities. He has a substantial income today at the age of 50 but has never taken a systematic approach to his retirement planning. He is not interested in putting in a qualified retirement plan. If he simply purchases a nonqualified annuity contract for himself and contributes a monthly amount of $300 until he reaches age 65, he will have accumulated approximately $88,000 in his annuity, assuming an interest rate of 6%. If he annuitizes the contract using a life income settlement option, he will receive approximately $588 each month for the remainder of his life.

One question that most small business owners ask about this type of approach is whether the business can pay the premium and, if so, whether the business can take an income tax deduction for the premium payment. With a nonqualified annuity, there is no income tax deduction available for the premiums as they are paid into the annuity. This is true no matter who pays the premium, Mr. Smith or his company. There is no reason why the business cannot pay the premium, but there is no particular advantage to doing so. If the business does pay the premium on an annuity that is owned personally by an employee-shareholder, the amount of the premium payment will be considered income taxable to the employee-shareholder as additional compensation. A deduction from income will be available to the business for this compensation amount as it would be with any reasonable salary payment made to an employee.[37] But, there is no special deduction available simply because the business pays the premium on a personally-owned annuity.

Another question that frequently arises with this planning technique is whether the business can or should own the annuity. Since the Tax Reform Act of 1986, the answer to this question is almost always no. Although there is nothing to prohibit a corporation from owning a nonqualified annuity, there is a disadvantage from an income tax viewpoint. As discussed in Chapter 7, the "nonnatural" person rule applies to annuities owned by corporations, and generally states that if any contributions are made after February 28, 1986, to a deferred annuity contract owned by a corporation or other entity that is not considered under the tax law to be a natural person, the interest earned each year on the funds inside the annuity is taxable.[38] In other words, the advantage of income tax deferral is lost for annuities owned by corporations.

Nonqualified Deferred Compensation Plans

Prior to enactment of the Tax Reform Act of 1986, annuities were often used as a funding vehicle for nonqualified deferred compensation plans. The enactment of the "nonnatural" person rule has made this practice much less attractive from a income tax point of view.

As mentioned above, the nonnatural person rule states that if any contributions are made after February 28, 1986, to a deferred annuity contract owned by a corporation or other entity not considered under the tax law to be a natural person, the interest earned each year on the funds inside the annuity is taxable.[39] The loss of the tax deferral on the interest earned on the annuity has significantly lessened the use of nonqualified annuities for funding deferred compensation plans. There is no actual prohibition against doing so. It simply is not as attractive from a financial perspective as it once was.

Sale of a Business

Often, as a business owner approaches retirement age, he realizes that the only source of retirement income available will be Social Security. With the realization that he will not be able to quit working, the business owner often looks toward the sale of all or perhaps only a portion of his business.

If a business is sold, the former owner may find himself in possession of a large amount of cash. Since these funds are intended to finance the owner's retirement years, a nonqualified annuity is often a good place to put the cash generated by the sale of a business interest. Frequently, a business that was largely dependent upon the efforts or special talents of the owner will be sold for a small purchase price with the former owner agreeing to act as a consultant for several years and receive either a salary for his efforts or a percentage of the company's sales or profits. If this is the case, a deferred annuity will be able to accept not only the initial purchase price but a portion of the amount that the former owner receives in each subsequent year.

Take the example of Mr. Jones, who owns a successful insurance agency. As he approaches age 65, Mr. Jones agrees to sell the agency to two individuals. Since many of his large accounts are personal friends and might not stay with the agency without his presence, Mr. Jones agrees to work for the new owners for a period of five years in return for a percentage of the commission earned by the agency each year. The initial purchase price paid to Mr. Jones is $25,000, an amount that could be placed in a variable annuity. In each of the next five years, he could place a part of the salary he earns from the new owners into the same variable annuity contract. At the end of five years, when he is 70 years old and ready to retire completely, Mr. Jones could annuitize the variable annuity contract, selecting a life income settlement option, and receive a check each month for the remainder of his life. Figure 6.04 shows one possible outcome of this approach which would give Mr. Jones a lifetime income from a single source plus control over how much of his salary he places into the annuity, the type of investments his funds are in, and finally, the timing of the onset of annuity benefits. If Mr. Jones should die prior to the end of the five year period, his beneficiary under the annuity contract would receive a death benefit equal to at least the amount of money that had been invested in the annuity contract up to the time of Mr. Jones' death. At age 70, the accumulation value of the annuity would provide Mr. Jones with a monthly income for life of $895.

Figure 6.04

Sale of Mr. Jones' Business			
	Mr. Jones' Income	Amount Placed in Variable Annuity	Value at Year End*
Initial Purchase Price		$25,000	$ 26,500
Year 1	$40,000	$15,000	$ 43,990
Year 2	$36,500	$12,000	$ 59,349
Year 3	$27,000	$12,000	$ 75,630
Year 4	$32,000	$15,000	$ 96,068
Year 5	$28,000	$12,000	$114,552

*Assumes an interest rate of 6%.

Bonus Plan

Occasionally, an annuity is used in place of a life insurance policy in a type of nonqualified employee benefit plan referred to as a Bonus Plan or a Section 162 Bonus Plan. Although this type of plan is not a true "plan" it does provide a benefit. Under a Section 162 Bonus Plan, a corporation selects certain employees, usually top-level executives, to receive a salary increase or bonus. This salary increase is deductible from income by the corporation under IRC Section 162 (hence the name of the plan) and must be included in income by the employee. Once the increase is in the hands of the executive he uses the amount to pay the premium on a life insurance policy insuring his life and owned by him personally.

Although a life insurance policy is usually used in this type of plan, an annuity may be substituted in certain instances such as when the executive cannot purchase insurance (i.e., is uninsurable) due to health problems.

ALTERNATIVES TO ANNUITIES

As mentioned in Chapter 1, the primary use of a nonqualified annuity is to accumulate a sum of money that will be paid out over a certain period of years, often over the lifetime of the annuity holder. Although the annuity does offer certain advantages, it is not the only method by which a sum of money can be accumulated or paid out.

In addition to the other retirement planning vehicles discussed earlier in this chapter (IRAs, qualified retirement plans, and TSAs), other financial tools used to accumulate funds for some future purpose include bank savings accounts, certificates of deposit, and mutual funds. The characteristics of these additional alternatives are summarized below.

Bank Savings Account

A savings account at a bank, savings and loan, or a credit union is simply an account that holds money for the depositor.

Periodically, the bank credits interest at a pre-determined rate on the funds in the account. A true savings account does not offer any check-writing privileges. The account holder must go to the bank and make a withdrawal in order to obtain funds from the account. (Of course, the withdrawal may be made at an automated teller machine or electronically over the phone.)

A savings account is generally considered a safe place to keep funds, because banks do not usually invest in financial arrangements that carry a large degree of risk. In addition, deposits in many banks are insured by the Federal Deposit Insurance Corporation (FDIC) or a similar state institution.

Although a savings account is a low-risk financial vehicle allowing easy access to funds without penalty, interest earned on the savings account funds is taxed to the account holder at the time it is earned. The savings account does not allow deferral of the tax until the funds are withdrawn, as does the nonqualified annuity.

For example, if Mrs. Smith places $5,000 in a savings account earning interest at the rate of 3% for one year, the interest credited to her account must be included in her taxable income in the year it is paid. Assuming that Mrs. Smith makes a withdrawal from her account in an amount equal to the tax due on the interest earned, in the next year interest will be credited on the $5,000 plus the interest remaining after the tax was withdrawn. This is in contrast to an annuity, where the interest on Mrs. Smith's $5,000 would not be taxed in the year it was credited and would remain in the annuity to be credited with interest during the next year. In other words, a savings account effectively earns interest on the prior year's interest less the tax due while an annuity earns interest on the full amount of the prior year's interest. Over a number of years, this difference in the timing of the taxation can result in a significant difference in accumulation. Of course, as discussed throughout this book, most annuities do place restrictions, in the form of surrender charges, on the accessibility of funds placed in an annuity.

From a financial planning perspective, placing funds in an annuity to the exclusion of placing funds in a vehicle such as a savings account that offers immediate and penalty-free access to the funds is not a recommended course of action. Many financial planners counsel their clients to keep an "emergency fund" equal to three to six months' income in a savings-account type of fund. The emergency fund should be well-established before funds are channeled into less accessible vehicles such as annuities.

Certificates of Deposit

In contrast to the easy accessibility of a savings account, funds placed in a certificate of deposit, or CD, are available only at maturity without penalty. A CD is a vehicle, offered by a financial institution, into which an individual places funds for a certain length of time and, in return, receives interest at a set rate. The interest rate is usually higher than the rate of interest paid on a savings account and, often, the financial institution will require a minimum amount to purchase a CD. If a CD holder wishes to withdraw all or a portion of the CD funds prior to the end of the CD period, usually a certain portion of the interest earned on the funds will be forfeited to the bank.

Most banks and other institutions offer CDs for various lengths of time and, usually, the longer the time frame, the higher the interest rate that the CD holder will receive on his money. For example, a six-month CD might pay interest at 3.5% while a 24-month CD pays interest at a rate of 3.75%. The bank is willing to pay a higher rate because it anticipates having the use of the funds in the 24-month CD for a longer period of time.

From an income tax perspective, CDs are taxed like savings accounts. The interest earned is taxed in the year in which it is credited to the CD.

Mutual Funds

A mutual fund operates as a pool into which investors may place their funds. The mutual fund issues each investor a certain number of shares according to the amount of his investment. Then the mutual fund invests all the funds from all its investors in various investment vehicles available in the financial marketplace. By pooling their funds, the investors in a mutual fund create a much larger amount of money to invest than any single investor could muster. This allows the mutual fund to diversify its investments to a much greater extent than could a lone investor and, thus, lessen the risk to all investors.

There are many different types of mutual funds, some investing in only one type of investment such as growth stocks, some investing in a single industry such as health care and some offering a "family" of funds each with a different emphasis. Most funds, known as open-ended funds, will buy an investor's shares in the fund back at any time, making this type of investment a fairly liquid one.

Many funds charge investors a fee which consists of a stated percentage of the investors's account, a flat fee, or both. There are a significant number of funds that do not charge sales fees, called "no-load" funds. "Load" is another term used to describe a sales fee.

Returns from a mutual fund must be reported as taxable income by the investor currently. There is no income tax deferral offered by most mutual funds.

As discussed in Chapter 4, mutual funds may be purchased under the umbrella of a variable annuity.

ENDNOTES

1. See, generally, IRC Sec. 401.
2. IRC Sec. 408A.
3. See IRC Sec. 219(b), as amended by the Economic Growth and Tax Relief Reconciliation Act of 2001 (EGTRRA 2001). The $3,000 limit is increased to $4,000 for 2005 through 2007, and $5,000 for 2008. The $5,000 amount will be indexed for inflation in increments of $500 for 2009 and 2010. The $500 catch-up amount increases to $1,000 for 2006 through 2010. Note that all provisions of EGTRRA 2001 are scheduled to sunset, or expire, after December 31, 2010.
4. IRC Sec. 408A(c).
5. IRC Sec. 219(g).
6. IRC Sec. 408A(c), as amended by EGTRRA 2001. The $3,000 limit is increased to $4,000 for 2005 through 2007, and $5,000 for 2008. The $5,000 amount will be indexed for inflation in increments of $500 for 2009 and 2010. The $500 catch-up amount increases to $1,000 for 2006 through 2010.

7. IRC Sec. 408A(d)(1).
8. IRC Secs. 408A(d)(2), 408A(d)(5).
9. IRC Sec. 72(t).
10. IRC Sec. 408(d).
11. IRC Secs. 408(a)(6), 408(b)(3), 401(a)(9).
12. IRC Sec. 408A(c)(5).
13. IRC Secs. 403(b), 501(c)(3).
14. Rev. Rul. 68-116, 1968-1 CB 177.
15. Treas. Reg. §1.403(b)-1(c)(3).
16. Treas. Reg. §1.403(b)-1(b)(3).
17. IRC Sec. 403(b)(1).
18. IRC Sec. 403(b)(1)(D).
19. IRC Sec. 72(t).
20. IRC Sec. 403(b)(10).
21. IRC Sec. 403(b)(1).
22. IRC Sec. 2503(b). The $10,000 annual exclusion from the gift tax is adjusted for inflation after 1998. See Chapter 9.
23. IRC Sec. 2522. See Chapter 9.
24. IRC Sec. 72(e)(4)(C).
25. See, generally, IRC Secs. 170, 664.
26. IRC Sec. 170(f)(2)(A).
27. IRC Sec. 664(d)(2).
28. IRC Sec. 664(d)(1).
29. IRC Sec. 170(f)(2)(B).
30. Rev. Rul. 85-49, 1985-1 CB 330.
31. IRC Sec. 642(c)(5).
32. Treas. Reg. §1.642(c)-6(a)(2); see IRC Sec. 170.
33. IRC Sec. 642(c)(5); Treas. Reg. §1.642(c)-5.
34. Rev. Rul. 90-103, 1990-2 CB 159, as modified by Rev. Rul. 92-81, 1992-2 CB 119.
35. IRC Sec. 72(q).
36. IRC Sec. 2503. Gifts by a grandparent to a grandchild are also subject to generation-skipping transfer tax except to the extent an exclusion or exemption is available.
37. IRC Sec. 162.
38. IRC Sec. 72(u).
39. Ibid.

Chapter 7

INCOME TAXATION OF ANNUITIES

PREMIUMS

Generally, premiums (or deposits) paid into an annuity are not deductible from the annuity holder's income. Thus, if a married couple in their 50's decides to place a certain sum of money into a deferred annuity contract each month as part of their overall retirement plan, the monthly amount will not generate any income tax savings currently, although the interest earned on the funds once they are inside the annuity will be income-tax deferred. This general rule of non-deductibility applies whether the premium is a single payment or paid in installments over many years.

Contributions to certain types of annuities may be deductible from income tax if certain requirements are met. For example, contributions to a traditional Individual Retirement Annuity (IRA) may be deducted by the owner if neither the husband nor the wife participates in an employer-provided retirement plan. It may also be deductible even though one or both participate in such a plan as long as the couple's gross income falls within certain limits.[1] Also, a Tax Sheltered Annuity (TSA) plan is available to employees of certain tax-exempt employers and may receive employee contributions on a pre-tax basis. However, the general rule is that premiums used to purchase an individual annuity, whether for retirement planning or other purposes, will not be tax deductible.

CASH VALUE BUILD-UP

Natural Persons

If an annuity contract meets certain requirements of the Internal Revenue Code[2] the interest earned on the funds inside the annuity contract will not be taxed at the time it is credited. This is true only if the owner of the annuity is a natural person, as discussed below. However, the income tax on the annuity funds must be paid at some point. This occurs when the funds are paid out of the contract (i.e., the contract is annuitized) or the contract is surrendered for its full cash value.

Nonnatural Persons

Prior to 1986, the interest earned inside an annuity was tax deferred no matter who or what entity owned the annuity. However, in 1986, Congress enacted legislation designed to prevent corporations and other entities from taking advantage of this provision. Now, if any contributions are made after February 28, 1986 to a deferred annuity contract that is owned by a corporation or other entity that is not considered under the tax law to be a natural person, the interest earned each year on the funds inside the annuity is taxable.[3]

Generally, the amount of interest earned is referred to as "income on the contract." Technically, it is calculated by taking the sum of the net surrender value of the contract at the end of the taxable year and any amounts distributed under the contract during the taxable year and any prior taxable year and subtracting the sum of the net premiums for the taxable year and prior taxable years and any amounts includable in gross income for prior taxable years under this requirement.[4]

There are some types of annuities to which this rule, which is often referred to as "the nonnatural person" rule, does not apply.[5] These include any annuity contract that is:

1. Acquired by a person's estate at the person's death;

2. Held under a qualified retirement plan, a Tax Sheltered Annuity (TSA), or an Individual Retirement Arrangement (IRA);

3. Purchased by an employer upon the termination of a qualified retirement plan or TSA program and held by the employer until all amounts under the contract are distributed to the employee for whom the contract was purchased or to his beneficiary;

4. An immediate annuity (an annuity which is purchased with a single premium and begins payments within a year); and

5. A qualified funding asset (an annuity contract issued by a licensed insurance company which is purchased to fund payments for damages resulting from personal physical injury or sickness).

As with all rules regarding taxation, there is an exception to this general rule. When an annuity contract is held by a trust, corporation, or other "nonnatural" person *as an agent for* a natural person, the contract will be treated as an annuity and the interest earned will be income-tax deferred.[6]

Since this rule was created in 1986, there have been many questions about its application to certain types of trusts. Generally, the IRS has indicated that it views most types of trusts that have natural persons as beneficiaries as acting as an agent for the natural persons.[7] However, there are likely to be exceptions to this general outlook.[8]

Another item to remember about the "nonnatural person" rule is that it applies only to contributions made to annuity contracts after February 28, 1986.[9] Thus, it seems clear that if all contributions to the annuity are made after this date, the "nonnatural person" rule will apply to the contract. It also seems clear that if no contributions are made after this date, a contract held by a nonnatural person is treated for tax purposes as an annuity contract and therefore the interest earned inside the annuity is tax deferred. However, if contributions have been made both before and after this date to contracts held by nonnatural persons, it is not clear how the situation will be viewed by the Internal Revenue Service.

LOANS AND ASSIGNMENTS

Another area of annuity taxation that is somewhat confusing, and can cause some unexpected and sometimes unfortunate income tax results, concerns loans made from annuity contracts or the assignment of the values in an annuity contract as security for a loan. Generally, any amount received as a loan or the value of any part of an annuity contract pledged or assigned under a contract entered into after August 13, 1982 is taxable. The amount included in income and, therefore, taxable is calculated by taking the cash value of the contract immediately before the loan or assignment and subtracting the investment in the contract, which is generally equal to the amount of premium that has been paid into the annuity.[10]

The following example illustrates the surprise that awaits an annuity holder who uses his contract as security for a loan. Assume that Mr. Jones purchased an annuity contract in 1988 with a single premium of $50,000. Currently, the annuity's cash surrender value is $75,000. Mr. Jones wishes to borrow from his local bank to assist his twin sons with their educational expenses. He assigns to the bank an interest in the full value of the annuity. At the time of the assignment, Mr. Jones will have taxable income of approximately $25,000. This is calculated by taking the cash surrender value of the annuity immediately prior to the assignment ($75,000) and subtracting Mr. Jones' investment in the contract ($50,000).

It should be noted that loans made from certain specialized types of annuities and plans, such as Tax Sheltered Annuities and qualified retirement plans, are subject to different rules and that loans from Individual Retirement Annuities (IRAs) are prohibited.

Another situation that can result in taxable income to an annuity holder involves an owner who assigns the right to receive the annuity payments to another person while still retaining ownership of the contract. For example, such an assignment might be attractive to Mrs. Smith who has just re-married. Mrs. Smith lost her first husband ten years ago and, with the proceeds of his life insurance, purchased a single premium immediate annuity that pays her $800 each month. After the marriage, Mrs. Smith wishes to assign the monthly payment to her daughter, Jean. If the assignment is made, Jean will receive the $800 each month. However, without the transfer of the underlying contract, the gratuitous assignment of the income from Mrs. Smith's annuity will not shift the *taxability* of the income away from Mrs. Smith who is still the owner of the contract.[11] Thus, the annuity payments will be taxable to the owner, Mrs. Smith, even though they are paid to a third party, her daughter. (In a situation such as this, the gift tax consequences of the transfer of the annuity payment each month should also be considered. These are discussed in Chapter 9.)

PARTIAL WITHDRAWALS

Contract Surrender Charges

Most annuity contracts impose a surrender charge if funds are removed from the contract by either full or partial surrender within a certain number of years after the annuity contract is purchased. Often, the charges decline slightly each year and eventually no longer apply. For example, an annuity contract might impose a surrender charge of 8% of the amount surrendered during the first contract year, 7% during the second year, 6% in the third year and so on until the charge drops to 1% in the eighth year and then to zero in the ninth year. Imposition of these surrender charges is one reason why annuities must be looked upon as long-term purchases.

The surrender charges imposed by the annuity contract itself are separate from and should not be confused with the 10% penalty tax imposed on premature distributions by the Internal Revenue Code, discussed in the following section.[12] Since this penalty tax generally applies to distributions received prior to age 59½ and the contract surrender charges apply during the first few years after the annuity is purchased, an individual may incur one or both of the penalties, depending on the circumstances. For example, assume that Mr. Jones, age 65, purchased a deferred annuity last year. If he surrenders the contract this year, he will incur the second year contract surrender charge (7% in the example above) but he will not be subject to the tax code's 10% penalty tax because he is older than age 59½ at the time of the surrender. However, if Mrs. Smith, age 44, surrenders a deferred annuity contract purchased for her by her parents 20 years ago, it is not likely that any contract surrender charges will still be applicable, but the tax code's 10% penalty will still apply because Mrs. Smith is younger than 59½.

One final example illustrates the potential cost of surrendering an annuity contract subject to both contract and tax code surrender charges. Assume that Mr. Johnson purchased a deferred annuity three years ago when he took early retirement at age 55. To date, he has paid $15,000 into the contract. If he surrenders the contract now, he will receive the gross surrender value of the contract, $25,000. However, he will lose 6% of this amount, $1,500, due to the imposition of the contract surrender charge. In addition, he must pay $1,000, 10% of the taxable portion of the premature distribution, under the tax code's penalty tax. (The taxable portion of the surrender would be $10,000. This figure is arrived at by subtracting Mr. Johnson's investment in the contract of $15,000 from the $25,000 received upon surrender of the contract.) In all, Mr. Johnson will retain only $22,500 of the $25,000 gross surrender value after paying the surrender charge and penalty tax.

10% Premature Distribution Penalty Tax

In order to discourage the use of annuity contracts as short term tax sheltered investments, a 10% tax is imposed on certain "premature" payments under annuity contracts.[13] The 10% tax applies to the portion of any payment that is taxable. For example, if an annuity contract is surrendered for $50,000 and only $30,000 of this amount is includable in the income of the owner of the contract, then the 10% applies only to the $30,000 amount. Thus, the amount of the penalty tax is $3,000 (and not $5,000).

The 10% penalty tax on premature distributions from annuity contracts does not apply to any payment:[14]

1. Made after the taxpayer reaches age 59½;

2. Attributable to the taxpayer's disability;

3. Allocable to investment in the contract before August 14, 1982, including earnings on pre-August 14, 1982 investment;

4. Made from a qualified retirement plan (or under a contract purchased by this type of plan) or under a Tax Sheltered Annuity, or from an Individual Retirement Arrangement (but note that payments from these types of contracts are subject to similar penalties);

5. Made after the death of the annuity holder;

6. Made under an immediate annuity contract;

7. Made from an annuity purchased and held by an employer upon the termination of a qualified retirement plan;

8. Under a qualified funding asset (i.e., any annuity contract which is purchased as a result of a liability to pay for damages which resulted from physical injury or sickness); or

9. Which is part of a series of substantially equal periodic payments made (not less frequently than annually) for the life or life expectancy of the taxpayer or the joint lives or joint life expectancies of the taxpayer and his designated beneficiary.

The exception listed under number 9 above is one of the most-commonly used methods to take money out of a deferred annuity without incurring the 10% penalty tax. Basically, this exception allows an annuity holder of any age to begin receiving annuity payments from a contract that will be of the same amount. This amount is calculated using the taxpayer's life expectancy or, in the alternative, the joint life expectancies of the taxpayer and his or her beneficiary. Often this second alternative is used by married couples. Despite its usefulness, this exception for payments received over the taxpayer's lifetime carries some limitations. Basically, payments received under this exception may be "recaptured" if the series of payments is modified for reasons other than the death or disability of the taxpayer. If the modification takes place either before the taxpayer reaches age 59½ or before the end of a five-year period beginning at the time of the first payment (even if the taxpayer has reached age 59½), the tax on the amount recaptured is imposed in the first taxable year of the modification and is equal to the tax which would have been imposed plus interest had the exception not applied.[15]

Taxation of Withdrawals

The taxation of an amount received from an annuity that can be categorized as a partial withdrawal or partial surrender has been complicated by changes in the tax law over the last several decades. Looking to the date upon which the annuity contract was entered into is the first step in determining the income tax treatment of a partial surrender from an annuity. In general terms, if an annuity was entered into after August 13, 1982, a partial surrender will be taxed under what is usually referred to as the "interest first" rule while an annuity entered into prior to this date is taxed under the "cost recovery" rule. These rules, which are explained below, are named for that part of the annuity value that the annuity holder is deemed to have received first. Under the "interest first" rule, the annuity holder is deemed to receive the interest earned inside the annuity contract before he recovers his cost in the contract, thus receiving taxable income earlier rather than later. In contrast, under "the cost recovery" rule, the annuity holder is deemed to have received the cost of the annuity before he receives any interest that has accumulated within the contract, thus receiving taxable income later, not earlier.

More specifically, the interest first rule states that amounts received on partial surrender under annuity contracts entered into after August 13, 1982, are taxable as income to the extent that the cash value of the contract immediately before the payment exceeds the investment in the contract.[16] To the extent the amount received is greater than the excess of cash surrender value over the investment in the contract, the amount will be treated as a tax-free return of investment. In effect, these amounts are treated as distributions of interest first and only second as recovery of cost.

Cash withdrawals and amounts received on partial surrender under annuity contracts which were entered into before August 14, 1982 (and allocable to investment in the contract made before August 14, 1982) are taxed under the "cost recovery rule." Under the cost recovery rule, the taxpayer may receive all such amounts tax-free until he has received tax-free amounts equal to his pre-August 14, 1982 investment in the contract; the amounts are taxable only after such basis has been fully recovered.[17]

A simplified example illustrates the difference in the application of these two rules. Assume that Mrs. Smith purchased an annuity for a single premium payment of $50,000. The value of the annuity today is $80,000, resulting in interest earned in the contract of $30,000 ($80,000 surrender value minus the $50,000 single premium). Mrs. Smith decides to make a partial surrender of $20,000. If the contract falls under the interest first rule, Mrs. Smith will pay income tax on the full $20,000 received as a result of the partial surrender. This is true because amounts coming out of the annuity first are deemed to be interest, so until the partial surrender amount exceeds the interest in the annuity of $30,000, the partial surrender amount will be fully taxable.

In contrast, if the partial surrender is subject to the cost recovery rule, Mrs. Smith will not pay income tax on any of the $20,000 that she receives. This is so because no amount received upon surrender is considered taxable until an amount equal to Mrs. Smith's cost (the single premium of $50,000) is withdrawn from the annuity. Since the surrender amount of $20,000 is less than the cost amount of $50,000, no income tax is due. Mrs. Smith is deemed to be simply recovering the amount that the annuity cost her to purchase. If, on the other hand, the partial surrender amount is $60,000, rather than $20,000, the excess of the $60,000 surrender amount over the $50,000 cost will be taxable income to Mrs. Smith where the annuity is taxed under the cost recovery rule.

The cash value of an annuity is determined without regard to any surrender charge[18] and the investment in the contract is, under the general rule, the cost of the annuity less any amounts previously received from the annuity that were properly excluded from income. Further, investment in the contract is increased by loans treated as distributions to the extent the amount is includable in income.[19]

The purpose behind the "interest first" rule applicable to investment in contracts after August 13, 1982, is to limit the tax advantages of deferred annuity contracts to long term investment goals, such as income security, and to prevent the use of tax deferred inside build-up as a method of sheltering income on freely withdrawable short term investments.

As with any change in the tax law that divides contracts into those issued before a certain date and those issued after the date, there are questions about how to treat contracts that have one foot on each side of the date. Regarding the taxation of partial surrenders from annuities, the question arises about how to treat a partial surrender from an annuity that was issued prior to the 1982 cut-off date but that received premium payments after 1982. According to the Internal Revenue Code, amounts received from a partial surrender that are allocable to premiums paid after August 13, 1982 in an annuity contract entered into before August 14, 1982 are treated as received under a contract entered into after August 13, 1982 and are subject to the above "interest first" rule.[20] If an annuity contract has income allocable to earnings on pre-August 14, 1982 and post-August 13, 1982 investments, the amount received is allocable first to investments made prior to August 14, 1982, then to income accumulated with respect to such investments (under the "cost recovery" rule), then to income accumulated with respect to investments made after August 13, 1982 and finally to investments made after August 13, 1982 (under the "interest first" rule).[21]

As a final word on partial surrenders and withdrawals, it is important to note that for the taxation of withdrawals from annuity contracts, as with other taxation issues, different rules apply to amounts received under qualified retirement plans, Tax Sheltered Annuities, and Individual Retirement Arrangements.

Multiple Annuity Contracts

All annuity contracts entered into after October 21, 1988, that are issued by the same company to the same policyholder during any calendar year will be treated as one annuity contract for purposes of determining the amount of any distribution that is includable in income.[22] This aggregation rule does not apply to distributions received under qualified retirement plans, Tax Sheltered Annuities, or from an Individual Retirement Arrangement.[23] Apparently, it does not apply to immediate annuities either.[24]

Effect of a Tax Free Exchange

In order to give effect to the grandfathering of pre-August 14, 1982, annuity contracts, a replacement contract obtained in a tax free exchange of annuity contracts succeeds to the status of the surrendered contract, for purposes of determining when amounts are to be considered invested and for computing the taxability of any withdrawals.[25] Investment in the replacement contract is considered made on, before or after August 13, 1982 to the same extent the investment was made on, before or after August 13, 1982 in the replaced contract. For example, assume that Ms. Jones purchased an annuity with a single premium of $10,000 in 1981 and then, at some point after 1982, exchanged the annuity, via a Code section 1035 exchange, for another annuity. Even though the newly-received annuity was issued after the 1982 cut-off date, it keeps its right for partial surrenders to be taxed under the more-favorable cost recovery rule rather than the less-favorable interest first rule usually applicable to annuities issued after 1982.

COMPLETE SURRENDER OF THE ANNUITY

Generally, if an annuity holder surrenders the annuity and receives the complete surrender value available under the contract, the holder must pay income tax on the difference between the amount he has received and his basis in the annuity. (In most instances, the annuity holder's basis will be equal to the amount of premiums paid into the annuity, but to be fully accurate in this calculation, the premiums paid figure must be reduced by any amounts previously received from the annuity that were properly excluded from the annuity holder's income.) In terms of the rules applicable to partial surrenders discussed above, a complete or full surrender of an annuity is taxed under the cost recovery rule.[26]

For example, assume that Mr. Smith owns an annuity with a cash surrender value of $50,000 and his basis, or the amount of premiums that he has paid into the contract, equals $20,000. Upon complete surrender of the annuity, Mr. Smith will pay income tax on $30,000. This figure is arrived at by subtracting the $20,000 basis in the annuity from the $50,000 amount received upon surrendering the contract.

EXCHANGES – SECTION 1035

On occasion, an annuity holder may wish to trade or exchange the annuity contract that he currently has for an annuity contract issued by another company. There are several reasons why an annuity holder would be interested in such an exchange, including the solvency of the current company, the interest rates currently offered by various companies, and the desire for additional investment alternatives not offered under the current contract.

The Internal Revenue Code does provide for an exchange of one annuity contract for another, subject to certain requirements, in Code section 1035.[27] If the requirements are met, the annuity holder may exchange one annuity contract for another without incurring any current income taxation. Despite the language of Code section 1035 which states that a permissible exchange is of "... an annuity contract for another annuity...," the Internal

Revenue Service has concluded, in a private letter ruling, that the exchange of one annuity contract for two annuity contracts is a proper exchange under Section 1035.[28]

Code section 1035 exchanges are generally available to nonqualified annuity contracts. Annuities used in Individual Retirement Annuities (IRAs) and Tax Sheltered Annuities may be exchanged under certain circumstances but are generally subject to different rules.

Code section 1035 deals not only with the exchange of annuities but also with the exchange of life insurance policies. Generally, the section provides that the following exchanges may be made without current income taxation:

1. An annuity contract for another annuity contract;

2. A life insurance policy for an annuity contract;

3. An endowment contract for an annuity contract;

4. A life insurance policy for another life insurance policy;

5. A life insurance policy for an endowment contract; and

6. An endowment contract for an endowment contract which will begin making payments no later than payments would have commenced under the old contract.

One type of exchange is not included in the list; the exchange of an annuity for a life insurance policy. This exchange is not permitted by Code section 1035.[29] The reasoning behind this policy is assumed to be that allowing such an exchange would enable an annuity holder to transfer funds from the annuity, which incurs income tax on at least a portion of the benefits paid out under the contract, to a life insurance policy, which pays death benefits free of income tax. In other words, an annuity to insurance exchange would move from a tax-deferred item to a tax-free item. While the Internal Revenue Code is willing to allow policy holders to exchange policies, it is not willing to allow an exchange which will improve the income taxation of the benefits.

Whether the annuity contract received in exchange for a life insurance policy, an endowment contract, or fixed annuity contract is a variable annuity contract makes no difference. Such an exchange qualifies as a tax free exchange under Section 1035, whether the new contract is issued by the same company or a different company.[30] Although there are no rulings to date, it is generally assumed that the same rules would apply to an equity-indexed annuity issued as part of a Section 1035 exchange.

If an annuity is exchanged for another annuity, both contracts must be payable to the same person or persons. Otherwise, the exchange does not qualify as a tax free exchange under Section 1035.[31] The Code defines an annuity for this purpose as a contract with an insurance company which may be payable during the life of the annuitant only in installments.[32]

Within the confines of the Section 1035 exchange, the distinction between an "exchange" and a surrender and purchase is not always clear. If the annuity contracts are properly exchanged, there is no income tax due. However, if one contract is surrendered and then a new contract is subsequently purchased there will more than likely be some income tax due as a result of the surrender of the old contract. Generally, where the annuity contract of one insurer is assigned, prior to maturity, to another insurer for a new contract of the second insurer, the transaction is considered an "exchange."[33]

After a Section 1035 exchange takes place, the cost basis of the new annuity will be generally the same as the cost basis of the old annuity. (To the basis in the old annuity, future premiums paid must be added and any excludable amounts received after the exchange must be subtracted.)

This is true if no cash or property other than the new annuity contract is received in connection with the exchange. However, if cash or other property is received as a part of the exchange, any gain will be recognized to the extent of the cash or other property received.[34]

Further, the existence of a loan against an annuity at the time of an exchange can affect the income tax outcome, although this situation does not arise often where annuities are concerned.[35]

A question often asked when the exchange of one annuity contract for another is contemplated is whether the exchange will cause an annuity which is currently "grandfathered" for purposes of the taxation of withdrawals from the contract to lose this status. (Generally, withdrawals from annuities issued prior to August 14, 1982, are taxed under the cost recovery rule which states that the annuity holder may receive funds out of the contract on a tax free basis until he has received tax free amounts equal to his basis in the contract. Withdrawals from annuities issued after this date are taxed under the less-favorable interest first rule, as discussed earlier under the heading of "Taxation of Withdrawals.") In order to give effect to this grandfathering, a replacement contract obtained in a tax free exchange of annuity contracts will succeed to the status of the surrendered contract. In other words, if the old annuity contract was grandfathered, the new annuity contract received in a Section 1035 exchange will also be grandfathered.[36]

GIFT OF AN ANNUITY

It is not uncommon for an annuity holder to decide that she wishes to give the annuity to another person. Take, for example, Mrs. Tucker who purchased a deferred annuity as a funding vehicle for her daughter's college education but was happy to learn that her daughter had been awarded a full scholarship to college. Since the funds were ear-marked for the daughter's education but not needed for this purpose, Mrs. Tucker may decide to give these funds to the daughter.

The most obvious manner in which to transfer the funds is for Mrs. Tucker to surrender the annuity and give the cash to the daughter. However, this will result in an income tax cost to Mrs. Tucker equal to the amount received upon the surrender of the annuity less the amount she had contributed to the annuity over the years. Plus, this method has the further disadvantage of not providing the daughter with the benefit of the income tax deferral on the interest earned on the funds after she receives them that continuing the annuity would have offered.

A second alternative is for Mrs. Tucker to transfer ownership of the annuity contract to the daughter. After the gift, the contract will continue in existence with the daughter as owner. However, unlike the gift of some types of property, the gift of an annuity contract carries some immediate income tax consequences. Generally, an individual who makes a gift of an annuity contract that was issued after April 22, 1987 is treated as having received an amount equal to the cash surrender value of the contract at the time of the gift minus the annuity holder's investment in the annuity. This amount is then added to the investment in the contract for the recipient of the gift.[37] To illustrate, assume that Mrs. Tucker had paid $1,000 each year into the college-expense annuity for 15 years. At the time she wishes to make a gift of the annuity to her daughter, the cash surrender value in the annuity contract is $22,000. Thus, at the time of the gift, Mrs. Tucker will have taxable income of $7,000. (This figure is arrived at by subtracting the $15,000 that Mrs. Tucker put into the annuity from the $22,000 cash surrender value.) Mrs. Tucker's investment in the contract will then be increased by $7,000 to $22,000. Generally, this rule does not apply to a transfer between spouses or former spouses that is incident to a divorce.[38]

The treatment of the gift of an annuity issued before 1988 differs from the treatment of an annuity issued after this date, as discussed above. If the cash surrender value of an annuity contract issued prior to April 23, 1987 at the time of the gift exceeds the cost basis of the person making the gift, and the person receiving the gift surrenders the contract sometime after receiving it, the person who made the gift must report as taxable income in the year of the surrender the "gain" that existed at the time of gift. To put this rule in terms of the college funding example used above, assume that Mrs. Tucker made the gift of the annuity to her daughter when she completed college at age 22. The daughter did not surrender the annuity contract until she reached age 28 and needed the funds for the purchase of a house. Mrs. Tucker would not be taxed on the difference between the $15,000 premiums she paid and the $22,000 cash surrender value of the contract until the year the annuity was surrendered, five years after the gift was made. The balance of the gain, if any, would be taxed to the daughter. The difficult aspect of this pre-1988 rule is that the proper year for Mrs. Tucker to include the gain in her gross income is the year in which the contract is *surrendered* by the daughter, not the year in which the gift is actually made.[39]

If a person who has received a gift of an annuity contract does not surrender the contract but instead chooses to begin receiving annuity payments under the contract, the payments are taxed under the general annuity rules which call for the application of an exclusion ratio resulting in the taxation of a portion of each annuity payment. With respect to gifts of annuities issued after April 22, 1987, the person receiving the gift of the annuity takes as his basis in the contract the same basis as the person making the gift held at the time of the transfer plus any amount included in the donor's income due to the gift.[40]

SALE OF AN ANNUITY

The Seller

At times, the owner of an annuity contract may wish to sell the contract to another individual or perhaps even to a business entity. If such a sale takes place, the gain is taxed to the seller as ordinary income—not as capital gain.[41] The amount of taxable gain resulting from the sale of an annuity is determined in the same way as upon surrender of a contract. In other words, gain is determined by subtracting the amount that the annuity owner had paid into the contract from the sale price.

However, where an annuity contract is sold after maturity, for purposes of determining the seller's gain, the cost basis of the contract (the amount the annuity owner has paid into the contract) must be reduced by the total of the portions of the annuity payments that have been received and were excluded from income. The adjusted basis cannot be reduced below zero.[42]

Where an annuity contract is sold for less than its cost basis, apparently the seller realizes an ordinary loss.

As it relates to an annuity contract, a loss deduction can be claimed only if the loss is incurred in connection with the taxpayer's trade or business or in a transaction entered into for profit.[43]

Generally, the purchase of a personal annuity contract is considered a transaction entered into for profit. Consequently, if a taxpayer sustains a loss upon surrender of an annuity contract, he may claim a deduction for the loss, regardless of whether he purchased the contract in connection with his trade or business or as a personal investment. The amount of the loss is determined by subtracting the cash surrender value from the taxpayer's basis for the contract, which is generally equal to the amount he has paid into the annuity contract. The loss is an ordinary loss, not a capital one.[44]

However, if the taxpayer purchased the contract for purely personal reasons, and not for profit, no loss deduction will be allowed.[45]

The Purchaser

If the purchaser of an annuity contract receives lifetime proceeds under the contract he is taxed in the same way as the original owner would have been taxed. His cost basis is, generally, the sales price that he paid for the contract plus any premiums he paid into the annuity after the purchase. If the contract is purchased after payments commence under a life income or installment option, a new exclusion ratio must be determined.[46]

If the purchaser of an annuity is a corporation or other "nonnatural" entity, the income tax deferral on the interest earned inside the annuity contract may be lost, as discussed earlier in this chapter under the heading of "Nonnatural Persons."

TAXATION OF ANNUITY BENEFIT PAYMENTS

The Basic Rule

The basic rule for the income taxation of payments received from an annuity contract is designed to return the purchaser's investment in equal tax-free amounts over the payment period. The balance of each payment received must be included in gross income. Each payment, therefore, is generally part nontaxable return of cost and part taxable income. Any excess interest or dividends added to the guaranteed payments is taxed as income in the year it is received.

The Exclusion Ratio

To determine what portion of the annuity payment is taxed and what portion is not, an exclusion ratio must be determined for the contract. The exclusion ratio may be expressed as a fraction or as a percentage and is arrived at by dividing the investment in the contract by the expected return. This exclusion ratio is applied to each annuity payment to find the portion of the payment that is excludable from gross income; the balance of the guaranteed annuity payment is includable in gross income for the year received.[47]

Figure 7.01 illustrates the use of an exclusion ratio. In this calculation, Mr. Baker, age 58, begins to receive annuity payments that will extend over his lifetime. At the time the payments commence, Mr. Baker has paid $100,000 into the annuity contract. Of the $700 payment that Mr. Baker will receive each month, 54% ($378 for the month or $4,536 for the year) must be included in his income for the year. The remaining 46% of the payment ($322 for the month or $3,864 for the year) in not taxable.

In Figure 7.01, the 46% exclusion ratio is arrived at by taking the investment in the contract of $100,000 and dividing by the expected return of $217,560. (The expected return amount of $217,560 is calculated by multiplying the $700 monthly payment by 12 to arrive at a yearly amount of $8,400 and then multiplying this amount by Mr. Baker's life expectancy of 25.9 years.)

Figure 7.01

FIXED LEVEL ANNUITY PAYABLE OVER A SINGLE LIFE		
Birthdate:	January 1, 1944 (Age: 58)	Sex: Male
Monthly Payment:	$700	Investment: $100,000
First Payment:	January 1, 2002	Guarantee: None
		Unisex
		Annuity Table
Percentage Includable in Income:		54.0%
Percentage Excludable from Income:		46.0%
Amount Includable - First Year:		$4,536
Amount Excludable - First Year:		$3,864
Amount Includable - Succ. Years:		$4,536
Amount Excludable - Succ. Years:		$3,864
Cost Recovered in Payment Made:		11/01/2027
After cost fully recovered, all amounts are includable.		

In the unusual instance where the investment in the contract is greater than the annuity holder's expected return, the full amount of each payment is received tax-free.[48]

The number of months or years for which the exclusion ratio applies is governed by the "annuity starting date," which is the first day of the first period for which an annuity payment is received.[49] If the annuity starting date is after December 31, 1986, the exclusion ratio applies to payments received until the investment in the contract is fully recovered. Payments received after this point are fully includable in income.[50] Referring again to Figure 7.01, because the annuity starting date is after 1986, Mr. Baker will no longer be able to exclude 46% of the monthly annuity payment from income beginning in November of 2027.

If, on the other hand, the annuity starting date was before January 1, 1987, the exclusion ratio applies to all payments received throughout the entire payment period, even if the annuitant has recovered his investment. Thus, it is possible for a long-lived annuitant to receive tax-free amounts that total more than he put into the annuity contract.

The Investment in the Contract

Generally speaking, the investment in the contract is the gross premium cost or other consideration paid for the annuity contract. To be fully accurate in this calculation the gross premium cost must be reduced by any amounts previously received from the annuity to the extent that these amounts were properly excluded from the annuity holder's income.[51]

In the case of a participating annuity contract, dividends must be taken into account for purposes of calculating the investment in the contract. If dividends have been received in cash or used to reduce premiums, the total amount of these dividends received or credited before the annuity payments commenced must be subtracted from gross premiums to the extent the dividends were excluded from the annuity holder's income.[52] But if excludable dividends have been left on deposit with the insurance company to accumulate at interest, and the dividends and interest are used to produce larger annuity payments, such dividends are not subtracted from gross premiums but are considered part of the cost of the larger payments. In this situation, gross premiums plus accumulated interest equal the cost of the contract.

It is helpful to remember that there are different rules that apply in computing the investment in the contract with respect to employee annuities such as IRAs, TSAs, and qualified retirement plans.

If the annuity is a life annuity with a refund or period-certain guarantee, a special adjustment must be made to the investment in the contract. The value of the refund or period-certain guarantee, as determined under certain rules, must be subtracted from the investment in the contract. It is this adjusted investment in the contract that is used in the exclusion ratio.[53]

The Expected Return

The expected return from an annuity contract, as discussed above, is the figure into which the investment in the contract is divided when calculating the annuity's exclusion ratio. Generally speaking, expected return is the total amount that the annuitant (or annuitants) can expect to receive under the contract.

More specifically, if payments are for a fixed period or a fixed amount with no life expectancy involved, expected return is the sum of the guaranteed payments.[54]

If payments are to continue for a life or lives, expected return is arrived at by multiplying the sum of one year's annuity payments by the life expectancy of the measuring life or lives. The life expectancy multiple or multiples must be taken from the Annuity Tables set forth by the IRS.[55] The IRS Annuity Tables are reproduced in the Appendix A.

Figure 7.02 shows a sample annuity exclusion ratio calculation and the applicable annuity table, Table V, is displayed in Figure 7.03. In Figure 7.02, a 50-year-old male will begin receiving annuity payments over his life time from an annuity into which he has paid $50,000. He will receive monthly annuity payments of $300 or $3,600 annually. Each year he will exclude from income $1,512, or 42%, and include in income the remaining $2,088, or 58%. The exclusion ratio was arrived at by dividing the investment in the contract of $50,000 by the expected return of $119,160. The expected return was calculated by taking the monthly annuity payment of $300 and multiplying it by 12 months to arrive at $3,600 and then multiplying this amount by the annuitant's life expectancy figure from Table V of 33.1 years.

Figure 7.02

FIXED LEVEL ANNUITY PAYABLE OVER A SINGLE LIFE	
Birthdate: January 1, 1952 (Age: 50) Sex: Male	
Monthly Payment: $300 Investment: $50,000	
First Payment: January 1, 2002 Guarantee: None	
	Unisex Annuity Table
Percentage Includable in Income:	58.0%
Percentage Excludable from Income:	42.0%
Amount Includable - First Year:	$2,088
Amount Excludable - First Year:	$1,512
Amount Includable - Succ. Years:	$2,088
Amount Excludable - Succ. Years:	$1,512
Cost Recovered in Payment Made:	1/01/2035
After cost fully recovered, all amounts are includable.	

Figure 7.03

Table V — Ordinary Life Annuities — One Life — Expected Return Multiples					
Age	Multiple	Age	Multiple	Age	Multiple
5	76.6	42	40.6	79	10.0
6	75.6	43	39.6	80	9.5
7	74.7	44	38.7	81	8.9
8	73.7	45	37.7	82	8.4
9	72.7	46	36.8	83	7.9
10	71.7	47	35.9	84	7.4
11	70.7	48	34.9	85	6.9
12	69.7	49	34.0	86	6.5
13	68.8	50	33.1	87	6.1
14	67.8	51	32.2	88	5.7
15	66.8	52	31.3	89	5.3
16	65.8	53	30.4	90	5.0
17	64.8	54	29.5	91	4.7
18	63.9	55	28.6	92	4.4
19	62.9	56	27.7	93	4.1
20	61.9	57	26.8	94	3.9
21	60.9	58	25.9	95	3.7
22	59.9	59	25.0	96	3.4
23	59.0	60	24.2	97	3.2
24	58.0	61	23.3	98	3.0
25	57.0	62	22.5	99	2.8
26	56.0	63	21.6	100	2.7
27	55.1	64	20.8	101	2.5
28	54.1	65	20.0	102	2.3
29	53.1	66	19.2	103	2.1
30	52.2	67	18.4	104	1.9
31	51.2	68	17.6	105	1.8
32	50.2	69	16.8	106	1.6
33	49.3	70	16.0	107	1.4
34	48.3	71	15.3	108	1.3
35	47.3	72	14.6	109	1.1
36	46.4	73	13.9	110	1.0
37	45.4	74	13.2	111	.9
38	44.4	75	12.5	112	.8
39	43.5	76	11.9	113	.7
40	42.5	77	11.2	114	.6
41	41.5	78	10.6	115	.5

The Annuity Tables

The life expectancy for a single life is found in Table I or in Table V, whichever is applicable, according to when amounts were paid into the annuity. The life expectancy multiples for joint and survivor annuities are taken from Tables II and IIA or Tables VI and VIA, whichever are applicable.[56] The annuity tables are entered with the age of the measuring life as of his or her birthday nearest the annuity starting date. The annuity tables are reproduced in Appendix A.

Generally, gender-based Tables I - IV are to be used if the investment in the annuity contract does not include a post-June 30, 1986 investment. Unisex Tables V - VIII are to be used if the investment in the contract does include a post-June 30, 1986 investment. However, transitional rules permit an irrevocable election to use the unisex tables even where there is no post-June 1986 investment and, if investment in the contract includes both a pre-July 1986 investment and a post-June 1986 investment, an election may be made in some situations to make separate computations with respect to each portion of the aggregate investment in the contract using with respect to each portion the tables applicable to it.[57] Specific examples of these calculations appear in Appendix B.

For example, a female annuitant, age 63, with an annuity into which all premiums have been paid after 1986 would look to Table V for a life expectancy of 21.6 years. A male annuitant, age 63, would also use a life expectancy figure of 21.6 years, taken from Table V. However, an annuity into which all premiums were paid prior to 1986 with a female annuitant of age 63 would look to Table I for a life expectancy figure of 19.6 years while an annuity owned by a male, age 63, with all pre-1986 premiums would use a life expectancy figure from Table I of 16.2 years.

Taxation of Variable Annuity Benefit Payments

As discussed in Chapter 4, variable annuities are similar to fixed annuities in some respects and yet different in other respects. The same is true regarding the taxation of fixed and variable annuities. In some respects taxation is the same while in other instances the taxation differs.

One area where fixed and variable annuities are taxed similarly is the deferral of income tax on the interest earned inside the annuity. Generally, an annuity owner who is a natural person will pay no income tax until he either surrenders the annuity for cash or begins to receive an income under the contract.

However, in order to receive this deferral of income tax, a variable annuity must meet one additional requirement. Beginning on January 1, 1984, a variable annuity contract will not be treated as an annuity and taxed as such unless the underlying investments of the segregated asset account are "adequately diversified," according to regulations prescribed by the Internal Revenue Service.[58]

Both fixed dollar and variable annuity payments are subject to the same basic tax rule: a fixed portion of each annuity payment is excludable from gross income as a tax-free recovery of the purchaser's investment, and the balance is taxable as ordinary income. However, the rules for these types of annuities differ in that with a variable annuity the excludable portion is not determined by calculating an "exclusion ratio" as it is for a fixed dollar annuity. Since the expected return under a variable annuity is unknown, it is deemed to be equal to the investment in the contract. Thus, the excludable portion is determined by dividing the investment in the contract by the number of years over which it is anticipated the annuity will be paid.[59]

If payments are to be made for a fixed number of years without regard to life expectancy, the divisor is the fixed number of years. If payments are to be made for a single life, the divisor is the appropriate life expectancy multiple from Table I or Table V, whichever is applicable (depending on when the investment in the contract was made, as explained in Appendix A).[60]

Remember that, as discussed earlier, the amount determined using the exclusion ratio may be excluded from gross income each year for as long as the payments are received if the annuity payments began before January 1, 1987. If the annuity payments begin after 1986, the amount determined may be excluded from gross income only until the investment in the contract is recovered.[61]

There is one other income tax "quirk" that applies to variable annuities, but not fixed annuities, purchased some years back. If the owner of a variable annuity contract acquired prior to October 21, 1979, dies before the annuity payments begin, the contract acquires a new cost basis rather than retaining as its cost basis the amount which has been paid into the annuity. The basis of the contract in the hands of the beneficiary will be the value of the contract at the date of the annuitant's death. Therefore, this "quirk" in the law provides a possible income tax savings in that if the annuity's basis equals the amount received by the beneficiary there will be no income taxable gain and the appreciation in the value of the contract while owned by the deceased will escape income tax entirely.[62] However, the Internal Revenue Service has indicated its general opinion that if a variable annuity contract purchased before October 21, 1979 is exchanged, via Code section 1035, for another variable annuity contract issued after October 20, 1979 and the annuity owner dies before the annuity payments begin, the beneficiary will not be entitled to this "step-up" in basis.[63]

DEATH OF THE ANNUITY OWNER

An annuity is usually purchased on the assumption that the annuity owner will live long enough for the annuitant to begin receiving annuity payments. In reality, of course, this does not always happen. When the owner dies before the entire interest in the contract has been paid out certain distributions from the annuity must be made. These rules are intended to prevent deferral of income tax on the gain in the annuity for an indefinite period of time through successive ownership of the annuity.

The Internal Revenue Code mandates that an annuity issued after January 18, 1985, will not be treated as an annuity contract and, thus, receive the income tax deferral associated with an annuity unless the contract provides two items. First, the annuity must provide that if any owner dies after the annuity has begun making annuity payments (i.e., after the annuity starting date) but before the entire interest in the contract has been distributed, the remaining portion must be distributed at least as rapidly as under the method of distribution being used at the owner's death. Second, the annuity must provide that if the owner dies before the annuity payments have started, the entire interest in the contract must be distributed within the five years following the owner's death.[64] In the case of joint owners of an annuity issued after April 22, 1987, these distribution requirements are applied at the first death.[65]

For purposes of meeting these distribution requirements, if any portion of the owner's interest is to be distributed to a designated beneficiary over the beneficiary's life (or over a period not extending beyond the life expectancy of the beneficiary) and the distribution begins within one year after the owner's death, that portion will be treated as distributed on the day such distribution begins.

For example assume that Mr. Robins, age 50, buys an annuity contract and is the owner. He names his son, Mr. Robins, Jr., age 25, as the annuitant, with annuity payments to begin when his son becomes age 45. The father dies at age 58 and the son (now age 33) becomes the new owner of the contract. Under the provisions discussed above, there must be a distribution of the entire interest in the contract within five years of the father's death or there must be annuitization of the contract within one year of such date.[66]

If the designated beneficiary (that is, the person who becomes the new owner) is the surviving spouse of the owner, then the distribution requirements are applied by treating the spouse as the owner.[67] In effect, this allows a surviving spouse to "step into the shoes" of the deceased spouse and carry the annuity along without any change. For example, assume that Mr. Smith purchased a single premium deferred annuity five years prior to his death, naming himself as owner and annuitant and his wife, Mrs. Smith, as the designated beneficiary. He had not yet started to receive payments from the annuity contract at his death. Since Mrs. Smith would be treated as the annuity contact owner upon his death, the distribution requirements would allow her to continue the annuity in its accumulation phase for the time being.

For the purpose of these distribution requirements which take effect upon the death of the annuity owner, some provision must be made when the annuity owner is an entity such as a trust or corporation. The Internal Revenue Code provides that where the owner of a contract issued after April 22, 1987, is a corporation or other nonnatural person, the primary annuitant will be treated as the owner of the contract. The primary annuitant is the individual whose life is of primary importance in affecting the timing or amount of the payout under the contract (e.g., the measuring life).[68] For purposes of these distribution requirements, a change in the primary annuitant of such a contract is treated as the death of the owner.[69]

If an annuity contract which is issued after January 18, 1985 is received in exchange for one issued prior to that date it will be considered a new contract and, thus, subject to these distribution requirements.[70]

DEATH OF THE ANNUITANT

Often it is the same person who is named as both the owner and the annuitant of an annuity contract. Thus, when the annuitant dies, the owner also dies and the annuity is subject to the distribution requirements discussed above. However, there are times when one person is named as the annuity contract owner and another individual is named as the annuitant. One example of this is grandparents who buy an annuity for a grandchild naming one of the grandparents as owner of the contract and the grandchild as the annuitant.

If the annuitant dies before the deferred annuity matures, the amount payable at his death is generally subject to income tax. Usually, an annuity contract provides that if the annuitant dies before the annuity payments begin, the beneficiary will be paid a death benefit equal to the amount of premiums paid or the accumulation value of the contract. The gain, if any, is taxable as ordinary income to the beneficiary.

The death benefit under an annuity contract is not excludable from income under Code section 101(a) as life insurance proceeds payable by reason of insured's death. The gain in an annuity contract is measured by subtracting the total premiums from the death benefit received. (Aggregate dividends and any other amounts that have been received under the contract which were excludable from gross income must be added to the death benefit received amount as a part of this calculation.)[71]

Thus, continuing with the grandparents/grandchild example mentioned earlier, if the grandchild dies and the grandparent is still living, a death benefit amount will be paid to the grandparent. If the death benefit paid equals $25,000 and the grandparents have paid $20,000 into the annuity, then the gain of $5,000 must be included in the grandparent's income for the year.

There is one election open to the annuity owner at the time of the annuitant's death that may help to minimize the income tax consequences of the annuitant's death. The beneficiary of the death benefit will not be taxed on the gain in the year of death if he elects, within 60 days after the annuitant's death, to apply the death benefit under a life income or installment option.[72] The periodic payments will then be taxable to the beneficiary under the regular annuity rules.[73]

Another question that arises in relationship to an annuity when investment results have not met expectations is whether there is a deductible loss sustained under a straight life annuity if the annuitant dies before the total annuity payments received equal the annuitant's cost. If the annuity contract began making annuity payments before July 2, 1986, there is no deductible loss since the annuitant has received all that the contract called for.[74] The result is the same for one who purchases an annuity on the life of another person who dies prematurely.[75] If the annuity payments began after July 1, 1986, a deduction may be taken on the individual's final income tax return for the unrecovered investment in the contract.[76]

ENDNOTES

1. IRC Sec. 219.
2. IRC Sec. 72.
3. IRC Sec. 72(u).
4. IRC Sec. 72(u)(2).
5. IRC Sec. 72(u)(3).
6. IRC Sec. 72(u)(1), flush language; H.R. Conf. Rep. No. 99-841 (TRA '86) *reprinted in* 1986-3 CB 401.
7. Let. Ruls. 9639057, 9316018, 9204014, 9204010, 9120024.
8. See Let. Rul. 9009047.
9. Tax Reform Act of 1986 (TRA '86), Section 1135(b).
10. IRC Sec. 72(e)(4)(A).
11. See *Helvering v. Eubank*, 311 U.S. 112 (1940); *Lucas v. Earl*, 281 U.S. 111 (1930); *Van Brunt v. Comm.*, 11 BTA 406 (1928).
12. IRC Sec. 72(q).
13. Ibid.
14. IRC Sec. 72(q)(2).
15. IRC Sec. 72(q)(3); H.R. Conf. Rep. No. 99-841 (TRA '86) *reprinted in* 1986-3 CB 403.
16. IRC Secs. 72(e)(2), 72(e)(3).
17. IRC Sec. 72(e)(5)(B).
18. IRC Sec. 72(e)(3).
19. IRC Sec. 72(e)(4)(A), flush language.
20. IRC Sec. 72(e)(5)(B).
21. Rev. Rul. 85-159, 1985-2 CB 29.
22. IRC Sec. 72(e)(11).
23. IRC Sec. 72(e)(11)(A), flush language.
24. Conference Report on Omnibus Budget Reconciliation Act of 1989 (OBRA '89) for Act sec. 7815(a)(3) and (5), amending Code sec. 72(e)(11)(A).
25. Rev. Rul. 85-159, 1985-2 CB 29.
26. IRC Sec. 72(e)(5)(E).
27. IRC Sec. 1035. As of August 5, 1997, the Section 1035 rules do not apply to any exchange having the effect of transferring property to any non-United States person. IRC Sec. 1035(c).
28. Let. Rul. 9644016. See also Let. Rul. 9708016.
29. Treas. Reg. §1.1035-1; Rev. Rul. 54-264, 1954-2 CB 57; *Barrett v. Comm.*, 348 F.2d 916 (1st Cir. 1965) *aff'g* 42 TC 993.
30. Rev. Rul. 72-358, 1972-2 CB 473; Rev. Rul. 68-235, 1968-1 CB 360.
31. Treas. Reg. §1.1035-1.
32. IRC Sec. 1035(b)(2).
33. Rev. Rul. 72-358, 1972-2 CB 473.
34. Treas. Reg. §1.1031(b)-1(a).
35. Treas. Reg. §1.1031(b)-1(c).
36. Rev. Rul. 85-159, 1985-2 CB 29.
37. IRC Sec. 72(e)(4)(C).
38. IRC Secs. 72(e)(4)(C)(ii), 1041.
39. Rev. Rul. 69-102, 1969-1 CB 32.
40. IRC Sec. 72(e)(4)(C)(iii).

41. *First Nat'l Bank of Kansas City v. Comm.*, 309 F.2d 587 (8th Cir. 1962) *aff'g Michael Katz v. Comm.*, TC Memo 1961-270; *Roff v. Comm.*, 304 F.2d 450 (3rd Cir. 1962) *aff'g* 36 TC 818 (1961); *Arnfeld v. U.S.*, 163 F. Supp. 865 (Ct. Cl. 1958), *cert. denied* 359 U.S. 943 (1959).
42. IRC Sec. 1021.
43. IRC Sec. 165.
44. Rev. Rul. 61-201, 1961-2 CB 46; *Cohan v. Comm.*, 39 F.2d 540 (2nd Cir. 1930), *aff'g* 11 BTA 743 (1928).
45. *Early v. Atkinson*, 175 F.2d 118 (4th Cir. 1949).
46. Treas. Regs. §§1.72-4(b)(2)(ii), 1.72-10(a).
47. IRC Sec. 72(b)(1).
48. Treas. Reg. §1.72-4(d)(2).
49. IRC Sec. 72(c)(4); Treas. Reg. §1.72-4(b).
50. IRC Sec. 72(b)(2).
51. IRC Sec. 72(c)(1).
52. Treas. Reg. §1.72-6(a).
53. IRC Sec. 72(c)(2); Treas. Reg. §1.72-7.
54. IRC Sec. 72(c)(3)(B); Treas. Regs. §§1.72-5(c), 1.72-5(d).
55. IRC Sec. 72(c)(3)(A).
56. Treas. Regs. §§1.72-5(a), 1.72-5(b).
57. Treas. Reg. §1.72-9.
58. IRC Sec. 817(h); Treas. Reg. §1.817-5.
59. Treas. Reg. §1.72-2(b)(3).
60. Treas. Regs. §§1.72-2(b)(3), 1.72-4(d)(3).
61. IRC Sec. 72(b)(2).
62. Rev. Rul. 79-335, 1979-2 CB 292.
63. TAM 9346002; Let. Rul. 9245035.
64. IRC Sec. 72(s)(1).
65. Tax Reform Act of 1986 (TRA '86), Sec. 1826(b)(2).
66. Example taken from the *General Explanation of the Deficit Reduction Act of 1984*, at p. 660.
67. IRC Sec. 72(s)(3).
68. IRC Sec. 72(s)(6).
69. IRC Sec. 72(s)(7).
70. The Report of the Conference Committee (TRA '84) H.R. Conf. Rep. No. 98-861 (TRA '84) *reprinted in* 1984-3 CB 331-332.
71. IRC Sec. 72(e)(5)(E); Treas. Reg. §1.72-11(c); Rev. Rul. 55-313, 1955-1 CB 219.
72. IRC Sec. 72(h).
73. Treas. Regs. §§1.72-11(a), 1.72-11(e).
74. *Industrial Trust Co. v. Broderick*, 94 F.2d 927 (1st Cir. 1938); Rev. Rul. 72-193, 1972-1 CB 58; see also *Est. of Lambert v. Comm.*, 40 BTA 802 (1939).
75. *Helvering v. Louis*, 77 F.2d 386 (D.C. App. Ct. 1935); *White v. U.S.*, 19 AFTR 2d 658 (N.D. Tex. 1966).
76. IRC Sec. 72(b)(3)(A).

Chapter 8

ESTATE TAXATION OF ANNUITIES

WHAT IS THE ESTATE TAX?

In arranging financial affairs, questions concerning the application of the estate tax are often raised. This federal system of taxation can diminish, often significantly, the amount of property and money that is passed from one family member to another at death. Because of this potential, the estate tax should be understood and evaluated, at least generally, with regard to nonqualified annuities. The estate tax is repealed for one year for decedents dying in 2010.

The estate tax system is a transfer tax that is applicable to the value of most property that a person owns at the time of his death and even to some property that the person has already given away. The amount of estate tax due the federal government is paid out of the value of the property before any distributions from the person's estate are made to his heirs.

HOW IS THE ESTATE TAX CALCULATED?

Generally speaking, if a person dies in 2002 owning property worth more than $1,000,000, his estate will pay some estate tax. The $1,000,000 figure is the dollar value sheltered by the "unified credit" in 2002. Applicable to both the estate tax and the gift tax, the unified credit essentially allows the estate to transfer property worth up to $1,000,000 (in 2002) to the person's heirs before any tax must be paid.[1] As it affects gifts of annuities, the unified credit is discussed in Chapter 9.

The estate tax is applied according to a graduated schedule which is set forth in Figure 8.01. The top estate tax rate is 50% (in 2002), a rate which can result in the loss of a substantial portion of the property that an individual has accumulated during his lifetime. It is no wonder that individuals are concerned with keeping as much of their property as possible from being subject to this tax.

Figure 8.01

GIFT AND ESTATE TAX TABLE
(Lower Brackets: 2001 - 2009, 2011)

Taxable Gift/Estate From	To	Tax on Col. 1	Rate on Excess
$ 0	$ 10,000	$ 0	18%
10,000	20,000	1,800	20%
20,000	40,000	3,800	22%
40,000	60,000	8,200	24%
60,000	80,000	13,000	26%
80,000	10,0000	18,200	28%
100,000	150,000	23,800	30%
150,000	250,000	38,800	32%
250,000	500,000	70,800	34%
500,000	750,000	155,800	37%
750,000	1,000,000	248,300	39%
1,000,000	1,250,000	345,800	41%
1,250,000	1,500,000	448,300	43%

GIFT AND ESTATE TAX TABLE
(Upper Brackets: 2001, 2011 and later)

Taxable Gift/Estate From	To	Tax on Col. 1	Rate on Excess
1,500,000	2,000,000	555,800	45%
2,000,000	2,500,000	780,800	49%
2,500,000	3,000,000	1,025,800	53%
3,000,000	10,000,000	1,290,800	55%
10,000,000	17,184,000	5,140,800	60%
17,184,000	....	9,451,200	55%

Figure 8.01 (cont'd)

GIFT AND ESTATE TAX TABLE (Upper Brackets: 2002)			
Taxable Gift/Estate		**Tax on**	**Rate on**
From	**To**	**Col. 1**	**Excess**
1,500,000	2,000,000	555,800	45%
2,000,000	2,500,000	780,800	49%
2,500,000	....	1,025,800	50%

GIFT AND ESTATE TAX TABLE (Upper Brackets: 2003)			
Taxable Gift/Estate		**Tax on**	**Rate on**
From	**To**	**Col. 1**	**Excess**
1,500,000	2,000,000	555,800	45%
2,000,000	....	780,800	49%

GIFT AND ESTATE TAX TABLE (Upper Brackets: 2004)			
Taxable Gift/Estate		**Tax on**	**Rate on**
From	**To**	**Col. 1**	**Excess**
1,500,000	2,000,000	555,800	45%
2,000,000	....	780,800	48%

GIFT AND ESTATE TAX TABLE (Upper Brackets: 2005)			
Taxable Gift/Estate		**Tax on**	**Rate on**
From	**To**	**Col. 1**	**Excess**
1,500,000	2,000,000	555,800	45%
2,000,000	....	780,800	47%

Figure 8.01 (cont'd)

GIFT AND ESTATE TAX TABLE (Upper Brackets: 2006)			
Taxable Gift/Estate		**Tax on**	**Rate on**
From	**To**	**Col. 1**	**Excess**
1,500,000	2,000,000	555,800	45%
2,000,000	....	780,800	46%

GIFT AND ESTATE TAX TABLE (Upper Bracket: 2007 - 2009)			
Taxable Gift/Estate		**Tax on**	**Rate on**
From	**To**	**Col. 1**	**Excess**
1,500,000	....	555,800	45%

IRC Secs. 2001(c), 2502.

To illustrate the effect of the estate tax, suppose that Mrs. Smith, a 70-year-old widow, owns property worth $1,350,000 and dies in 2002. At first glance, it may seem that a person owning property worth over one million dollars is extremely wealthy. However, an examination of the breakdown of her assets, set forth below, shows that while Mrs. Smith is certainly comfortably established, she is not a member of the ultra-rich.

Mrs. Smith's Assets

Asset	Current Net Value
Home	$ 235,000
Certificates of Deposit	$ 95,000
Mutual Funds	$ 165,000
Individual Retirement Annuity	$ 175,000
Life Insurance Death Benefits	$ 400,000
Family Business Interest	$ 280,000
	$1,350,000

Applying the estate tax rate schedule in Figure 8.01 to Mrs. Smith's estate, (and assuming that the estate would not have any deductions), she would owe estate tax of approximately $145,500 ($491,300 tentative tax minus $345,800 unified credit). Or stated another way, at Mrs. Smith's death, only about 89% of her assets would pass on to her children, with the other 11% going to the federal government.

DEDUCTIONS FROM THE ESTATE TAX

In the example above, it was assumed that Mrs. Smith's estate was not entitled to any deductions. However, this is not the case with most estates. There are several deductions that may be subtracted from the total value of the property which is subject to the estate tax, generally known as the gross estate. These deductions are used extensively in estate planning and offer the potential to move a significant amount of property beyond the estate tax's reach.

One of the most used deductions is the marital deduction. Generally, the value of any property that is included in the gross estate and that will pass to the spouse of the individual who has died, called the decedent, can be deducted from the amount that will be subject to the estate tax.[2] In the example concerning Mrs. Smith above, assume that she remarried before her death and that her home would pass to her second husband at her death. Her gross estate of $1,350,000 would be decreased by the amount of the marital deduction, $235,000 (the value of the home) and, thus, only $1,115,000 would be subject to the estate tax, assuming that no other deductions would be available. The tax is calculated by applying the rate schedule in Figure 8.01. Assuming no other deduction are available, the amount of tax due would be $47,150 ($392,950 tentative tax minus $345,800 unified credit), which is $98,350 less than the amount of tax due if the marital deduction had not been available.

Another estate tax deduction is the charitable deduction. The value of any property which will go to a charity after the decedent's death can be subtracted from the gross estate in calculating the amount of estate tax due.[3] If Mrs. Smith, mentioned above, had placed a bequest in her will of $25,000 to her church, this amount, in addition to the marital deduction, could be subtracted from her gross estate of $1,350,000. Thus, if Mrs. Smith could take advantage of both deductions, her taxable estate would equal $1,090,000, which is arrived at by subtracting the marital deduction of $235,000 and the charitable deduction of $25,000 from $1,350,000. Thus, the estate tax due on the estate would be $36,900 ($382,700 tentative tax minus $345,800 unified credit). The use of the two deductions would save Mrs. Smith's estate approximately $108,600, a significant sum of money.

Note that, if Mrs. Smith passed $350,000 ($1,350,000 gross estate minus $1,000,000 unified credit equivalent) to her spouse, her taxable estate would be equal to $1,000,000 and the estate tax would be $0 ($345,800 tentative tax minus $345,800 unified credit). This would save $145,500.

Finally, there are several other estate tax deductions available, including deductions for funeral expenses, administration expenses, claims against the estate, and for debts against property that is included in the gross estate.[4]

Figure 8.02 shows a sample estate tax calculation which takes into account the deductions and credits mentioned above plus some items of a more technical nature.

ANNUITY CONTRACTS OWNED AT DEATH

One of the most common estate tax questions concerning annuities is whether an annuity owned by a person at his death must be included in the estate for purposes of calculating the amount of estate tax due. The answer differs depending upon whether the annuity contract had not yet commenced benefit payments (i.e., was is the accumulation phase) or had already begun benefit payments (i.e., was in the annuitization phase) at the time of the annuity holder's death.

In the Accumulation Phase

Although it is probably not expected at the time a nonqualified annuity is purchased, there are times when the annuity holder dies before annuitizing the contract and beginning to receive

Figure 8.02

FEDERAL ESTATE TAX CALCULATION		
Year of Death		2002
Gross Estate		$2,000,000
Less:Funeral and Administration Expenses	$25,000	
Claims Against Estate and Certain Debt	$0	
Uncompensated Losses During Administration	$5,000	($30,000)
Adjusted Gross Estate		$1,970,000
Less:Charitable Deduction	$50,000	
Marital Deduction	$750,000	($800,000)
Taxable Estate		$1,170,000
Adjusted Taxable Gifts		$0
Tentative Tax on Computation Base of $1,170,000		$415,500
Gift Tax Payable on Post-1976 Gifts		($0)
Gross Regular Federal Estate Tax		$415,500
Less:Unified Credit	$345,800	
Credit for State Death Taxes	$32,460	
Credit for Certain Pre-1977 Gift Taxes	$0	
Credit for Foreign Death Taxes	$0	
Credit for Tax on Prior Transfers	$0	($378,260)
Regular Federal Estate Tax		$37,240

benefit payments from the annuity. If this happens, generally the value of the annuity contract must be included in the gross estate of the annuity holder.[5]

As discussed in Chapter 7, most nonqualified annuity contracts pay a death benefit equal to at least the amount of premiums that the annuity holder has paid into the contract prior to his death. Although the nonqualified annuity contract does pay a benefit at death, in this instance, this benefit is not considered to be the same as a "death benefit" that is paid under a life insurance policy. If the annuity death benefit is payable to the annuity holder's estate, its value must be included in his gross estate.[6] This is true since the value of the annuity's death benefit is considered to be property owned by the annuity holder at the time of his death.

Even if the death benefit is payable to a beneficiary designated by the annuity holder, the value of the death benefit generally must be included in the annuity holder's gross estate whether or not the annuity holder had reserved the right to change the beneficiary.[7] For example, assume that Mr. Jones, age 60, purchased an annuity contract some years ago that would begin paying benefits to him when he retired at age 65. The annuity has a current value of $40,000. If Mr. Jones does not live until age 65 as he expected, the value of the death benefit paid from the annuity to either Mr. Jones' estate or his beneficiary would be included in Mr. Jones' gross estate.

However, if an annuity was a gift for another person from the person who has died (the decedent) and the decedent did not retain any interest in the annuity contract or payments, the value of annuity will ordinarily not be included in the decedent's gross estate.

In the Annuitization Phase

If the person was receiving payments under a straight life annuity, there will be no more payments from the annuity after the annuity holder's death, under the terms of this settlement option. Thus, there is no property interest remaining to be included in his gross estate and nothing will be added to the gross estate as a result of owning the annuity contract. To illustrate, assume that Mr. Smith, age 80, owns property worth approximately $750,000 and receives a payment of $900 each month from a single premium immediate annuity that he bought twenty years ago with funds inherited from his favorite uncle. Mr. Smith is both the owner and the annuitant of this contract. Since the annuity settlement option is a single life (sometimes called a straight life) annuity, once the single life (Mr. Smith's) has ended, the contract is also at an end and no more payments will be made. Thus, ownership of the annuity contract would not add anything to the gross estate of Mr. Smith.

As discussed in Chapter 3, there are usually several settlement options available under a nonqualified annuity contract including a refund life annuity, a joint and survivor life annuity, a fixed period annuity, and a fixed amount annuity. If an annuity settlement option was elected by the annuity holder prior to his death that includes some type of survivor benefit, such as under the refund life annuity or joint and survivor annuity, determining what amount must be included in the estate of the annuity holder following his death is slightly more complicated. Generally, if the survivor's benefit is payable to the estate of the annuity holder, the value of the payments to be made after the annuity holder's death must be included in the annuity holder's estate.[8] This is so, because the value of the post-death payments are considered to be "property" owned by the annuity holder at his death.

To illustrate, assume that Mr. Jones purchased a single premium deferred annuity and began receiving monthly benefit payments of $500 seven years ago. If Mr. Jones had elected a single life annuity settlement option, at his death after seven years of benefit payments, no further payments would be due. Thus, no amount would be included in his estate as a result of owning the annuity. However, if Mr. Jones elected a ten year certain settlement option, at his death after only seven years, another three years of monthly benefit payments would remain to be paid. The value of these remaining payments would be included in Mr. Jones' estate.

Generally speaking, the estate tax results are the same when an annuity's survivor benefit will be paid to the annuity holder's beneficiary rather than to his estate. To continue with Mr. Jones' example above, if the remaining three years of annuity payments were to go to Mr. Jones' daughter, the value of the remaining three years worth of benefit payments would be included in his gross estate.[9] Another step may be added to the calculation if the annuity holder did not furnish the entire purchase price of the annuity. In this case, only a portion of the value of the remaining benefit payments would be included in the annuity holder's gross estate.

For example, assume that Mr. and Mrs. Smith purchased a joint and survivor annuity with a single premium of $50,000, each contributing one-half, or $25,000, to the purchase price. At Mr. Smith's death several years later, the value of the benefit that will be paid to the survivor, Mrs. Smith, is $35,000. Since Mr. Smith contributed one-half of the annuity's purchase price, at his death, one-half of the value of the survivor's benefit, or $17,500, must be included in his gross estate. Since the survivor's benefit, in this example, will go to the spouse of the decedent, it should qualify for the marital deduction and thus not be included in the estate values upon which the amount of estate tax due is calculated.[10] If the annuity had been purchased in the same manner by Mr. Smith and his daughter, the marital deduction would not have this effect.

The value for estate tax purposes of the survivor's annuity under a joint and survivor annuity contract is generally equal to the amount the same insurance company would charge the survivor to purchase a single life annuity at the time of the first annuitant's death.[11] However, if the length of time that the particular survivor is expected to live is less than the statistical average for a person of that age, it may be possible to obtain a lower valuation amount.[12]

If the beneficiary that will receive the refund or survivor's benefit is a charitable organization, the estate will be able to take a deduction for the value of the transfer to the charity.[13]

It is important to remember that other types of annuities and retirement plans, such as Individual Retirement Annuities (IRAs), Tax Sheltered Annuities (TSAs), and annuities that are part of qualified retirement plans, are not treated in exactly the same manner as nonqualified annuities for purposes of the estate tax.

OWNER AND ANNUITANT ARE NOT THE SAME PERSON

While the more usual scenario casts the same individual as both the owner and the annuitant of a nonqualified annuity contract, there is no particular requirement that this be so. Fairly often, nonqualified annuity contracts are purchased by one individual who names a second person as the annuitant. From an estate tax perspective, what is the effect on the amount of estate tax due if an individual owns an annuity at the time of his death, but someone else, who is still living, is named as the annuitant?

Where an individual owns an annuity contract at the time of his death, but another individual is named as the annuitant, the value of the annuity is included in the owner's gross estate for purposes of determining the amount of estate tax due.[14] The value of the contract is apparently the amount that it would cost to purchase a comparable annuity contract at the time of the annuity owner's death.[15]

Such a situation might arise where an annuity had been purchased for an aging parent by an adult child. Assume that Greg Smith purchased an annuity, naming himself as the owner of the contract. Since the contract was purchased for the benefit of his mother, Rose Smith, Greg named her as the annuitant. If Greg died before his mother, the value of the annuity would be included in Greg's estate for estate tax purposes.

ANNUITY CONTRACTS PURCHASED AS GIFTS

If an annuity is given to someone as a gift and the purchaser does not retain any ownership interest in the contract after its purchase, the value of the annuity will ordinarily not be included in the purchaser's gross estate.[16] This will generally be true whether the purchaser named the person receiving the gift as both the owner and the annuitant or, instead, named a third person as the annuitant. Continuing with the example of Greg Smith and his mother from above, if Greg purchased a nonqualified annuity and named his mother as both the owner and the annuitant, at his death, no portion of the value of the annuity would be included in his gross estate.

PRIVATE ANNUITIES

As discussed in Chapter 4, a private annuity does not involve an annuity contract purchased from an insurance company. Rather, it is an arrangement between two individuals in which one individual transfers property to the other in return for a promise that the person receiving the property will pay an annuity for life to the person making the transfer.

In a private annuity arrangement, the transfer of the property given in exchange for the promise to pay the annuity is complete and absolute and the annuity payments generally stop upon the death of the person receiving them (the annuitant). Thus, there is generally no property interest to be included in the gross estate of the individual who was receiving the private annuity payments for purposes of the estate tax.[17]

ENDNOTES

1. IRC Sec. 2010. The amount of the estate tax unified credit (and the corresponding exemption equivalent or applicable exclusion amount) is scheduled to be $345,800 ($1,000,000) in 2002 and 2003; $555,800 ($1,500,000) in 2004 and 2005; $780,800 ($2,000,000) in 2006 to 2008; $1,455,800 ($3,500,000) in 2009; and $345,800 ($1,000,000) in 2011. The estate tax (but not the gift tax) is repealed for one year in 2010. However, the gift tax unified credit exemption equivalent is only $1,000,000 for such years.
2. IRC Sec. 2056(a). If the surviving spouse is not a United States citizen, a qualified domestic trust is generally required to take advantage of the marital deduction. IRC Secs. 2056(d), 2056A.
3. IRC Sec. 2055.
4. IRC Sec. 2053(a).
5. IRC Secs. 2033, 2039. See Treas. Reg. §20.2039-1(d).
6. IRC Sec. 2033.
7. IRC Sec. 2039.
8. IRC Sec. 2033.
9. IRC Sec. 2039(a).
10. See IRC Sec. 2056.
11. Treas. Reg. §20.2031-8; *Est. of Mearkle v. Comm.*, 129 F.2d 386 (3rd Cir. 1942); *Est. of Pruyn v. Comm.*, 12 TC 754 (1949).
12. *Est. of Jennings v. Comm.*, 10 TC 323 (1948); *Est. of Dalton v. Comm.*, 52 AFTR 1919 (S.D. Ind. 1956).
13. IRC Sec. 2055.
14. IRC Secs. 2033, 2039.
15. IRC Sec. 2031; Treas. Reg. §20.2031-(1)(b).
16. See *Wishard v. U.S.*, 143 F.2d 704 (7th Cir. 1944).
17. See, generally, IRC Sec. 2033.

Chapter 9

GIFT TAXATION OF ANNUITIES

WHAT IS THE GIFT TAX?

The federal gift tax is an excise tax which is levied upon gifts of money or property that are made during an individual's lifetime.[1] Although it may seem hard to accept, it is true that the federal government can assess a tax on the right of an individual to give away his property. Actually, the federal gift tax and the federal estate tax together form a unified tax system that imposes a tax on the transfer of property both during a person's life and at his death. The federal estate tax, particularly as it affects nonqualified annuities, is discussed in Chapter 8.

The gift tax can enter the annuity picture in several ways, including the gift of an annuity contract itself, the gift of funds for the purchase of an annuity, and certain beneficiary and settlement option choices. One aspect of the gift tax that seems unusual to some is that it is the responsibility of the person making the gift, not the person receiving the gift, to pay the gift tax.[2] However, if the person making the gift does not do so, the person receiving the gift will be held responsible for paying the tax, at least up to the value of the gift he has received.[3]

HOW IS THE GIFT TAX CALCULATED?

The gift tax is imposed on the fair market value of the total of all gifts made by an individual during one calendar year after all applicable exclusions and deductions are subtracted. The gift tax rate schedule, which appears in Figure 9.01, shows the range of rates. The gift tax is a cumulative tax in that gifts made in prior calendar years generally have the effect of causing gifts made in later years to be taxed at higher rate

Figure 9.01

GIFT AND ESTATE TAX TABLE (Lower Brackets: 2001 - 2009, 2011)			
Taxable Gift/Estate		**Tax on**	**Rate on**
From	**To**	**Col. 1**	**Excess**
$ 0	$ 10,000	$ 0	18%
10,000	20,000	1,800	20%
20,000	40,000	3,800	22%
40,000	60,000	8,200	24%
60,000	80,000	13,000	26%
80,000	10,0000	18,200	28%
100,000	150,000	23,800	30%
150,000	250,000	38,800	32%
250,000	500,000	70,800	34%
500,000	750,000	155,800	37%
750,000	1,000,000	248,300	39%
1,000,000	1,250,000	345,800	41%
1,250,000	1,500,000	448,300	43%

GIFT AND ESTATE TAX TABLE (Upper Brackets: 2001, 2011 and later)			
Taxable Gift/Estate		**Tax on**	**Rate on**
From	**To**	**Col. 1**	**Excess**
1,500,000	2,000,000	555,800	45%
2,000,000	2,500,000	780,800	49%
2,500,000	3,000,000	1,025,800	53%
3,000,000	10,000,000	1,290,800	55%
10,000,000	17,184,000	5,140,800	60%
17,184,000	....	9,451,200	55%

GIFT AND ESTATE TAX TABLE (Upper Brackets: 2002)			
Taxable Gift/Estate		**Tax on**	**Rate on**
From	**To**	**Col. 1**	**Excess**
1,500,000	2,000,000	555,800	45%
2,000,000	2,500,000	780,800	49%
2,500,000	....	1,025,800	50%

Figure 9.01 (cont'd)

GIFT AND ESTATE TAX TABLE (Upper Brackets: 2003)			
Taxable Gift/Estate From	To	Tax on Col. 1	Rate on Excess
1,500,000	2,000,000	555,800	45%
2,000,000	....	780,800	49%

GIFT AND ESTATE TAX TABLE (Upper Brackets: 2004)			
Taxable Gift/Estate From	To	Tax on Col. 1	Rate on Excess
1,500,000	2,000,000	555,800	45%
2,000,000	....	780,800	48%

GIFT AND ESTATE TAX TABLE (Upper Brackets: 2005)			
Taxable Gift/Estate From	To	Tax on Col. 1	Rate on Excess
1,500,000	2,000,000	555,800	45%
2,000,000	....	780,800	47%

GIFT AND ESTATE TAX TABLE (Upper Brackets: 2006)			
Taxable Gift/Estate From	To	Tax on Col. 1	Rate on Excess
1,500,000	2,000,000	555,800	45%
2,000,000	....	780,800	46%

GIFT AND ESTATE TAX TABLE (Upper Bracket: 2007 - 2009)			
Taxable Gift/Estate From	To	Tax on Col. 1	Rate on Excess
1,500,000	....	555,800	45%

Figure 9.01 (cont'd)

GIFT TAX ONLY TABLE (2010)			
Taxable Gift		**Tax on**	**Rate on**
From	**To**	**Col. 1**	**Excess**
$0	$10,000	$0	18%
10,000	20,000	1,800	20%
20,000	40,000	3,800	22%
40,000	60,000	8,200	24%
60,000	80,000	13,000	26%
80,000	10,0000	18,200	28%
100,000	150,000	23,800	30%
150,000	250,000	38,800	32%
250,000	500,000	70,800	34%
500,000	....	155,800	35%

IRC Secs. 2001(c), 2502.

The gift tax is calculated by first subtracting the available exclusions and deductions from the total amount of gifts made for the current calendar year. Next, the tax on the total gifts for the current year and all previous calendar years is calculated. Then, the tax is calculated on the gifts made in previous years only. The difference between the first figure and the second figure is the gift tax due for the current year except to the extent there is unified credit remaining to offset this amount.

For example, assume that Mrs. Smith has given property worth a total of $40,000 to her daughter in years prior to 2002 (i.e., taxable gifts prior to 2002 equal $40,000). In 2002, she makes a gift of some farm property worth $75,000 to her daughter. The amount of gift tax that Mrs. Smith must pay for 2002 will be calculated by first subtracting any available exclusions or deductions from gifts made in 2002. If the only exclusion or deduction available is the $11,000 (in 2002) annual exclusion (see below), the taxable gift amount for 2002 is $64,000 ($75,000 less $11,000). Next, the total gifts for 2002 of $64,000 are added to the total of the gifts made in years prior to 2002 for a total of $104,000 ($64,000 plus $40,000). Looking at the gift tax rate schedule reproduced in Figure 9.01, the gift tax due on this amount is $25,000. The gift tax due on the amount of gifts made in years prior to 2002, $40,000, is $8,200. Subtracting this figure of $8,200 from the amount of gift tax due on all gifts of $25,000, results in a gift tax due (before application of the unified credit) for 2002 of $16,800. To the extent that Mrs. Smith has unified credit (see below) remaining, the gift tax will be reduced.

THE ANNUAL EXCLUSION

There are several provisions in the federal gift tax that can help to lessen the tax bite due when a gift is made. One of the most useful is the annual exclusion, a provision which allows each individual to make gifts up to $10,000 as indexed ($11,000 in 2002) to any other one person during a single calendar year without incurring any gift tax. The $10,000 annual exclusion amount is adjusted for inflation after 1998.[4]

The effect of the annual exclusion can be amplified when two spouses agree to "split" a gift going to another individual. If the gift is split, a total of two times the current annual exclusion amount (i.e., $22,000 when the annual exclusion amount is $11,000) can be given to another person without incurring gift tax in the current year. Gift "splitting" is available only to spouses, not just to any two persons.[5]

The fact that amounts up to the annual exclusion figure can pass to one person without gift tax can be useful when dealing with nonqualified annuities. Suppose that a parent, Mr. Jones, wishes to give his adult daughter funds to begin her retirement planning. Giving the funds away will remove the funds from Mr. Jones' estate, if certain conditions are met, and give his daughter the benefit of the funds sooner than if they passed to her at her father's death. If Mr. Jones does not make a gift of more than the annual exclusion amount each year, there will be no gift tax due on the transfer. His daughter can take the gift each year and use the funds to make an annual premium payment into a deferred annuity which she will annuitize when she reaches retirement age.

The annual exclusion can also be used to avoid gift tax when a gift of an actual annuity contract itself is made. The greater the number of gift recipients, the greater the potential to maximize the effect of the annual exclusion. To illustrate, take the example of Mrs. Smith, a grandmother, who purchased an annuity on each of her three grandchildren at the time of their birth. In 2002, the youngest grandchild is age 18, and the older two are ages 20 and 23. The annuities are valued at $12,000, $14,000 and $16,000, respectively. If Mrs. Smith made a gift of the annuities to her grandchildren in 2002 without the benefit of the annual exclusion, she would have made a taxable gift of $42,000 (ignoring the possible use of the unified credit). Since the annual exclusion is available to Mrs. Smith in the amount of $33,000 (3 gifts x $11,000 annual exclusion in 2002), her taxable gift for the year is only $9,000. Note that if Mr. Smith were still living and had agreed to split the gifts with his wife, an annual exclusion of $22,000 (2 x $11,000 annual exclusion in 2002) would be available for each of three grandchildren for a total of $66,000 (3 x $22,000). Since the gifts total only $42,000, no gift tax would be due at all. This is shown in Figure 9.02.

There is one additional requirement that must be satisfied before a gift of property can qualify to take advantage of the annual exclusion. The gift must be of a "present interest," not a "future interest."[6] A present interest gift is one which the recipient can begin to enjoy or have control over immediately. Generally, a future interest is the right to use property at some point in the future, rather than currently. Often, the future interest question arises with gifts made in trust.

The gift tax annual exclusion is increased to $100,000 as indexed ($110,000 in 2002) for gifts to a spouse who is not a United States citizen if the gift would otherwise qualify for the marital deduction (see below).[7] However, the gift tax marital deduction is not available unless the spouse is a United States citizen.

THE UNIFIED CREDIT

Another important aspect of the gift tax is the unified credit. This credit can be used during an individual's lifetime to lessen the amount of gift tax due. The unified credit is so named because it can be used to offset the amount of gift tax due on gifts made

Figure 9.02

Mrs. Smith's Gifts to Grandchildren

Mrs. Smith

	Grandchild	Grandchild	Grandchild
Annuity Value	$12,000	$14,000	$16,000

**Total Gifts Without Use of
Annual Exclusion = $42,000**

Mrs. Smith

	Grandchild	Grandchild	Grandchild
Annuity Value	$12,000	$14,000	$16,000
Annual Exclusion	-$11,000	-$11,000	-$11,000
	$ 1,000	$ 3,000	$ 5,000

**Total Gifts With Use of $11,000
Annual Exclusion = $19,000**

Mrs. Smith

	Grandchild	Grandchild	Grandchild
Annuity Value	$12,000	$14,000	$16,000
Annual Exclusion	-$22,000	-$22,000	-$22,000
	$ 0	$ 0	$ 0

**Total Gifts With Use of $11,000
Annual Exclusion and Gift Splitting = $0**

during life as well as the amount of estate tax due on property passing to another at death. In other words, the unified credit applies to the tax imposed by the unified system of transfer taxation which encompasses both the gift tax and the estate tax.

The gift tax unified credit equals $345,800 in 2002.[8] Since it is a tax credit, this amount may be set off directly, or on a dollar-for-dollar basis, against the amount of tax due. It is the equivalent of $1,000,000 worth of property. In fact, the $1,000,000 figure is often referred to as the "exemption equivalent," which means that the unified credit of $345,800 is sufficient to exempt property worth $1,000,000 from tax.

Use of the gift tax unified credit in prior years reduces the amount of the gift tax unified credit available in the current year. For example, assume Mr. Jones made taxable gifts which used $200,000 of the gift tax unified credit prior to 2002. The gift tax unified credit available to Mr. Jones in 2002 is limited to $145,800 ($345,800 - $200,000).

The unified credit can be an extremely useful planning tool. For example, assume that, in 2002, a parent, Mr. Smith, wanted to make a gift of some family vacation property to his daughter, Susan. The property is currently worth approximately $1,200,000. Mr. Smith wants to give the property to his daughter now for two reasons. First, because of health reasons, he is no longer able to use the property. Second, he does not want to have the property included in his gross estate for purposes of the estate tax calculation at his death. Ignoring for simplicity any exclusions and deductions that might apply to such a gift, the amount of gift tax due (before application of the unified credit) on a taxable gift of $1,200,000 would be $427,800. However, since Mr. Smith has his full unified credit available he can subtract the $345,800 gift tax unified credit from the tentative tax of $427,800 and pay gift tax of only $82,000. Thus, the unified credit would save Mr. Smith $345,800 in gift tax on the transfer of the vacation property to his daughter.

DEDUCTIONS FROM THE GIFT TAX

Like most tax calculations, there are several deductions that may be taken in connection with the gift tax.

One of the most useful deductions is the marital deduction which basically provides that the full amount of a gift made from one spouse to another may be deducted from the taxable gift amount for the year.[9] In effect, this means that a spouse may make unlimited gifts to his or her spouse without paying gift tax on the transfers. Gifts of "terminable interests," which, very generally, are interests that end during the receiving spouse's lifetime, are able to qualify for the gift tax marital deduction only if certain requirements are met.[10]

The gift tax marital deduction is not available unless the spouse is a United States citizen. However, the gift tax annual exclusion (see above) is increased to $100,000 as indexed ($110,000 in 2002) for gifts to a spouse who is not a United States citizen if the gift would otherwise qualify for the marital deduction.[11]

To illustrate the effect that the availability of the marital deduction can have, assume that Mr. Jones wishes to pass on ownership of some property that has been in his family for several generations. If he gives the property, valued at approximately $1,500,000, to his wife, no gift tax will be due. If, instead, he chooses to pass the property along to his son, gift tax will be due on the entire $1,500,000 less any available exclusions and the unified credit.

A gift of an annuity contract from one spouse to another qualifies for the gift tax marital deduction if no other individual has any interest in the annuity.

A second deduction available from the gift tax is for gifts of property made to charitable organizations, i.e., a charitable deduction. Generally, a deduction is allowed for the value of a gift made to a charity.

Figure 9.03 shows the difference that taking advantage of the marital deduction and the charitable deduction can make in the

Figure 9.03

FEDERAL GIFT TAX CALCULATION		
Mr. Jones' Gifts to His Two Children		
Current Calendar Year		2002
Gifts Made During Current Calendar Year		$1,550,000
Less: Annual Exclusion(s)	$22,000	
Exclusions for Qualified Transfers	$0	
Charitable Deduction	$0	
Marital Deduction	$0	($22,000)
Taxable Gifts Made During Current Calendar Year		$1,528,000
Taxable Gifts Made During All Preceding Calendar Periods		$0
Gross Federal Gift Tax		$568,400
Unified Credit		($345,800)
Net Federal Gift Tax		$222,600
Mr. Jones' Gifts to Mrs. Jones and a Charity		
Current Calendar Year		2002
Gifts Made During Current Calendar Year		$1,550,000
Less: Annual Exclusion(s)	$0	
Exclusions for Qualified Transfers	$0	
Charitable Deduction	$50,000	
Marital Deduction	$1,500,000	($1,550,000)
Taxable Gifts Made During Current Calendar Year		$0
Taxable Gifts Made During All Preceding Calendar Periods		$0
Gross Federal Gift Tax		$0
Unified Credit		($0)
Net Federal Gift Tax		$0

amount of overall gift tax that is payable. Continuing with the example involving Mr. Jones and his gift of the family property to his wife, Figure 9.03 also assumes that Mr. Jones made a gift of $50,000 to his favorite charity in 2002. If the property and the $50,000 had been given to Mr. Jones' two children, the tax due would have been $222,600, even after application of the full unified credit amount. If the property and the cash were given to Mrs. Jones and the charity, respectively, then no gift tax would be due because of the marital and charitable deductions.

As discussed in Chapter 6, there are several trust arrangements that are commonly used in the charitable planning area. Generally, no charitable deduction from the gift tax is allowed for the lead interest in a trust unless the payments to the charity are made as a guaranteed annuity or as a fixed percentage of the property's fair market value. Further, no charitable deduction is available for a remainder interest in a trust unless the trust qualifies as either a charitable remainder annuity trust, a charitable remainder unitrust, or a pooled income fund.[12]

A gift tax charitable deduction is allowed for a charitable gift annuity, (i.e., a gift to a charity which is made in exchange for an annuity to be paid by the charity) if the value of the gift exceeds the value of the annuity, and the annuity is payable out of the general funds of the charity.[13]

Figure 9.04 shows a sample gift tax calculation which takes into account the deductions and credits mentioned above.

Figure 9.04

FEDERAL GIFT TAX CALCULATION		
Current Calendar Year		2002
Gifts Made During Current Calendar Year		$300,000
Less: Annual Exclusion(s)	$11,000	
Exclusions for Qualified Transfers	$0	
Charitable Deduction	$0	
Marital Deduction	$125,000	($136,000)
Taxable Gifts Made During Current Calendar Year		$164,000
Taxable Gifts Made During All Preceding Calendar Periods		$100,000
Gross Federal Gift Tax		$51,760
Unified Credit		($51,760)
Net Federal Gift Tax		$0

WHAT CONSTITUTES A GIFT?

Gift of an Annuity Contract

If an individual purchases an annuity contract and the annuity benefit payments will be paid to a beneficiary other than the purchaser or his estate, the annuity purchaser is considered to have made a gift of the annuity contract. The gift is considered to have been made if the purchaser of the annuity does not retain any interest in the annuity for either himself or his estate and does not retain the power to change the beneficiary designation.

For example, if Mr. Smith purchases a single premium deferred annuity for $25,000 and names his son, Junior, as the irrevocable beneficiary of the annuity, Mr. Smith has made a gift of $25,000 to Junior. As discussed above, Mr. Smith can take advantage of the annual exclusion provision to keep at least a portion of the gift from being subject to the gift tax and may be able to use a portion of his unified credit to keep the remaining amount beyond the reach of the gift tax. It should be noted that a gift is considered to have been made only if Mr. Smith does not retain any interest in the annuity and has named his son as the beneficiary of the contract irrevocably.

Purchase of a Joint and Survivor Annuity

Another scenario involving an annuity which may result in a gift being made is the purchase of a joint and survivor annuity. A joint and survivor annuity is one which pays a benefit during the lives of both annuitants and then pays either the same benefit or a benefit of a lesser amount to the survivor of the two for the remainder of his lifetime. The purchase of this type of annuity may result in a gift being made if the purchaser does not retain the right to change the individual who is designated to receive the payments made to the survivor of the two annuitants.[14] In other words, the purchaser of the annuity will have made a gift if he makes an irrevocable beneficiary designation. Thus, if a father purchases a joint and survivor annuity naming himself and his son as the annuitants, he will have made a gift to his son if he does not keep the right to change the designation of who will receive the survivor's benefit. Of course, if the joint and survivor annuity is purchased by a husband and wife, as is often the case, the gift tax marital deduction will generally eliminate any gift tax being due.

Assignment of an Annuity Contract

The same result is true if an individual absolutely assigns an annuity contract to another. The individual making the assignment (the assignor) will be considered to have made a gift of the annuity to the person receiving the assignment (the assignee).[15] The assignment of an annuity contract also carries some possible adverse income tax consequences which are discussed in Chapter 7.

Payment of an Annuity Premium

If an individual pays a premium on an annuity contract which he does not own, he is considered to have made a gift of the premium amount.[16] As discussed earlier, if an individual wishes to fund an annuity for another, he may make a gift to that person each year of up to the annual exclusion amount without incurring any gift tax.

This technique of making a gift of the premium amount is used more often to fund the purchase of a life insurance policy on the life of a parent that is owned by a child than it is used to facilitate the purchase of an annuity. The gift of the life insurance premium (if it is less than the annual exclusion amount each year) is not subject to gift tax when made and the child receives the face amount of the life insurance policy at the death of the parent free of income tax, and possibly free of estate tax. Thus, the child receives a much greater amount than the sum of the premium payments and the parents profit since neither the premium payments, if certain requirements are met, nor the death benefit of the life insurance policy owned by the child is part of the parent's estate for estate tax purposes.

There is no reason why the same technique cannot be used with a nonqualified annuity. The gift of an annuity premium that is less than the annual exclusion amount will not be subject to gift tax. However, the main difference in using a life insurance policy as opposed to an annuity is that the life insurance policy will pay a much larger amount to the child at the death of the parent. With an annuity which names the parent as the annuitant, the child will receive an amount equal to approximately the sum of the annuity premiums paid, and not the much larger life insurance death benefit.

Naming an Irrevocable Beneficiary

When an annuity purchaser chooses how he will receive the benefit payments from the annuity, he usually has a choice of several settlement options. Several of his choices, such as the life with period certain guarantee option, offer a refund type feature. The purchaser must name a beneficiary who will receive the refund payments should they become payable. For instance, if Mr. Jones purchases a single premium immediate annuity with a 10 year period certain settlement option, his beneficiary will receive the remainder of ten year's worth of payments if Mr. Jones, the annuitant, dies within ten years after he purchases the annuity. In other words, if Mr. Jones receives six years of payments from the annuity and then dies, the remaining four years of payments in the guarantee period will be paid to the beneficiary he has named.

If Mr. Jones names his son as beneficiary, but does not do so irrevocably, no gift has been made. His son has no rights under the annuity contract because Mr. Jones can change his mind at any time and name another as beneficiary. However, if Mr. Jones makes his son the beneficiary irrevocably, a gift has been made. An irrevocable beneficiary designation cannot be changed after it is made. A gift is considered to have been made even though the refund beneficiary, Mr. Jones' son, will get nothing unless Mr. Jones dies before receiving payments for ten years. However, it should be noted that since the gift is contingent upon Mr. Jones' death within ten years, it is considered a gift of a future interest and does not qualify for the annual exclusion.[17] The value of the gift is the present value of the son's contingent right to receive any remaining payments upon the death of Mr. Jones.

HOW IS THE GIFT OF AN ANNUITY VALUED?

If an individual purchases an annuity, names himself as the annuitant, and immediately gives the annuity contract to another person, the value of the gift is considered to be the amount of premium paid for the annuity. So, for example, if Mrs. Smith purchases a single premium annuity for $35,000, naming herself as both the owner and the annuitant and then immediately transfers ownership of the annuity to her daughter, the value of the gift she has made to her daughter will be $35,000. The value would be the same if Mrs. Smith had purchased the annuity, naming herself as the annuitant but naming her daughter as the annuity's owner from the beginning. The value of the gift would also be the premium paid for the contract, $35,000, if Mrs. Smith purchased a single premium annuity and named her daughter as both owner and annuitant.

The valuation figure is arrived at in a slightly more compli-cated manner if the purchaser of the annuity holds the contract for a period of time before making a gift of it to another individual. In this instance, the gift tax value is the single premium that the life insurance company that issued the contract would charge for an annuity that would pay the same benefits provided on the life of a person who is the same age as the annuitant when the gift is made.[18]

Where an individual purchases a joint and survivor annuity naming himself and one other person as the annuitants, the gift tax value is the cost of the joint and survivor annuity minus the cost of a single life annuity for the person making the purchase.[19] For example, if Mrs. Jones purchases a joint and survivor annuity contract which will pay a monthly annuity of $400 during her lifetime, and the same amount to her sister if she survives her, the gift will be equal to the amount needed to purchase an annuity contract that would pay a benefit of $400 only during Mrs. Jones' life subtracted from the premium paid for the joint and survivor annuity.

ENDNOTES

1. IRC Sec. 2501(a)(1).
2. IRC Sec. 2502(c).
3. IRC Sec. 6324(b); see *Comm. v. Chase Manhattan Bank*, 259 F.2d 231 (5th Cir. 1958).
4. IRC Sec. 2503(b).
5. IRC Sec. 2513.
6. IRC Sec. 2503(b).
7. IRC Sec. 2523(i).
8. IRC Sec. 2505(a). While the amount of the gift tax unified credit exemption equivalent is $1,000,000 after 2001, the amount of the gift tax unified credit is $345,800 in 2001 to 2009, and in 2011 and later; but only $330,800 in 2010, because of changes in tax rates. See Chapter 8 regarding the amount of the estate tax unified credit and its exemption equivalent.
9. IRC Sec. 2523(a).
10. See, generally, IRC Sec. 2523.
11. IRC Sec. 2523(i).
12. IRC Sec. 2522(c).
13. IRC Sec. 2522(a); Rev. Rul. 80-281, 1980-2 CB 282.
14. Rev. Rul. 55-388, 1955-1 CB 233; Treas. Reg. §25.2511-1.
15. See Treas. Reg. §25.2511-1(h)(8); *Fletcher Trust Co. v. Comm.*, 1 TC 798 (1943), aff'd 141 F.2d 36 (7th Cir. 1944).
16. Ibid.
17. *Morrow v. Comm.*, 2 TC 210 (1943).
18. Treas. Reg. §25.2512-6.
19. Ibid.

Appendix A

ACTUARIAL TABLES FOR TAXING ANNUITIES

As referenced in various places throughout the text of this publication, the tables used for taxing annuities appear on the following pages. Included here are gender-based Tables I, II, IIA, and III and unisex Tables V, VI, VIA, and VII. The gender-based tables are to be used if the investment in the contract does not include a post-June 30, 1986 investment in the contract. The unisex tables are to be used if the investment in the contract does include a post-June 30, 1986 investment in the contract.

However, even if there is no investment in the contract after June 30, 1986, an annuitant receiving annuity payments after June 30, 1986 (regardless of when they first began) may elect to treat his entire investment in the contract as post-June 30, 1986 and apply Tables V-VII. This election may be made for any taxable year in which such amounts are received by the taxpayer; it is irrevocable and applies with respect to all amounts the taxpayer receives as an annuity under the contract in the taxable year for which the election is made or in any subsequent tax year.

If investment in the contract includes both a pre-July 1986 investment and a post-June 1986 investment, an election may be made to make separate computations with respect to each portion of the aggregate investment in the contract using with respect to each portion the tables applicable to it. The amount excludable is the sum of the amounts determined under the separate computations. However, the election is not available (i.e., the entire investment must be treated as post-June 1986 investment) if the annuity starting date is after June 30, 1986 and the contract provides an option (whether or not it is exercised) to receive amounts under the contract other than in the form of a life annuity. Reg. §1.72-6(d).

Treasury regulations extend some of the tables to higher and lower ages, but the partial tables contained here are adequate for all practical purposes. The multiples in Tables I, II, and IIA or V, VI, and VIA need not be adjusted for monthly payments. For quarterly, semi-annual or annual payments, they must be adjusted according to the Frequency of Payment Adjustment Table, below. Table III and Table VII multiples, giving the percentage value of refund features, are never adjusted.

All tables are entered with the age of the annuitant at his or her birthday nearest the annuity starting date.

Frequency of Payment Adjustment Table

If the number of whole months from the annuity starting date to the first payment date is	0-1	2	3	4	5	6	7	8	9	10	11	12
And payments under the contract are to be made: Annually	+0.5	+0.4	+0.3	+0.2	+0.1	0	0	-0.1	-0.2	-0.3	-0.4	-0.5
Semiannually	+ .2	+ .1	0	0	- .1	- .2	....	....	....	....	....	....
Quarterly	+ .1	0	- .1	....	....	....	....	....	....	....	....	....

Example. Ed Black bought an annuity contract on January 1 which provides him with an *annual* payment of $4,000 payable on December 31st of each year. His age on birthday nearest the annuity starting date (January 1) is 66. The multiple from Table V for male age 66, is 19.2. This multiple must be adjusted for annual payment by subtracting .5 (19.2 - .5 = 18.7). Thus, his total expected return is $74,800 (18.7 x $4,000). See Treas. Reg. §1.72-5(a)(2).

Table I — Ordinary Life Annuities — One Life — Expected Return Multiples

Male	Female (Ages)	Multiples	Male	Female (Age)	Multiples
6	11	65.0	59	64	18.9
7	12	64.1	60	65	18.2
8	13	63.2	61	66	17.5
9	14	62.3	62	67	16.9
10	15	61.4	63	68	16.2
11	16	60.4	64	69	15.6
12	17	59.5	65	70	15.0
13	18	58.6	66	71	14.4
14	19	57.7	67	72	13.8
15	20	56.7	68	73	13.2
16	21	55.8	69	74	12.6
17	22	54.9	70	75	12.1
18	23	53.9	71	76	11.6
19	24	53.0	72	77	11.0
20	25	52.1	73	78	10.5
21	26	51.1	74	79	10.1
22	27	50.2	75	80	9.6
23	28	49.3	76	81	9.1
24	29	48.3	77	82	8.7
25	30	47.4	78	83	8.3
26	31	46.5	79	84	7.8
27	32	45.6	80	85	7.5
28	33	44.6	81	86	7.1
29	34	43.7	82	87	6.7
30	35	42.8	83	88	6.3
31	36	41.9	84	89	6.0
32	37	41.0	85	90	5.7
33	38	40.0	86	91	5.4
34	39	39.1	87	92	5.1
35	40	38.2	88	93	4.8
36	41	37.3	89	94	4.5
37	42	36.5	90	95	4.2
38	43	35.6	91	96	4.0
39	44	34.7	92	97	3.7
40	45	33.8	93	98	3.5
41	46	33.0	94	99	3.3
42	47	31.2	96	101	2.9
44	49	30.4	97	102	2.7
45	50	29.6	98	103	2.5
46	51	28.7	99	104	2.3
47	52	27.9	100	105	2.1
48	53	27.1	101	106	1.9
49	54	26.3	102	107	1.7
50	55	25.5	103	108	1.5
51	56	24.7	104	109	1.3
52	57	24.0	105	110	1.2
53	58	23.2	106	111	1.0
54	59	22.4	107	112	.8
55	60	21.7	108	113	.7
56	61	21.0	109	114	.6
57	62	20.3	110	115	.5
58	63	19.6	111	116	.0

Table II — Ordinary Joint Life and Last Survivor Annuities — Two Lives — Expected Return Multiples

Male (Ages)	Male / Female	35 / 40	36 / 41	37 / 42	38 / 43	39 / 44	40 / 45	41 / 46	42 / 47	43 / 48	44 / 49	45 / 50	46 / 51	47 / 52
35	40	46.2	45.7	45.3	44.8	44.4	44.0	43.6	43.3	43.0	42.6	42.3	42.0	41.8
36	41	...	45.2	44.8	44.3	43.9	43.5	43.1	42.7	42.3	42.0	41.7	41.4	41.1
37	42	...	...	44.3	43.8	43.4	42.9	42.5	42.1	41.8	41.4	41.1	40.7	40.4
38	43	...	...	...	43.3	42.9	42.4	42.0	41.6	41.2	40.8	40.5	40.1	39.8
39	44	...	...	...	...	42.4	41.9	41.5	41.0	40.6	40.2	39.9	39.5	39.2
40	45	...	...	...	...	...	41.4	41.0	40.5	40.1	39.7	39.3	38.9	38.6
41	46	...	...	...	...	...	...	40.5	40.0	39.6	39.2	38.8	38.4	38.0
42	47	...	...	...	...	...	...	...	39.6	39.1	38.7	38.2	37.8	37.5
43	48	...	...	...	...	...	...	...	...	38.6	38.2	37.7	37.3	36.9
44	49	...	...	...	...	...	...	...	...	...	37.7	37.2	36.8	36.4
45	50	...	...	...	...	...	...	...	...	...	...	36.8	36.3	35.9
46	51	...	...	...	...	...	...	...	...	...	...	...	35.9	35.4
47	52	...	...	...	...	...	...	...	...	...	...	...	...	35.0

Male (Ages)	Male / Female	48 / 53	49 / 54	50 / 55	51 / 56	52 / 57	53 / 58	54 / 59	55 / 60	56 / 61	57 / 62	58 / 63	59 / 64	60 / 65
35	40	41.5	41.3	41.0	40.8	40.6	40.4	40.4	40.1	40.0	39.8	39.7	39.6	39.5
36	41	40.8	40.6	40.3	40.1	39.9	39.7	39.5	39.3	39.2	39.0	38.9	38.8	38.6
37	42	40.2	39.9	39.6	39.4	39.2	39.0	38.8	38.6	38.4	38.3	38.1	38.0	37.9
38	43	39.5	39.2	39.0	38.7	38.5	38.3	38.1	37.9	37.7	37.5	37.3	37.2	37.1
39	44	38.9	38.6	38.3	38.0	37.8	37.6	37.3	37.1	36.9	36.8	36.6	36.4	36.3
40	45	38.3	38.0	37.7	37.4	37.1	36.9	36.6	36.4	36.2	36.0	35.9	35.7	35.5
41	46	37.7	37.3	37.0	36.7	36.5	36.2	36.0	35.7	35.5	35.3	35.1	35.0	34.8
42	47	37.1	36.8	36.4	36.1	35.8	35.6	35.3	35.1	34.8	34.6	34.4	34.2	34.1
43	48	36.5	36.2	35.8	35.5	35.2	34.9	34.7	34.4	34.2	33.9	33.7	33.5	33.3
44	49	36.0	35.6	35.3	34.9	34.6	34.3	34.0	33.8	33.5	33.3	33.0	32.8	32.6
45	50	35.5	35.1	34.7	34.4	34.0	33.7	33.4	33.1	32.9	32.6	32.4	32.2	31.9
46	51	35.0	34.6	34.2	33.8	33.5	33.1	32.8	32.5	32.2	32.0	31.7	31.5	31.3
47	52	34.5	34.1	33.7	33.3	32.9	32.6	32.2	31.9	31.6	31.4	31.1	30.9	30.6
48	53	34.0	33.6	33.2	32.8	32.4	32.0	31.7	31.4	31.1	30.8	30.5	30.2	30.0
49	54	...	33.1	32.7	32.3	31.9	31.5	31.2	30.8	30.5	30.2	29.9	29.6	29.4
50	55	...	...	32.3	31.8	31.4	31.0	30.6	30.3	29.9	29.6	29.3	29.0	28.8
51	56	...	...	...	31.4	30.9	30.5	30.1	29.8	29.4	29.1	28.8	28.5	28.2
52	57	...	...	...	...	30.5	30.1	29.7	29.3	28.9	28.6	28.2	27.9	27.6
53	58	...	...	...	...	...	29.6	29.2	28.8	28.4	28.1	27.7	27.4	27.1
54	59	...	...	...	...	...	...	28.8	28.3	27.9	27.6	27.2	26.9	26.5
55	60	...	...	...	...	...	...	...	27.9	27.5	27.1	26.7	26.4	26.0
56	61	...	...	...	...	...	...	...	...	27.1	26.7	26.3	25.9	25.5
57	62	...	...	...	...	...	...	...	...	...	26.2	25.8	25.4	25.1
58	63	...	...	...	...	...	...	...	...	...	...	25.4	25.0	24.6
59	64	...	...	...	...	...	...	...	...	...	...	...	24.6	24.2
60	65	...	...	...	...	...	...	...	...	...	...	...	...	23.8

Table II — Ordinary Joint Life and Last Survivor Annuities — Two Lives — Expected Return Multiples — Continued

Ages Male Male	Female	61 66	62 67	63 68	64 69	65 70	66 71	67 72	68 73	69 74	70 75	71 76	72 77	73 78
35	40	39.4	39.3	39.2	39.1	39.0	38.9	38.9	38.8	38.8	38.7	38.7	38.6	38.6
36	41	38.5	38.4	38.3	38.2	38.2	38.1	38.0	38.0	37.9	37.9	37.8	37.8	37.7
37	42	37.7	37.6	37.5	37.4	37.3	37.3	37.2	37.1	37.1	37.0	36.9	36.9	36.9
38	43	36.9	36.8	36.7	36.6	36.5	36.5	36.4	36.4	36.3	36.2	36.2	36.1	36.0
39	44	36.2	36.0	35.9	35.8	35.7	35.6	35.5	35.5	35.4	35.3	35.3	35.2	35.2
40	45	35.4	35.3	35.1	35.0	34.9	34.8	34.7	34.6	34.6	34.5	34.4	34.4	34.3
41	46	34.6	34.5	34.4	34.2	34.1	34.0	33.9	33.8	33.8	33.7	33.6	33.5	33.5
42	47	33.9	33.7	33.6	33.5	33.4	33.2	33.1	33.0	33.0	32.9	32.8	32.7	32.7
43	48	33.2	33.0	32.9	32.7	32.6	32.5	32.4	32.3	32.2	32.1	32.0	31.9	31.9
44	49	32.5	32.3	32.1	32.0	31.8	31.7	31.6	31.5	31.4	31.3	31.2	31.1	31.1
45	50	31.8	31.6	31.4	31.3	31.1	31.0	30.8	30.7	30.6	30.5	30.4	30.4	30.3
46	51	31.1	30.9	30.7	30.5	30.4	30.2	30.1	30.0	29.9	29.8	29.7	29.6	29.5
47	52	30.4	30.2	30.0	29.8	29.7	29.5	29.4	29.3	29.1	29.0	28.9	28.8	28.7
48	53	29.8	29.5	29.3	29.2	29.0	28.8	28.7	28.5	28.4	28.3	28.2	28.1	28.0
49	54	29.1	28.9	28.7	28.5	28.3	28.1	28.0	27.8	27.7	27.6	27.5	27.4	27.3
50	55	28.5	28.3	28.1	27.8	27.6	27.5	27.3	27.1	27.0	26.9	26.7	26.6	26.5
51	56	27.9	27.7	27.4	27.2	27.0	26.8	26.6	26.5	26.3	26.2	26.0	25.9	25.8
52	57	27.3	27.1	26.8	26.6	26.4	26.2	26.0	25.8	25.7	25.5	25.4	25.2	25.1
53	58	26.8	26.5	26.2	26.0	25.8	25.6	25.4	25.2	25.0	24.8	24.7	24.6	24.4
54	59	26.2	25.9	25.7	25.4	25.2	25.0	24.7	24.6	24.4	24.2	24.0	23.9	23.8
55	60	25.7	25.4	25.1	24.9	24.6	24.4	24.1	23.9	23.8	23.6	23.4	23.3	23.1
56	61	25.2	24.9	24.6	24.3	24.1	23.8	23.6	23.4	23.2	23.0	22.8	22.6	22.5
57	62	24.7	24.4	24.1	23.8	23.5	23.3	23.0	22.8	22.6	22.4	22.2	22.0	21.9
58	63	24.3	23.9	23.6	23.3	23.0	22.7	22.5	22.2	22.0	21.8	21.6	21.4	21.3
59	64	23.8	23.5	23.1	22.8	22.5	22.2	21.9	21.7	21.5	21.2	21.0	20.9	20.7
60	65	23.4	23.0	22.7	22.3	22.0	21.7	21.4	21.2	20.9	20.7	20.5	20.3	20.1
61	66	23.0	22.6	22.2	21.9	21.6	21.3	21.0	20.7	20.4	20.2	20.0	19.8	19.6
62	67	...	22.2	21.8	21.5	21.1	20.8	20.5	20.2	19.9	19.7	19.5	19.2	19.0
63	68	...	...	21.4	21.1	20.7	20.4	20.1	19.8	19.5	19.2	19.0	18.7	18.5
64	69	...	...	...	20.7	20.3	20.0	19.6	19.3	19.0	18.7	18.5	18.2	18.0
65	70	...	...	...	...	19.9	19.6	19.2	18.9	18.6	18.3	18.0	17.8	17.5
66	71	...	...	...	...	...	19.2	18.8	18.5	18.2	17.9	17.6	17.3	17.1
67	72	...	...	...	...	...	...	18.5	18.1	17.8	17.5	17.2	16.9	16.7
68	73	...	...	...	...	...	...	...	17.8	17.4	17.1	16.8	16.5	16.2
69	74	...	...	...	...	...	...	...	...	17.1	16.7	16.4	16.1	15.8
70	75	...	...	...	...	...	...	...	...	...	16.4	16.1	15.8	15.5
71	76	...	...	...	...	...	...	...	...	...	...	15.7	15.4	15.1
72	77	...	...	...	...	...	...	...	...	...	...	...	15.1	14.8
73	78	...	...	...	...	...	...	...	...	...	...	...	...	14.4

Ages Male Male	Female	74 79	75 80	76 81	77 82	78 83	79 84	80 85	81 86	82 87	83 88	84 89	85 90
35	40	38.6	38.5	38.5	38.5	38.4	38.4	38.4	38.4	38.4	38.4	38.3	38.3
36	41	37.7	37.6	37.6	37.6	37.5	37.5	37.5	37.5	37.5	37.5	37.5	37.4
37	42	36.8	36.8	36.7	36.7	36.7	36.7	36.6	36.6	36.6	36.6	36.6	36.6
38	43	36.0	35.9	35.9	35.8	35.8	35.8	35.8	35.8	35.7	35.7	35.7	35.7
39	44	35.1	35.1	35.0	35.0	35.0	34.9	34.9	34.9	34.9	34.8	34.8	34.8
40	45	34.3	34.2	34.2	34.2	34.1	34.1	34.1	34.0	34.0	34.0	34.0	34.0
41	46	33.4	33.4	33.3	33.3	33.3	33.2	33.2	33.2	33.2	33.1	33.1	33.1
42	47	32.6	32.6	32.5	32.5	32.4	32.4	32.4	32.3	32.3	32.3	32.3	32.3
43	48	31.8	31.8	31.7	31.7	31.6	31.6	31.5	31.5	31.5	31.5	31.4	31.4
44	49	31.0	30.9	30.9	30.8	30.8	30.8	30.8	30.7	30.7	30.7	30.6	30.6
45	50	30.2	30.1	30.1	30.0	30.0	30.0	29.9	29.9	29.9	29.8	29.8	29.8
46	51	29.4	29.4	29.3	29.2	29.2	29.2	29.1	29.1	29.0	29.0	29.0	28.9
47	52	28.7	28.6	28.5	28.5	28.4	28.4	28.3	28.3	28.2	28.2	28.2	28.1
48	53	27.9	27.8	27.8	27.7	27.6	27.6	27.5	27.5	27.5	27.4	27.4	27.4
49	54	27.2	27.1	27.0	26.9	26.9	26.8	26.8	26.7	26.7	26.6	26.6	26.6
50	55	26.4	26.3	26.3	26.2	26.1	26.1	26.0	26.0	25.9	25.9	25.8	25.8
51	56	25.7	25.6	25.5	25.5	25.4	25.3	25.3	25.2	25.2	25.1	25.1	25.0
52	57	25.0	24.9	24.8	24.7	24.7	24.6	24.5	24.5	24.4	24.4	24.3	24.3
53	58	24.3	24.2	24.1	24.0	23.9	23.9	23.8	23.7	23.7	23.6	23.6	23.5
54	59	23.6	23.5	23.4	23.3	23.2	23.2	23.1	23.0	23.0	23.0	22.9	22.8
55	60	22.9	22.9	22.8	22.7	22.6	22.5	22.4	22.3	22.3	22.2	22.2	22.1
56	61	22.3	22.2	22.1	22.0	21.9	21.8	21.7	21.6	21.6	21.5	21.5	21.4
57	62	21.7	21.6	21.5	21.3	21.2	21.1	21.1	21.0	20.9	20.8	20.8	20.7
58	63	21.1	21.0	20.8	20.7	20.6	20.5	20.4	20.3	20.2	20.2	20.1	20.0
59	64	20.5	20.4	20.2	20.1	20.0	19.9	19.8	19.7	19.6	19.5	19.4	19.4
60	65	19.9	19.8	19.6	19.5	19.4	19.3	19.1	19.0	19.0	18.9	18.8	18.7
61	66	19.4	19.2	19.1	18.9	18.8	18.7	18.5	18.4	18.3	18.3	18.2	18.1
62	67	18.8	18.7	18.5	18.3	18.2	18.1	18.0	17.8	17.7	17.7	17.6	17.5
63	68	18.3	18.1	18.0	17.8	17.6	17.5	17.4	17.3	17.2	17.1	17.0	16.9
64	69	17.8	17.6	17.4	17.3	17.1	17.0	16.8	16.7	16.6	16.5	16.4	16.3
65	70	17.3	17.1	16.9	16.7	16.6	16.4	16.3	16.2	16.0	15.9	15.8	15.8
66	71	16.9	16.6	16.4	16.3	16.1	15.9	15.8	15.6	15.5	15.4	15.3	15.2
67	72	16.4	16.2	16.0	15.8	15.6	15.4	15.3	15.1	15.0	14.9	14.8	14.7
68	73	16.0	15.7	15.5	15.3	15.1	15.0	14.8	14.6	14.5	14.4	14.3	14.2
69	74	15.6	15.3	15.1	14.9	14.7	14.5	14.3	14.2	14.0	13.9	13.8	13.7
70	75	15.2	14.9	14.7	14.5	14.3	14.1	13.9	13.7	13.6	13.4	13.3	13.2
71	76	14.8	14.5	14.3	14.1	13.8	13.6	13.5	13.3	13.1	13.0	12.8	12.7
72	77	14.5	14.2	13.9	13.7	13.5	13.2	13.0	12.9	12.7	12.5	12.4	12.3
73	78	14.1	13.8	13.6	13.3	13.1	12.9	12.7	12.5	12.3	12.1	12.0	11.8
74	79	13.8	13.5	13.2	13.0	12.7	12.5	12.3	12.1	11.9	11.7	11.6	11.4
75	80	...	13.2	12.9	12.6	12.4	12.2	11.9	11.7	11.5	11.4	11.2	11.0
76	81	...	...	12.6	12.3	12.1	11.8	11.6	11.4	11.2	11.0	10.8	10.7
77	82	...	...	...	12.1	11.8	11.5	11.3	11.1	10.8	10.7	10.5	10.3
78	83	...	...	...	...	11.5	11.2	11.0	10.7	10.5	10.3	10.1	10.0
79	84	...	...	...	...	...	11.0	10.7	10.5	10.2	10.0	9.8	9.6
80	85	...	...	...	...	...	...	10.4	10.2	10.0	9.7	9.5	9.3
81	86	...	...	...	...	...	...	...	9.9	9.7	9.5	9.3	9.1
82	87	...	...	...	...	...	...	...	...	9.4	9.2	9.0	8.8
83	88	...	...	...	...	...	...	...	...	...	9.0	8.7	8.5
84	89	...	...	...	...	...	...	...	...	...	...	8.5	8.3
85	90	...	...	...	...	...	...	...	...	...	...	...	8.1

Table IIA—Annuities for Joint Life Only — Two Lives — Expected Return Multiples

Ages Male	Ages Female	35 40	36 41	37 42	38 43	39 44	40 45	41 46	42 47	43 48	44 49	45 50	46 51	47 52
35	40	30.3	29.9	29.4	29.0	28.5	28.0	27.5	27.0	26.5	26.0	25.5	24.9	24.4
36	41	...	29.5	29.0	28.6	28.2	27.7	27.2	26.7	26.2	25.7	25.2	24.7	24.2
37	42	...	...	28.6	28.2	27.8	27.3	26.9	26.4	25.9	25.5	25.0	24.4	23.9
38	43	...	...	...	27.8	27.4	27.0	26.5	26.1	25.6	25.2	24.7	24.2	23.7
39	44	...	...	...	...	27.0	26.6	26.2	25.8	25.3	24.8	24.4	23.9	23.4
40	45	...	...	...	...	...	26.2	25.8	25.4	25.0	24.5	24.1	23.6	23.1
41	46	...	...	...	...	...	...	25.4	25.0	24.6	24.2	23.8	23.3	22.9
42	47	...	...	...	...	...	...	...	24.6	24.2	23.8	23.4	23.0	22.6
43	48	...	...	...	...	...	...	...	...	23.9	23.5	23.1	22.7	22.2
44	49	...	...	...	...	...	...	...	...	...	23.1	22.7	22.3	21.9
45	50	...	...	...	...	...	...	...	...	...	...	22.4	22.0	21.6
46	51	...	...	...	...	...	...	...	...	...	...	...	21.6	21.2
47	52	...	...	...	...	...	...	...	...	...	...	...	...	20.9

Ages Male	Ages Female	48 53	49 54	50 55	51 56	52 57	53 58	54 59	55 60	56 61	57 62	58 63	59 64	60 65
35	40	23.8	23.3	22.7	22.1	21.6	21.0	20.4	19.8	19.3	18.7	18.1	17.5	17.0
36	41	23.6	23.1	22.5	22.0	21.4	20.8	20.3	19.7	19.1	18.6	18.0	17.4	16.9
37	42	23.4	22.9	22.3	21.8	21.2	20.7	20.1	19.6	19.0	18.4	17.9	17.3	16.8
38	43	23.2	22.6	22.1	21.6	21.1	20.5	20.0	19.4	18.9	18.3	17.8	17.2	16.7
39	44	22.9	22.4	21.9	21.4	20.9	20.3	19.8	19.3	18.7	18.2	17.7	17.1	16.6
40	45	22.7	22.2	21.7	21.2	20.7	20.1	19.6	19.1	18.6	18.0	17.5	17.0	16.5
41	46	22.4	21.9	21.4	20.9	20.4	19.9	19.4	18.9	18.4	17.9	17.4	16.9	16.3
42	47	22.1	21.6	21.2	20.7	20.2	19.7	19.2	18.7	18.2	17.7	17.2	16.7	16.2
43	48	21.8	21.4	20.9	20.5	20.0	19.5	19.0	18.6	18.1	17.6	17.1	16.6	16.1
44	49	21.5	21.1	20.6	20.2	19.8	19.3	18.8	18.4	17.9	17.4	16.9	16.4	15.9
45	50	21.2	20.8	20.4	19.9	19.5	19.1	18.6	18.1	17.7	17.2	16.7	16.3	15.8
46	51	20.9	20.5	20.1	19.7	19.2	18.8	18.4	17.9	17.5	17.0	16.6	16.1	15.6
47	52	20.5	20.1	19.8	19.4	19.0	18.5	18.1	17.7	17.3	16.8	16.4	15.9	15.5
48	53	20.2	19.8	19.4	19.1	18.7	18.3	17.9	17.5	17.0	16.6	16.2	15.7	15.3
49	54	...	19.5	19.1	18.8	18.4	18.0	17.6	17.2	16.8	16.4	16.0	15.5	15.1
50	55	...	...	18.8	18.4	18.1	17.7	17.3	16.9	16.6	16.2	15.8	15.3	14.9
51	56	...	...	...	18.1	17.8	17.4	17.0	16.7	16.3	15.9	15.5	15.1	14.7
52	57	...	...	...	...	17.4	17.1	16.8	16.4	16.0	15.7	15.3	14.9	14.5
53	58	...	...	...	...	...	16.8	16.4	16.1	15.8	15.4	15.1	14.7	14.3
54	59	...	...	...	...	...	...	16.1	15.8	15.5	15.1	14.8	14.4	14.1
55	60	...	...	...	...	...	...	...	15.5	15.2	14.9	14.5	14.2	13.9
56	61	...	...	...	...	...	...	...	...	14.9	14.6	14.3	13.9	13.6
57	62	...	...	...	...	...	...	...	...	...	14.3	14.0	13.7	13.4
58	63	...	...	...	...	...	...	...	...	...	...	13.7	13.4	13.1
59	64	...	...	...	...	...	...	...	...	...	...	...	13.1	12.8
60	65	...	...	...	...	...	...	...	...	...	...	...	...	12.6

Ages Male	Ages Female	61 66	62 67	63 68	64 69	65 70	66 71	67 72	68 73	69 74	70 75	71 76	72 77	73 78
35	40	16.4	15.8	15.3	14.7	14.2	13.7	13.1	12.6	12.1	11.6	11.1	10.7	10.2
36	41	16.3	15.8	15.2	14.7	14.1	13.6	13.1	12.6	12.1	11.6	11.1	10.6	10.2
37	42	16.2	15.7	15.1	14.6	14.1	13.6	13.0	12.5	12.0	11.5	11.1	10.6	10.1
38	43	16.1	15.6	15.1	14.5	14.0	13.5	13.0	12.5	12.0	11.5	11.0	10.6	10.1
39	44	16.0	15.5	15.0	14.5	13.9	13.4	12.9	12.4	11.9	11.5	11.0	10.5	10.1
40	45	15.9	15.4	14.9	14.4	13.9	13.4	12.9	12.4	11.9	11.4	11.0	10.5	10.0
41	46	15.8	15.3	14.8	14.3	13.8	13.3	12.8	12.3	11.8	11.4	10.9	10.5	10.0
42	47	15.7	15.2	14.7	14.2	13.7	13.2	12.7	12.3	11.8	11.3	10.9	10.4	10.0
43	48	15.6	15.1	14.6	14.1	13.6	13.1	12.7	12.2	11.8	11.3	10.8	10.4	9.9
44	49	15.5	15.0	14.5	14.0	13.5	13.1	12.6	12.1	11.7	11.2	10.8	10.3	9.9
45	50	15.3	14.8	14.4	13.9	13.4	13.0	12.5	12.0	11.6	11.1	10.7	10.3	9.8
46	51	15.2	14.7	14.2	13.8	13.3	12.9	12.4	12.0	11.5	11.1	10.6	10.2	9.8
47	52	15.1	14.6	14.1	13.7	13.2	12.8	12.3	11.9	11.4	11.0	10.6	10.1	9.7
48	53	14.9	14.4	14.0	13.5	13.1	12.6	12.2	11.8	11.3	10.9	10.5	10.1	9.7
49	54	14.7	14.3	13.8	13.4	13.0	12.5	12.1	11.7	11.3	10.8	10.4	10.0	9.6
50	55	14.5	14.1	13.7	13.3	12.8	12.4	12.0	11.6	11.2	10.7	10.3	9.9	9.5
51	56	14.3	13.9	13.5	13.1	12.7	12.3	11.9	11.5	11.1	10.7	10.3	9.9	9.5
52	57	14.1	13.7	13.3	12.9	12.5	12.1	11.7	11.3	10.9	10.6	10.2	9.8	9.4
53	58	13.9	13.6	13.2	12.8	12.4	12.0	11.6	11.2	10.8	10.5	10.1	9.7	9.3
54	59	13.7	13.4	13.0	12.6	12.2	11.9	11.5	11.1	10.7	10.3	10.0	9.6	9.2
55	60	13.5	13.2	12.9	12.4	12.1	11.7	11.3	11.0	10.6	10.2	9.9	9.5	9.1
56	61	13.3	12.9	12.6	12.2	11.9	11.5	11.2	10.8	10.3	10.1	9.9	9.4	9.0
57	62	13.0	12.7	12.4	12.1	11.7	11.4	11.0	10.7	10.3	10.0	9.6	9.3	8.9
58	63	12.8	12.5	12.2	11.8	11.5	11.2	10.9	10.3	10.0	9.8	9.5	9.2	8.8
59	64	12.6	12.3	11.9	11.6	11.3	11.0	10.7	10.4	10.0	9.7	9.4	9.1	8.7
60	65	12.3	12.0	11.7	11.4	11.1	10.8	10.3	10.2	9.9	9.6	9.3	8.9	8.6
61	66	12.0	11.8	11.5	11.2	10.9	10.6	10.3	10.0	9.7	9.4	9.1	8.8	8.5
62	67	...	11.5	11.2	11.0	10.7	10.4	10.1	9.8	9.6	9.3	9.0	8.7	8.4
63	68	...	...	11.0	10.7	10.5	10.2	9.9	9.7	9.4	9.1	8.8	8.5	8.2
64	69	...	...	...	10.5	10.2	10.0	9.7	9.5	9.2	9.0	8.7	8.1	8.1
65	70	...	...	...	...	10.0	9.9	9.5	9.3	9.0	8.8	8.5	8.3	8.0
66	71	...	...	...	...	...	9.5	9.3	9.1	8.8	8.6	8.3	8.1	7.8
67	72	...	...	...	...	...	...	9.1	8.9	8.6	8.4	8.1	7.9	7.7
68	73	...	...	...	...	...	...	...	8.6	8.4	8.2	8.0	7.7	7.3
69	74	...	...	...	...	...	...	...	...	8.2	8.0	7.8	7.6	7.3
70	75	...	...	...	...	...	...	...	...	...	7.8	7.6	7.4	7.2
71	76	...	...	...	...	...	...	...	...	...	...	7.4	7.2	7.0
72	77	...	...	...	...	...	...	...	...	...	...	...	7.0	6.8
73	78	...	...	...	...	...	...	...	...	...	...	...	...	6.7

THE ANNUITY HANDBOOK

Table IIA — Annuities for Joint Life Only — Two Lives —
Expected Return Multiples — Continued

Ages Male	Female	74 79	75 80	76 81	77 82	78 83	79 84	80 85	81 86	82 87	83 88	84 89	85 90	86 91
35	40	9.7	9.3	8.9	8.5	8.1	7.7	7.3	6.9	6.6	6.2	5.9	5.6	5.3
36	41	9.7	9.3	8.9	8.4	8.0	7.7	7.3	6.9	6.6	6.2	5.9	5.6	5.3
37	42	9.7	9.3	8.8	8.4	8.0	7.6	7.3	6.9	6.5	6.2	5.9	5.6	5.3
38	43	9.7	9.2	8.8	8.4	8.0	7.6	7.2	6.9	6.5	6.2	5.9	5.6	5.3
39	44	9.6	9.2	8.8	8.4	8.0	7.6	7.2	6.9	6.5	6.2	5.9	5.6	5.3
40	45	9.6	9.2	8.8	8.4	8.0	7.6	7.2	6.9	6.5	6.2	5.9	5.5	5.2
41	46	9.6	9.2	8.7	8.3	7.9	7.6	7.2	6.8	6.5	6.2	5.8	5.5	5.2
42	47	9.5	9.1	8.7	8.3	7.9	7.5	7.2	6.8	6.5	6.2	5.8	5.5	5.2
43	48	9.5	9.1	8.7	8.3	7.9	7.5	7.2	6.8	6.5	6.1	5.8	5.5	5.2
44	49	9.5	9.0	8.6	8.2	7.9	7.5	7.1	6.8	6.4	6.1	5.8	5.5	5.2
45	50	9.4	9.0	8.6	8.2	7.8	7.5	7.1	6.8	6.4	6.1	5.8	5.5	5.2
40	51	9.4	9.0	8.6	8.2	7.8	7.4	7.1	6.7	6.4	6.1	5.8	5.5	5.2
47	52	9.3	8.9	8.5	8.1	7.8	7.4	7.1	6.7	6.4	6.1	5.8	5.5	5.2
48	53	9.3	8.9	8.5	8.1	7.7	7.4	7.0	6.7	6.4	6.0	5.7	5.4	5.1
49	54	9.2	8.8	8.4	8.1	7.7	7.3	7.0	6.7	6.3	6.0	5.7	5.4	5.1
50	55	9.1	8.8	8.4	8.0	7.7	7.3	7.0	6.6	6.3	6.0	5.7	5.4	5.1
51	56	9.1	8.7	8.3	8.0	7.6	7.3	6.9	6.6	6.3	6.0	5.7	5.4	5.1
52	57	9.0	8.6	8.3	7.9	7.6	7.2	6.9	6.6	6.2	5.9	5.6	5.4	5.1
53	58	8.9	8.6	8.2	7.9	7.5	7.2	6.9	6.5	6.2	5.9	5.6	5.3	5.1
54	59	8.9	8.5	8.2	7.8	7.5	7.1	6.8	6.5	6.2	5.9	5.6	5.3	5.0
55	60	8.8	8.4	8.1	7.7	7.4	7.1	6.8	6.4	6.1	5.8	5.6	5.3	5.0
56	61	8.7	8.4	8.0	7.7	7.3	7.0	6.7	6.4	6.1	5.8	5.5	5.3	5.0
57	62	8.6	8.3	7.9	7.6	7.3	7.0	6.7	6.4	6.1	5.8	5.5	5.2	5.0
58	63	8.5	8.2	7.9	7.5	7.2	6.9	6.6	6.3	6.0	5.7	5.5	5.2	4.9
59	64	8.4	8.1	7.8	7.5	7.1	6.8	6.5	6.3	6.0	5.7	5.4	5.2	4.9
60	65	8.3	8.0	7.7	7.4	7.1	6.8	6.5	6.2	5.9	5.6	5.4	5.1	4.9
61	66	8.2	7.9	7.6	7.3	7.0	6.7	6.4	6.1	5.9	5.6	5.3	5.1	4.8
62	67	8.1	7.8	7.5	7.2	6.9	6.6	6.4	6.1	5.8	5.5	5.3	5.0	4.8
63	68	8.0	7.7	7.4	7.1	6.8	6.6	6.3	6.0	5.7	5.5	5.2	5.0	4.7
64	69	7.8	7.6	7.3	7.0	6.7	6.5	6.2	5.9	5.7	5.4	5.2	4.9	4.7
65	70	7.7	7.4	7.2	6.9	6.6	6.4	6.1	5.9	5.6	5.4	5.1	4.9	4.7
66	71	7.6	7.3	7.1	6.8	6.5	6.3	6.0	5.8	5.5	5.3	5.1	4.8	4.6
67	72	7.4	7.2	6.9	6.7	6.4	6.2	6.0	5.7	5.5	5.2	5.0	4.8	4.6
68	73	7.3	7.0	6.8	6.6	6.3	6.1	5.9	5.6	5.4	5.2	4.9	4.7	4.5
69	74	7.1	6.9	6.7	6.4	6.2	6.0	5.8	5.5	5.3	5.1	4.9	4.7	4.5
70	75	7.0	6.8	6.5	6.3	6.1	5.9	5.7	5.4	5.2	5.0	4.8	4.6	4.4
71	76	6.8	6.6	6.4	6.2	6.0	5.8	5.6	5.3	5.1	4.9	4.7	4.5	4.3
72	77	6.6	6.4	6.3	6.1	5.9	5.7	5.5	5.3	5.0	4.9	4.7	4.5	4.3
73	78	6.5	6.3	6.1	5.9	5.7	5.5	5.3	5.1	5.0	4.8	4.6	4.4	4.2
74	79	6.3	6.1	6.0	5.8	5.6	5.4	5.2	5.0	4.9	4.7	4.5	4.3	4.1
75	80	..	6.0	5.8	5.6	5.5	5.3	5.1	4.9	4.8	4.6	4.4	4.2	4.1
76	81	..	..	5.6	5.5	5.3	5.2	5.0	4.8	4.7	4.5	4.3	4.1	4.0
77	82	..	..	..	5.3	5.2	5.0	4.9	4.7	4.5	4.4	4.2	4.1	3.9
78	83	..	..	..	..	5.0	4.9	4.7	4.6	4.4	4.3	4.1	4.0	3.8
79	84	..	..	..	..	..	4.7	4.6	4.5	4.3	4.2	4.0	3.9	3.7
80	85	..	..	..	..	..	..	4.5	4.3	4.2	4.1	3.9	3.8	3.6
81	86	..	..	..	..	..	..	..	4.2	4.1	3.9	3.8	3.7	3.6
82	87	..	..	..	..	..	..	..	..	4.0	3.8	3.7	3.6	3.5
83	88	..	..	..	..	..	..	..	..	..	3.7	3.6	3.5	3.4
84	89	..	..	..	..	..	..	..	..	..	..	3.5	3.4	3.3
85	90	..	..	..	..	..	..	..	..	..	..	..	3.3	3.2
86	91	..	..	..	..	..	..	..	..	..	..	..	..	3.1

Table III — Percent Value of Refund Feature

| Ages | | Duration of guaranteed amount | | | | | | | | | | | |
Male	Female	1 Yr %	2 Yrs %	3 Yrs %	4 Yrs %	5 Yrs %	6 Yrs %	7 Yrs %	8 Yrs %	9 Yrs %	10 Yrs %	11 Yrs %	12 Yrs %
6	11	..	..	..	..	..	..	..	..	1	1	1	1
7	12	..	..	..	..	..	..	..	..	1	1	1	1
8	13	..	..	..	..	..	..	..	..	1	1	1	1
9	14	..	..	..	..	..	..	..	1	1	1	1	1
10	15	..	..	..	..	..	..	..	1	1	1	1	1
11	16	..	..	..	..	..	..	..	1	1	1	1	1
12	17	..	..	..	..	..	..	..	1	1	1	1	1
13	18	..	..	..	..	..	..	..	1	1	1	1	1
14	19	..	..	..	..	..	..	..	1	1	1	1	1
15	20	..	..	..	..	..	..	..	1	1	1	1	1
16	21	..	..	..	..	..	..	..	1	1	1	1	1
17	22	..	..	..	..	..	..	..	1	1	1	1	1
18	23	..	..	..	..	..	..	..	1	1	1	1	1
19	24	..	..	..	..	..	..	..	1	1	1	1	1
20	25	..	..	..	..	..	..	..	1	1	1	1	1
21	26	..	..	..	..	..	..	..	1	1	1	1	1
22	27	..	..	..	..	..	..	1	1	1	1	1	1
23	28	..	..	..	..	..	..	1	1	1	1	1	1
24	29	..	..	..	..	..	..	1	1	1	1	1	1
25	30	..	..	..	..	..	..	1	1	1	1	1	1
26	31	..	..	..	..	..	1	1	1	1	1	1	1
27	32	..	..	..	..	..	1	1	1	1	1	1	1
28	33	..	..	..	..	..	1	1	1	1	1	1	1
29	34	..	..	..	..	..	1	1	1	1	1	1	1
30	35	..	..	..	..	1	1	1	1	1	1	1	2
31	36	..	..	..	..	1	1	1	1	1	1	1	2
32	37	..	..	..	..	1	1	1	1	1	1	2	2
33	38	..	..	..	1	1	1	1	1	1	1	2	2
34	39	..	..	..	1	1	1	1	1	1	2	2	2
35	40	..	..	..	1	1	1	1	1	2	2	2	2
36	41	..	..	..	1	1	1	1	1	2	2	2	2
37	42	..	..	1	1	1	1	1	2	2	2	2	3
38	43	..	..	1	1	1	1	1	2	2	2	2	3
39	44	..	..	1	1	1	1	2	2	2	2	3	3
40	45	..	..	1	1	1	1	2	2	2	3	3	3
41	46	..	..	1	1	1	1	2	2	2	3	3	3
42	47	..	..	1	1	1	2	2	2	3	3	3	4
43	48	..	1	1	1	1	2	2	2	3	3	4	4
44	49	..	1	1	1	1	2	2	3	3	4	4	4
45	50	..	1	1	1	2	2	2	3	3	4	4	5
46	51	..	1	1	1	2	2	3	3	4	4	5	5
47	52	..	1	1	1	2	2	3	3	4	4	5	5
48	53	..	1	1	2	2	2	3	3	4	5	5	6
49	54	..	1	1	2	2	3	3	4	4	5	5	6
50	55	..	1	1	2	2	3	3	4	5	5	6	7
51	56	..	1	1	2	2	3	3	4	5	6	6	7
52	57	1	1	2	2	3	3	4	5	5	6	7	8
53	58	1	1	2	2	3	4	4	5	6	7	7	8
54	59	1	1	2	2	3	4	5	5	6	7	8	9
55	60	1	1	2	3	3	4	5	6	7	8	8	9
56	61	1	1	2	3	4	4	5	6	7	8	9	10
57	62	1	1	2	3	4	5	6	7	8	9	10	11
58	63	1	2	2	3	4	5	6	7	8	9	10	12
59	64	1	2	3	4	5	6	7	8	9	10	11	12
60	65	1	2	3	4	5	6	7	8	10	11	12	13
61	66	1	2	3	4	5	6	8	9	10	11	12	13
62	67	1	2	3	4	6	7	8	10	11	12	14	15
63	68	1	2	4	5	6	7	9	10	12	13	15	16
64	69	1	3	4	5	7	8	9	11	13	14	16	17
65	70	1	3	4	6	7	9	10	12	13	15	17	19
66	71	1	3	4	6	8	9	11	13	14	16	18	20
67	72	2	3	5	6	8	10	12	14	15	17	19	21
68	73	2	3	5	7	9	11	13	14	16	18	21	23
69	74	2	4	6	7	9	11	13	16	18	20	22	24
70	75	2	4	6	8	10	12	14	17	19	21	23	26
71	76	2	4	6	9	11	13	15	18	20	22	25	27
72	77	2	5	7	9	12	14	16	19	21	24	26	29
73	78	2	5	7	10	12	15	18	20	23	25	28	30
74	79	3	5	8	11	13	16	19	22	24	27	30	32
75	80	3	6	8	11	14	17	20	23	26	29	31	34
76	81	3	6	9	12	15	18	21	24	27	30	33	36
77	82	3	7	10	13	16	20	23	26	29	32	35	38
78	83	4	7	11	14	17	21	24	28	31	34	37	40
79	84	4	8	11	15	19	22	26	29	33	36	39	42
80	85	4	8	12	16	20	24	27	31	34	38	41	44
81	86	4	9	13	17	21	25	29	33	36	40	43	46
82	87	5	9	14	18	23	27	31	35	38	42	45	48
83	88	5	10	15	19	24	28	33	37	40	44	47	50
84	89	5	11	16	21	26	30	34	38	42	46	49	52
85	90	6	11	17	22	27	32	36	41	44	48	51	55

Table III — Percent Value of Refund Feature — Continued

Ages		Duration of guaranteed amount											
Male	Female	13 Yrs %	14 Yrs %	15 Yrs %	16 Yrs %	17 Yrs %	18 Yrs %	19 Yrs %	20 Yrs %	21 Yrs %	22 Yrs %	23 Yrs %	24 Yrs %
6	11	1	1	1	1	1	1	1	1	1	1	1	2
7	12	1	1	1	1	1	1	1	1	1	1	1	2
8	13	1	1	1	1	1	1	1	1	1	1	1	2
9	14	1	1	1	1	1	1	1	1	1	1	1	2
10	15	1	1	1	1	1	1	1	1	1	1	2	2
11	16	1	1	1	1	1	1	1	1	1	1	2	2
12	17	1	1	1	1	1	1	1	1	1	1	2	2
13	18	1	1	1	1	1	1	1	1	1	2	2	2
14	19	1	1	1	1	1	1	1	1	1	2	2	2
15	20	1	1	1	1	1	1	1	1	1	2	2	2
16	21	1	1	1	1	1	1	1	1	2	2	2	2
17	22	1	1	1	1	1	1	1	1	2	2	2	2
18	23	1	1	1	1	1	1	1	1	2	2	2	2
19	24	1	1	1	1	1	1	2	2	2	2	2	2
20	25	1	1	1	1	1	1	2	2	2	2	2	2
21	26	1	1	1	1	1	2	2	2	2	2	2	2
22	27	1	1	1	1	1	2	2	2	2	2	2	3
23	28	1	1	1	1	2	2	2	2	2	2	2	3
24	29	1	1	1	2	2	2	2	2	2	2	3	3
25	30	1	1	1	2	2	2	2	2	2	3	3	3
26	31	1	1	2	2	2	2	2	2	3	3	3	3
27	32	1	2	2	2	2	2	2	3	3	3	3	3
28	33	1	2	2	2	2	2	3	3	3	3	3	4
29	34	2	2	2	2	2	2	3	3	3	3	4	4
30	35	2	2	2	2	2	3	3	3	3	3	4	4
31	36	2	2	2	2	3	3	3	3	4	4	4	5
32	37	2	2	2	3	3	3	3	4	4	4	5	5
33	38	2	2	3	3	3	3	4	4	4	5	5	5
34	39	2	3	3	3	3	4	4	4	5	5	5	6
35	40	2	3	3	3	4	4	4	5	5	5	6	6
36	41	3	3	3	4	4	4	5	5	5	6	6	7
37	42	3	3	3	4	4	4	5	5	6	6	7	7
38	43	3	3	4	4	4	5	5	6	6	7	7	8
39	44	3	4	4	4	5	5	6	6	7	7	8	8
40	45	4	4	4	5	5	6	6	7	7	8	8	9
41	46	4	4	4	5	6	6	7	7	8	8	9	9
42	47	4	5	5	5	6	6	7	8	8	9	9	10
43	48	4	5	5	6	6	7	8	8	9	9	10	11
44	49	5	5	6	6	7	7	8	9	9	10	11	12
45	50	5	6	6	7	7	8	9	9	10	11	12	12
46	51	5	6	7	7	8	9	9	10	11	12	12	13
47	52	6	7	7	8	9	9	10	11	12	12	13	14
48	53	6	7	8	8	9	10	11	12	12	13	14	15
49	54	7	8	8	9	10	11	11	12	13	14	15	16
50	55	7	8	9	10	11	11	12	13	14	15	16	17
51	56	8	9	10	10	11	12	13	14	15	16	17	18
52	57	8	9	10	11	12	13	14	15	16	17	18	20
53	58	9	10	11	12	13	14	15	16	17	19	20	21
54	59	10	11	12	13	14	15	16	17	18	20	21	22
55	60	10	11	13	14	15	16	17	18	20	21	22	24
56	61	11	12	13	15	16	17	18	20	21	22	24	25
57	62	12	13	14	16	17	18	20	21	22	24	25	27
58	63	13	14	15	17	18	19	21	22	24	25	27	28
59	64	14	15	16	18	19	21	22	24	25	27	28	30
60	65	15	16	18	19	20	22	24	25	27	28	30	32
61	66	16	17	19	20	22	23	25	27	28	30	32	33
62	67	17	18	20	22	23	25	27	28	30	32	33	35
63	68	18	20	21	23	25	26	28	30	32	33	35	37
64	69	19	21	23	24	26	28	30	32	33	35	37	39
65	70	20	22	24	26	28	30	32	33	35	37	39	41
66	71	22	24	26	28	29	31	33	35	37	39	41	43
67	72	23	25	27	29	31	33	35	37	39	41	43	45
68	73	25	27	29	31	33	35	37	39	41	43	45	47
69	74	26	28	30	33	35	37	39	41	43	45	47	48
70	75	28	30	32	34	37	39	41	43	45	47	49	50
71	76	29	32	34	36	39	41	43	45	47	49	51	52
72	77	31	34	36	38	41	43	45	47	49	51	53	54
73	78	33	35	38	40	43	45	47	49	51	53	55	56
74	79	35	37	40	42	45	47	49	51	53	55	57	58
75	80	37	39	42	44	47	49	51	53	55	57	58	60
76	81	39	41	44	46	49	51	53	55	57	59	60	62
77	82	41	43	46	48	51	53	55	57	59	61	62	64
78	83	43	45	48	50	53	55	57	59	61	62	64	65
79	84	45	48	50	53	55	57	59	61	63	64	66	67
80	85	47	50	52	55	57	59	61	63	64	66	67	69
81	86	49	52	54	57	59	61	63	65	66	68	69	70
82	87	51	54	56	59	61	63	65	66	68	69	71	72
83	88	53	56	58	61	63	65	66	68	70	71	72	73
84	89	55	58	60	63	65	67	68	70	71	73	74	75
85	90	57	60	62	65	67	68	70	71	73	74	75	76

Table III — Percent Value of Refund Feature — Continued

Ages		Duration of guaranteed amount										
Male	Female	25 Yrs %	26 Yrs %	27 Yrs %	28 Yrs %	29 Yrs %	30 Yrs %	31 Yrs %	32 Yrs %	33 Yrs %	34 Yrs %	35 Yrs %
6	11	2	2	2	2	2	2	2	2	2	2	2
7	12	2	2	2	2	2	2	2	2	2	2	3
8	13	2	2	2	2	2	2	2	2	2	3	3
9	14	2	2	2	2	2	2	2	2	3	3	3
10	15	2	2	2	2	2	2	2	2	3	3	3
11	16	2	2	2	2	2	2	2	2	3	3	3
12	17	2	2	2	2	2	2	2	3	3	3	3
13	18	2	2	2	2	2	2	2	3	3	3	3
14	19	2	2	2	2	2	2	3	3	3	3	3
15	20	2	2	2	2	2	3	3	3	3	3	3
16	21	2	2	2	2	3	3	3	3	3	3	4
17	22	2	2	2	2	3	3	3	3	3	4	4
18	23	2	2	2	3	3	3	3	3	4	4	4
19	24	2	2	3	3	3	3	3	4	4	4	4
20	25	2	3	3	3	3	3	4	4	4	4	5
21	26	3	3	3	3	3	4	4	4	4	5	5
22	27	3	3	3	3	4	4	4	4	5	5	5
23	28	3	3	3	3	4	4	4	5	5	5	5
24	29	3	3	3	4	4	4	5	5	5	5	6
25	30	3	3	4	4	4	5	5	5	6	6	6
26	31	3	4	4	4	5	5	5	6	6	6	7
27	32	4	4	4	5	5	5	6	6	6	7	7
28	33	4	4	5	5	5	6	6	6	7	7	8
29	34	4	5	5	5	6	6	6	7	7	8	8
30	35	5	5	5	6	6	6	7	7	8	8	9
31	36	5	5	6	6	6	7	7	8	8	9	9
32	37	5	6	6	7	7	7	8	8	9	10	10
33	38	6	6	7	7	7	8	8	9	10	10	11
34	39	6	7	7	8	8	9	9	10	10	11	12
35	40	7	7	8	8	9	9	10	10	11	12	12
36	41	7	8	8	9	9	10	10	11	12	13	13
37	42	8	8	9	9	10	11	11	12	13	13	14
38	43	8	9	9	10	11	11	12	13	13	14	15
39	44	9	9	10	11	11	12	13	14	14	15	16
40	45	9	10	11	11	12	13	14	15	15	16	17
41	46	10	11	11	12	13	14	15	16	16	17	18
42	47	11	12	12	13	14	15	16	17	18	18	19
43	48	12	12	13	14	15	16	17	18	19	20	21
44	49	12	13	14	15	16	17	18	19	20	21	22
45	50	13	14	15	16	17	18	19	20	21	22	23
46	51	14	15	16	17	18	19	20	21	22	24	25
47	52	15	16	17	18	19	20	21	23	24	25	26
48	53	16	17	18	19	20	22	23	24	25	26	28
49	54	17	18	19	21	22	23	24	25	27	28	29
50	55	18	20	21	22	23	24	26	27	28	29	31
51	56	20	21	22	23	25	26	27	28	30	31	32
52	57	21	22	23	25	26	27	29	30	31	33	34
53	58	22	24	25	26	28	29	30	32	33	34	36
54	59	24	25	26	28	29	31	32	33	35	36	38
55	60	25	26	28	29	31	32	34	35	36	38	39
56	61	27	28	29	31	32	34	35	37	38	40	41
57	62	28	30	31	33	34	36	37	39	40	41	43
58	63	30	31	33	34	36	37	39	40	42	43	45
59	64	31	33	35	36	38	39	41	42	44	45	47
60	65	33	35	36	38	40	41	43	44	46	47	48
61	66	35	37	38	40	41	43	44	46	47	49	50
62	67	37	38	40	42	43	45	46	48	49	51	52
63	68	39	40	42	44	45	47	48	50	51	52	54
64	69	41	42	44	46	47	49	50	52	53	54	55
65	70	42	44	46	47	49	50	52	53	55	56	57
66	71	44	46	48	49	51	52	54	55	56	58	59
67	72	46	48	50	51	53	54	56	57	58	59	61
68	73	48	50	52	53	55	56	57	59	60	61	62
69	74	50	52	53	55	56	58	59	60	62	63	64
70	75	52	54	55	57	58	60	61	62	63	64	65
71	76	54	56	57	59	60	61	63	64	65	66	67
72	77	56	58	59	60	62	63	64	65	66	67	68
73	78	58	59	61	62	64	65	66	67	68	68	70
74	79	60	61	63	64	65	66	67	68	69	70	71
75	80	62	63	64	66	67	68	69	70	71	72	72
76	81	63	65	66	67	68	69	70	71	72	73	..
77	82	65	66	68	69	70	71	72	73	74	..	..
78	83	67	68	69	70	71	72	73	74	..	..	..
79	84	68	70	71	72	73	74	75	..	..	..	..
80	85	70	71	72	73	74	75	..	..	..	..	..
81	86	72	73	74	75	75	..	..	..	..	..	..
82	87	73	74	75	76	..	..	..	..	..	..	..
83	88	74	75	76	..	..	..	..	..	..	..	..
84	89	76	77	..	..	..	..	..	..	..	..	..
85	90	77	..	..	..	..	..	..	..	..	..	..

Table V — Ordinary Life Annuities — One Life — Expected Return Multiples

Age	Multiple	Age	Multiple	Age	Multiple
5	76.6	42	40.6	79	10.0
6	75.6	43	39.6	80	9.5
7	74.7	44	38.7	81	8.9
8	73.7	45	37.7	82	8.4
9	72.7	46	36.8	83	7.9
10	71.7	47	35.9	84	7.4
11	70.7	48	34.9	85	6.9
12	69.7	49	34.0	86	6.5
13	68.8	50	33.1	87	6.1
14	67.8	51	32.2	88	5.7
15	66.8	52	31.3	89	5.3
16	65.8	53	30.4	90	5.0
17	64.8	54	29.5	91	4.7
18	63.9	55	28.6	92	4.4
19	62.9	56	27.7	93	4.1
20	61.9	57	26.8	94	3.9
21	60.9	58	25.9	95	3.7
22	59.9	59	25.0	96	3.4
23	59.0	60	24.2	97	3.2
24	58.0	61	23.3	98	3.0
25	57.0	62	22.5	99	2.8
26	56.0	63	21.6	100	2.7
27	55.1	64	20.8	101	2.5
28	54.1	65	20.0	102	2.3
29	53.1	66	19.2	103	2.1
30	52.2	67	18.4	104	1.9
31	51.2	68	17.6	105	1.8
32	50.2	69	16.8	106	1.6
33	49.3	70	16.0	107	1.4
34	48.3	71	15.3	108	1.3
35	47.3	72	14.6	109	1.1
36	46.4	73	13.9	110	1.0
37	45.4	74	13.2	111	.9
38	44.4	75	12.5	112	.8
39	43.5	76	11.9	113	.7
40	42.5	77	11.2	114	.6
41	41.5	78	10.6	115	.5

Table VI — Ordinary Joint Life and Last Survivor Annuities — Two Lives — Expected Return Multiples

AGES	35	36	37	38	39	40	41	42	43	44	45	46	47	48	49	50
35	54.0	...	...	...	...	...	...	...	...	...	...	...	...	...	...	...
36	53.5	53.0	...	...	...	...	...	...	...	...	...	...	...	...	...	...
37	53.0	52.5	52.0	...	...	...	...	...	...	...	...	...	...	...	...	...
38	52.6	52.0	51.5	51.0	...	...	...	...	...	...	...	...	...	...	...	...
39	52.2	51.6	51.0	50.5	50.0	...	...	...	...	...	...	...	...	...	...	...
40	51.8	51.2	50.6	50.0	49.5	49.0	...	...	...	...	...	...	...	...	...	...
41	51.4	50.8	50.2	49.6	49.1	48.5	48.0	...	...	...	...	...	...	...	...	...
42	51.1	50.4	49.8	49.2	48.6	48.1	47.5	47.0	...	...	...	...	...	...	...	...
43	50.8	50.1	49.5	48.8	48.2	47.6	47.1	46.6	46.0	...	...	...	...	...	...	...
44	50.5	49.8	49.1	48.5	47.8	47.2	46.7	46.1	45.6	45.1	...	...	...	...	...	...
45	50.2	49.5	48.8	48.1	47.5	46.9	46.3	45.7	45.1	44.6	44.1	...	...	...	...	...
46	50.0	49.2	48.5	47.8	47.2	46.5	45.9	45.3	44.7	44.1	43.6	43.1	...	...	...	...
47	49.7	49.0	48.3	47.5	46.8	46.2	45.5	44.9	44.3	43.7	43.2	42.6	42.1	...	...	...
48	49.5	48.8	48.0	47.3	46.6	45.9	45.2	44.5	43.9	43.3	42.7	42.2	41.7	41.2	...	...
49	49.3	48.5	47.8	47.0	46.3	45.6	44.9	44.2	43.6	42.9	42.3	41.8	41.2	40.7	40.2	...
50	49.2	48.4	47.6	46.8	46.0	45.3	44.6	43.9	43.2	42.6	42.0	41.4	40.8	40.2	39.7	39.2
51	49.0	48.2	47.4	46.6	45.8	45.1	44.3	43.6	42.9	42.2	41.6	41.0	40.4	39.8	39.3	38.7
52	48.8	48.0	47.2	46.4	45.6	44.8	44.1	43.3	42.6	41.9	41.3	40.6	40.0	39.4	38.8	38.3
53	48.7	47.9	47.0	46.2	45.4	44.6	43.9	43.1	42.4	41.7	41.0	40.3	39.7	39.0	38.4	37.9
54	48.6	47.7	46.9	46.0	45.2	44.4	43.6	42.9	42.1	41.4	40.7	40.0	39.3	38.7	38.1	37.5
55	48.5	47.6	46.7	45.9	45.1	44.2	43.4	42.7	41.9	41.2	40.4	39.7	39.0	38.4	37.7	37.1
56	48.3	47.5	46.6	45.8	44.9	44.1	43.3	42.5	41.7	40.9	40.2	39.5	38.7	38.1	37.4	36.8
57	48.3	47.4	46.5	45.6	44.8	43.9	43.1	42.3	41.5	40.7	40.0	39.2	38.5	37.8	37.1	36.4
58	48.2	47.3	46.4	45.5	44.7	43.8	43.0	42.1	41.3	40.5	39.7	39.0	38.2	37.5	36.8	36.1
59	48.1	47.2	46.3	45.4	44.5	43.7	42.8	42.0	41.2	40.4	39.6	38.8	38.0	37.3	36.6	35.9
60	48.0	47.1	46.2	45.3	44.4	43.6	42.7	41.9	41.0	40.2	39.4	38.6	37.8	37.1	36.3	35.6
61	47.9	47.0	46.1	45.2	44.3	43.5	42.6	41.7	40.9	40.0	39.2	38.4	37.6	36.9	36.1	35.4
62	47.9	47.0	46.0	45.1	44.2	43.4	42.5	41.6	40.8	39.9	39.1	38.3	37.5	36.7	35.9	35.1
63	47.8	46.9	46.0	45.1	44.2	43.3	42.4	41.5	40.6	39.8	38.9	38.1	37.3	36.5	35.7	34.9
64	47.8	46.8	45.9	45.0	44.1	43.2	42.3	41.4	40.5	39.7	38.8	38.0	37.2	36.3	35.5	34.8
65	47.7	46.8	45.9	44.9	44.0	43.1	42.2	41.3	40.4	39.6	38.7	37.9	37.0	36.2	35.4	34.6
66	47.7	46.7	45.8	44.9	44.0	43.1	42.2	41.3	40.4	39.5	38.6	37.8	36.9	36.1	35.2	34.4
67	47.6	46.7	45.8	44.8	43.9	43.0	42.1	41.2	40.3	39.4	38.5	37.7	36.8	36.0	35.1	34.3
68	47.6	46.7	45.7	44.8	43.9	42.9	42.0	41.1	40.2	39.3	38.4	37.6	36.7	35.8	35.0	34.2
69	47.6	46.6	45.7	44.8	43.8	42.9	42.0	41.1	40.2	39.3	38.4	37.5	36.6	35.7	34.9	34.1
70	47.5	46.6	45.7	44.7	43.8	42.9	41.9	41.0	40.1	39.2	38.3	37.4	36.5	35.7	34.8	34.0
71	47.5	46.6	45.6	44.7	43.8	42.8	41.9	41.0	40.1	39.1	38.2	37.3	36.5	35.6	34.7	33.9
72	47.5	46.6	45.6	44.7	43.7	42.8	41.9	40.9	40.0	39.1	38.2	37.3	36.4	35.5	34.6	33.8
73	47.5	46.5	45.6	44.7	43.7	42.8	41.8	40.9	40.0	39.0	38.1	37.2	36.3	35.4	34.6	33.7
74	47.5	46.5	45.6	44.7	43.7	42.7	41.8	40.8	39.9	39.0	38.1	37.2	36.3	35.4	34.5	33.6
75	47.4	46.5	45.5	44.7	43.6	42.7	41.8	40.8	39.9	39.0	38.1	37.1	36.2	35.3	34.5	33.6
76	47.4	46.5	45.5	44.7	43.6	42.7	41.7	40.8	39.9	38.9	38.0	37.1	36.2	35.3	34.4	33.5
77	47.4	46.5	45.5	44.7	43.6	42.7	41.7	40.8	39.8	38.9	38.0	37.1	36.2	35.3	34.4	33.5
78	47.4	46.4	45.5	44.5	43.6	42.6	41.7	40.7	39.8	38.9	37.9	37.0	36.1	35.2	34.3	33.4
79	47.4	46.4	45.5	44.5	43.6	42.6	41.7	40.7	39.8	38.9	37.9	37.0	36.1	35.2	34.3	33.4
80	47.4	46.4	45.5	44.5	43.6	42.6	41.6	40.7	39.8	38.8	37.9	37.0	36.1	35.2	34.2	33.4
81	47.4	46.4	45.5	44.5	43.6	42.6	41.6	40.7	39.8	38.8	37.9	37.0	36.0	35.1	34.2	33.3
82	47.4	46.4	45.4	44.5	43.5	42.6	41.6	40.7	39.7	38.8	37.9	36.9	36.0	35.1	34.2	33.3
83	47.4	46.4	45.4	44.5	43.5	42.6	41.6	40.7	39.7	38.8	37.8	36.9	36.0	35.1	34.2	33.3
84	47.4	46.4	45.4	44.5	43.5	42.6	41.6	40.7	39.7	38.8	37.8	36.9	36.0	35.0	34.1	33.2
85	47.4	46.4	45.4	44.5	43.5	42.6	41.6	40.6	39.7	38.8	37.8	36.9	36.0	35.0	34.1	33.2
86	47.3	46.4	45.4	44.5	43.5	42.5	41.6	40.6	39.7	38.7	37.8	36.9	35.9	35.0	34.1	33.2
87	47.3	46.4	45.4	44.5	43.5	42.5	41.6	40.6	39.7	38.7	37.8	36.9	35.9	35.0	34.1	33.2
88	47.3	46.4	45.4	44.5	43.5	42.5	41.6	40.6	39.7	38.7	37.8	36.9	35.9	35.0	34.1	33.2
89	47.3	46.4	45.4	44.4	43.5	42.5	41.6	40.6	39.7	38.7	37.8	36.9	35.9	35.0	34.1	33.2
90	47.3	46.4	45.4	44.4	43.5	42.5	41.6	40.6	39.7	38.7	37.8	36.9	35.9	35.0	34.1	33.2

Table VI — Ordinary Joint Life and Last Survivor Annuities — Two Lives — Expected Return Multiples

AGES	51	52	53	54	55	56	57	58	59	60	61	62	63	64	65	66
51	38.2	...	...	...	...	...	...	...	...	...	...	...	...	...	...	...
52	37.8	37.3	...	...	...	...	...	...	...	...	...	...	...	...	...	...
53	37.3	36.8	36.3	...	...	...	...	...	...	...	...	...	...	...	...	...
54	36.9	36.4	35.8	35.3	...	...	...	...	...	...	...	...	...	...	...	...
55	36.5	55.9	35.4	34.9	34.4	...	...	...	...	...	...	...	...	...	...	...
56	36.1	35.6	35.0	34.4	33.9	33.4	...	...	...	...	...	...	...	...	...	...
57	35.8	35.2	34.6	34.0	33.5	33.0	32.5	...	...	...	...	...	...	...	...	...
58	35.5	34.8	34.2	33.6	33.1	32.5	32.0	31.5	...	...	...	...	...	...	...	...
59	35.2	34.5	33.9	33.3	32.7	32.1	31.6	31.1	30.6	...	...	...	...	...	...	...
60	34.9	34.2	33.6	32.9	32.3	31.7	31.2	30.6	30.1	29.7	...	...	...	...	...	...
61	34.6	33.9	33.3	32.6	32.0	31.4	30.8	30.2	29.7	29.2	28.7	...	...	...	...	...
62	34.4	33.7	33.0	32.3	31.7	31.0	30.4	29.9	29.3	28.8	28.3	27.8	...	...	...	...
63	34.2	33.5	32.7	32.0	31.4	30.7	30.1	29.5	28.9	28.4	27.8	27.3	26.9	...	...	...
64	34.0	33.2	32.5	31.8	31.1	30.4	29.8	29.2	28.6	28.0	27.4	26.9	26.4	25.9	...	...
65	33.8	33.0	32.3	31.6	30.9	30.2	29.5	28.9	28.2	27.6	27.1	26.5	26.0	25.5	25.0	...
66	33.6	32.9	32.1	31.4	30.6	29.9	29.2	28.6	27.9	27.3	26.7	26.1	25.6	25.1	24.6	24.1
67	33.5	32.7	31.9	31.2	30.4	29.7	29.0	28.3	27.6	27.0	26.4	25.8	25.2	24.7	24.2	23.7
68	33.4	32.5	31.8	31.0	30.2	29.5	28.8	28.1	27.4	26.7	26.1	25.5	24.9	24.3	23.8	23.3
69	33.2	32.4	31.6	30.8	30.1	29.3	28.6	27.8	27.1	26.5	25.8	25.2	24.6	24.0	23.4	22.9
70	33.1	32.3	31.5	30.7	29.9	29.1	28.4	27.6	26.9	26.2	25.6	24.9	24.3	23.7	23.1	22.5
71	33.0	32.2	31.4	30.5	29.7	29.0	28.2	27.5	26.7	26.0	25.3	24.7	24.0	23.4	22.8	22.2
72	32.9	32.1	31.2	30.4	29.6	28.8	28.1	27.3	26.5	25.8	25.1	24.4	23.8	23.1	22.5	21.9
73	32.8	32.0	31.1	30.3	29.5	28.7	27.9	27.1	26.4	25.6	24.9	24.2	23.5	22.9	22.2	21.6
74	32.8	31.9	31.1	30.2	29.4	28.6	27.8	27.0	26.2	25.5	24.7	24.0	23.3	22.7	22.0	21.4
75	32.7	31.8	31.0	30.1	29.3	28.5	27.7	26.9	26.1	25.3	24.6	23.8	23.1	22.4	21.8	21.1
76	32.6	31.8	30.9	30.1	29.2	28.4	27.6	26.8	26.0	25.2	24.4	23.7	23.0	22.3	21.6	20.9
77	32.6	31.7	30.8	30.0	29.1	28.3	27.5	26.7	25.9	25.1	24.3	23.6	22.8	22.1	21.4	20.7
78	32.5	31.7	30.8	29.9	29.1	28.2	27.4	26.6	25.8	25.0	24.2	23.4	22.7	21.9	21.2	20.5
79	32.5	31.6	30.7	29.9	29.0	28.2	27.3	26.5	25.7	24.9	24.1	23.3	22.6	21.8	21.1	20.4
80	32.5	31.6	30.7	29.8	29.0	28.1	27.3	26.4	25.6	24.8	24.0	23.2	22.4	21.7	21.0	20.2
81	32.4	31.5	30.7	29.8	28.9	28.1	27.2	26.4	25.5	24.7	23.9	23.1	22.3	21.6	20.8	20.1
82	32.4	31.5	30.6	29.7	28.9	28.0	27.2	26.3	25.5	24.6	23.8	23.0	22.3	21.5	20.7	20.0
83	32.4	31.5	30.6	29.7	28.8	28.0	27.1	26.3	25.4	24.6	23.8	23.0	22.2	21.4	20.6	19.9
84	32.3	31.4	30.6	29.7	28.8	27.9	27.1	26.2	25.4	24.5	23.7	22.9	22.1	21.3	20.5	19.8
85	32.3	31.4	30.5	29.6	28.8	27.9	27.0	26.2	25.3	24.5	23.7	22.8	22.0	21.3	20.5	19.7
86	32.3	31.4	30.5	29.6	28.7	27.9	27.0	26.1	25.3	24.5	23.6	22.8	22.0	21.2	20.4	19.6
87	32.3	31.4	30.5	29.6	28.7	27.8	27.0	26.1	25.3	24.4	23.6	22.8	21.9	21.1	20.4	19.6
88	32.3	31.4	30.5	29.6	28.7	27.8	27.0	26.1	25.2	24.4	23.5	22.7	21.9	21.1	20.3	19.5
89	32.3	31.4	30.5	29.6	28.7	27.8	26.9	26.1	25.2	24.4	23.5	22.7	21.9	21.1	20.3	19.5
90	32.3	31.3	30.5	29.5	28.7	27.8	26.9	26.1	25.2	24.3	23.5	22.7	21.8	21.0	20.2	19.4

Table VI — Ordinary Joint Life and Last Survivor Annuities — Two Lives — Expected Return Multiples

AGES	67	68	69	70	71	72	73	74	75	76	77	78	79	80	81	82
67	23.2	...	...	...	...	...	...	...	...	...	...	...	...	...	...	...
68	22.8	22.3	...	...	...	...	...	...	...	...	...	...	...	...	...	...
69	22.4	21.9	21.5	...	...	...	...	...	...	...	...	...	...	...	...	...
70	22.0	21.5	21.1	20.6	...	...	...	...	...	...	...	...	...	...	...	...
71	21.7	21.2	20.7	20.2	19.8	...	...	...	...	...	...	...	...	...	...	...
72	21.3	20.8	20.3	19.8	19.4	18.9	...	...	...	...	...	...	...	...	...	...
73	21.0	20.5	20.0	19.4	19.0	18.5	18.1	...	...	...	...	...	...	...	...	...
74	20.8	20.2	19.6	19.1	18.6	18.2	17.7	17.3	...	...	...	...	...	...	...	...
75	20.5	19.9	19.3	18.8	18.3	17.8	17.3	16.9	16.5	...	...	...	...	...	...	...
76	20.3	19.7	19.1	18.5	18.0	17.5	17.0	16.5	16.1	15.7	...	...	...	...	...	...
77	20.1	19.4	18.8	18.3	17.7	17.2	16.7	16.2	15.8	15.4	15.0	...	...	...	...	...
78	19.9	19.2	18.6	18.0	17.5	16.9	16.4	15.9	15.4	15.0	14.6	14.2	...	...	...	...
79	19.7	19.0	18.4	17.8	17.2	16.7	16.1	15.6	15.1	14.7	14.3	13.9	13.5	...	...	...
80	19.5	18.9	18.2	17.6	17.0	16.4	15.9	15.4	14.9	14.4	14.0	13.5	13.2	12.8	...	...
81	19.4	18.7	18.1	17.4	16.8	16.2	15.7	15.1	14.6	14.1	13.7	13.2	12.8	12.5	12.1	...
82	19.3	18.6	17.9	17.3	16.6	16.0	15.5	14.9	14.4	13.9	13.4	13.0	12.5	12.2	11.8	11.5
83	19.2	18.5	17.8	17.1	16.5	15.9	15.3	14.7	14.2	13.7	13.2	12.7	12.3	11.9	11.5	11.1
84	19.1	18.4	17.7	17.0	16.3	15.7	15.1	14.5	14.0	13.5	13.0	12.5	12.0	11.6	11.2	10.9
85	19.0	18.3	17.6	16.9	16.2	15.6	15.0	14.4	13.8	13.3	12.8	12.3	11.8	11.4	11.0	10.6
86	18.9	18.2	17.5	16.8	16.1	15.5	14.8	14.2	13.7	13.1	12.6	12.1	11.6	11.2	10.8	10.4
87	18.8	18.1	17.4	16.7	16.0	15.4	14.7	14.1	13.5	13.0	12.4	11.9	11.4	11.0	10.6	10.1
88	18.8	18.0	17.3	16.6	15.9	15.3	14.6	14.0	13.4	12.8	12.3	11.8	11.3	10.8	10.4	10.0
89	18.7	18.0	17.2	16.5	15.8	15.2	14.5	13.9	13.3	12.7	12.2	11.6	11.1	10.7	10.2	9.8
90	18.7	17.9	17.2	16.5	15.8	15.1	14.5	13.8	13.2	12.6	12.1	11.5	11.0	10.5	10.1	9.6

Table VI — Ordinary Joint Life and Last Survivor Annuities — Two Lives — Expected Return Multiples

AGES	83	84	85	86	87	88	89	90
83	10.8	...	...	...	...	...	...	...
84	10.5	10.2	...	...	...	...	...	...
85	10.2	9.9	9.6	...	...	...	...	...
86	10.0	9.7	9.3	9.1	...	...	...	...
87	9.8	9.4	9.1	8.8	8.5	...	...	...
88	9.6	9.2	8.9	8.6	8.3	8.0	...	...
89	9.4	9.0	8.7	8.3	8.1	7.8	7.5	...
90	9.2	8.8	8.5	8.2	7.9	7.6	7.3	7.1

Table VIA — Annuities for Joint Life Only — Two Lives — Expected Return Multiples

AGES	35	36	37	38	39	40	41	42	43	44	45	46	47	48	49	50
35	40.7	...	...	...	...	...	...	...	...	...	...	...	...	...	...	...
36	40.2	39.7	...	...	...	...	...	...	...	...	...	...	...	...	...	...
37	39.7	39.3	38.8	...	...	...	...	...	...	...	...	...	...	...	...	...
38	39.2	38.7	38.3	37.9	...	...	...	...	...	...	...	...	...	...	...	...
39	38.6	38.2	37.8	37.4	36.9	...	...	...	...	...	...	...	...	...	...	...
40	38.0	37.7	37.3	36.9	36.4	36.0	...	...	...	...	...	...	...	...	...	...
41	37.4	37.1	36.7	36.3	35.9	35.5	35.1	...	...	...	...	...	...	...	...	...
42	36.8	36.5	36.2	35.8	35.4	35.0	34.6	34.1	...	...	...	...	...	...	...	...
43	36.2	35.9	35.6	35.2	34.9	34.5	34.1	33.7	33.2	...	...	...	...	...	...	...
44	35.5	35.2	34.9	34.6	34.3	34.0	33.6	33.2	32.8	32.3	...	...	...	...	...	...
45	34.8	34.6	34.3	34.0	33.7	33.4	33.0	32.7	32.3	31.8	31.4	...	...	...	...	...
46	34.1	33.9	33.7	33.4	33.1	32.8	32.5	32.1	31.8	31.4	30.9	30.3	...	...	...	...
47	33.4	33.2	33.0	32.8	32.5	32.2	31.9	31.6	31.2	30.8	30.5	30.0	29.6	...	...	...
48	32.7	32.5	32.3	32.1	31.8	31.6	31.3	31.0	30.7	30.3	30.0	29.6	29.2	28.7	...	...
49	32.0	31.8	31.6	31.4	31.2	30.9	30.7	30.4	30.1	29.8	29.4	29.1	28.7	28.3	27.9	...
50	31.3	31.1	30.9	30.7	30.5	30.3	30.0	29.8	29.5	29.2	28.9	28.5	28.2	27.8	27.4	27.0
51	30.5	30.4	30.2	30.0	29.8	29.6	29.4	29.2	28.9	28.6	28.3	28.0	27.7	27.3	26.9	26.5
52	29.7	29.6	29.5	29.3	29.1	28.9	28.7	28.5	28.3	28.0	27.7	27.4	27.1	26.9	26.6	26.1
53	29.0	28.9	28.7	28.6	28.4	28.2	28.1	27.9	27.6	27.4	27.1	26.9	26.6	26.3	25.9	25.6
54	28.2	28.1	28.0	27.8	27.7	27.5	27.4	27.2	27.0	26.8	26.5	26.3	26.0	25.7	25.4	25.1
55	27.4	27.3	27.2	27.1	27.0	26.8	26.7	26.5	26.3	26.1	25.9	25.7	25.4	25.1	24.9	24.6
56	26.7	26.6	26.5	26.3	26.2	26.1	26.0	25.8	25.6	25.4	25.2	25.0	24.8	24.6	24.3	24.0
57	25.9	25.8	25.7	25.6	25.5	25.4	25.2	25.1	24.9	24.8	24.6	24.4	24.2	24.0	23.7	23.5
58	25.1	25.0	24.9	24.8	24.7	24.6	24.5	24.4	24.2	24.1	23.9	23.7	23.5	23.3	23.1	22.9
59	24.3	24.2	24.1	24.1	24.0	23.9	23.8	23.6	23.5	23.4	23.2	23.1	22.9	22.7	22.5	22.3
60	23.5	23.4	23.4	23.3	23.2	23.1	23.0	22.9	22.8	22.7	22.5	22.4	22.2	22.1	21.9	21.7
61	22.7	22.6	22.6	22.5	22.4	22.4	22.3	22.2	22.1	22.0	21.8	21.7	21.6	21.4	21.2	21.1
62	21.9	21.9	21.8	21.7	21.7	21.6	21.5	21.4	21.3	21.2	21.1	21.0	20.9	20.7	20.6	20.4
63	21.1	21.1	21.0	21.0	20.9	20.8	20.8	20.7	20.6	20.5	20.4	20.3	20.2	20.1	19.9	19.8
64	20.3	20.3	20.2	20.2	20.1	20.1	20.0	20.0	19.9	19.8	19.7	19.6	19.5	19.4	19.3	19.1
65	19.6	19.5	19.5	19.4	19.4	19.3	19.3	19.2	19.1	19.1	19.0	18.9	18.8	18.7	18.6	18.5
66	18.8	18.8	18.7	18.7	18.6	18.6	18.5	18.5	18.4	18.4	18.3	18.2	18.1	18.0	17.9	17.8
67	18.0	18.0	18.0	17.9	17.9	17.9	17.8	17.8	17.7	17.6	17.6	17.5	17.4	17.3	17.3	17.2
68	17.3	17.3	17.2	17.2	17.2	17.1	17.1	17.0	17.0	16.9	16.9	16.8	16.7	16.7	16.6	16.5
69	16.5	16.5	16.5	16.5	16.4	16.4	16.4	16.3	16.3	16.2	16.2	16.1	16.1	16.0	15.9	15.8
70	15.8	15.8	15.8	15.7	15.7	15.7	15.7	15.6	15.6	15.5	15.5	15.5	15.4	15.4	15.3	15.2
71	15.1	15.1	15.1	15.0	15.0	15.0	15.0	14.9	14.9	14.9	14.8	14.8	14.7	14.7	14.6	14.5
72	14.4	14.4	14.4	14.3	14.3	14.3	14.3	14.2	14.2	14.2	14.2	14.1	14.1	14.1	14.0	13.9
73	13.7	13.7	13.7	13.7	13.7	13.6	13.6	13.6	13.6	13.5	13.5	13.5	13.4	13.4	13.3	13.3
74	13.1	13.0	13.0	13.0	13.0	13.0	13.0	12.9	12.9	12.9	12.8	12.8	12.8	12.7	12.7	12.7
75	12.4	12.4	12.4	12.4	12.3	12.3	12.3	12.3	12.3	12.2	12.2	12.2	12.2	12.1	12.1	12.1
76	11.8	11.8	11.7	11.7	11.7	11.7	11.7	11.7	11.6	11.6	11.6	11.6	11.6	11.5	11.5	11.5
77	11.1	11.1	11.1	11.1	11.1	11.1	11.1	11.1	11.0	11.0	11.0	11.0	11.0	10.9	10.9	10.9
78	10.5	10.5	10.5	10.5	10.5	10.5	10.5	10.5	10.5	10.4	10.4	10.4	10.4	10.4	10.3	10.3
79	10.0	10.0	9.9	9.9	9.9	9.9	9.9	9.9	9.9	9.9	9.9	9.8	9.8	9.8	9.8	9.8
80	9.4	9.4	9.4	9.4	9.4	9.4	9.4	9.3	9.3	9.3	9.3	9.3	9.3	9.3	9.2	9.2
81	8.9	8.8	8.8	8.8	8.8	8.8	8.8	8.8	8.8	8.8	8.8	8.8	8.8	8.7	8.7	8.7
82	8.3	8.3	8.3	8.3	8.3	8.3	8.3	8.3	8.3	8.3	8.3	8.3	8.2	8.2	8.2	8.2
83	7.8	7.8	7.8	7.8	7.8	7.8	7.8	7.8	7.6	7.8	7.8	7.8	7.7	7.7	7.7	7.7
84	7.3	7.3	7.3	7.3	7.3	7.3	7.3	7.3	7.3	7.3	7.3	7.3	7.3	7.3	7.3	7.2
85	6.9	6.9	6.9	6.9	6.9	6.9	6.9	6.9	6.9	6.9	6.8	6.8	6.8	6.8	6.8	6.8
86	6.5	6.5	6.5	6.5	6.4	6.4	6.4	6.4	6.4	6.4	6.4	6.4	6.4	6.4	6.4	6.4
87	6.1	6.0	6.0	6.0	6.0	6.0	6.0	6.0	6.0	6.0	6.0	6.0	6.0	6.0	6.0	6.0
88	5.7	5.7	5.7	5.7	5.7	5.7	5.7	5.6	5.6	5.6	5.6	5.6	5.6	5.6	5.6	5.6
89	5.3	5.3	5.3	5.3	5.3	5.3	5.3	5.3	5.3	5.3	5.3	5.3	5.3	5.3	5.3	5.3
90	5.0	5.0	5.0	5.0	5.0	5.0	5.0	5.0	5.0	5.0	5.0	4.9	4.9	4.9	4.9	4.9

(Table VIA continues on the following page.)

Table VIA — Annuities for Joint Life Only — Two Lives — Expected Return Multiples

AGES	51	52	53	54	55	56	57	58	59	60	61	62	63	64	65	66
51	26.1	...	...	...	...	...	...	...	...	...	...	...	...	...	...	...
52	25.7	25.3	...	...	...	...	...	...	...	...	...	...	...	...	...	...
53	25.2	24.8	24.4	...	...	...	...	...	...	...	...	...	...	...	...	...
54	24.7	24.4	24.0	23.6	...	...	...	...	...	...	...	...	...	...	...	...
55	24.2	23.9	23.5	23.2	22.7	...	...	...	...	...	...	...	...	...	...	...
56	23.7	23.4	23.1	22.7	22.3	21.9	...	...	...	...	...	...	...	...	...	...
57	23.2	22.9	22.6	22.2	21.9	21.5	21.1	...	...	...	...	...	...	...	...	...
58	22.6	22.4	22.1	21.7	21.4	21.1	20.7	20.3	...	...	...	...	...	...	...	...
59	22.1	21.8	21.5	21.2	20.9	20.6	20.3	19.9	19.5	...	...	...	...	...	...	...
60	21.5	21.2	21.0	20.7	20.4	20.1	19.8	19.5	19.1	18.7	...	...	...	...	...	...
61	20.9	20.6	20.4	20.2	19.9	19.6	19.3	19.0	18.7	18.3	17.9	...	...	...	...	...
62	20.2	20.0	19.8	19.6	19.4	19.1	18.8	18.5	18.2	17.9	17.5	17.1	...	...	...	...
63	19.6	19.4	19.2	19.0	18.8	18.6	18.3	18.0	17.7	17.4	17.1	16.8	16.4	...	...	...
64	19.0	18.8	18.6	18.5	18.3	18.0	17.8	17.5	17.3	17.0	16.7	16.3	16.0	15.6	...	...
65	18.3	18.2	18.0	17.9	17.7	17.5	17.3	17.0	16.8	16.5	16.2	15.9	15.6	15.3	14.9	...
66	17.7	17.6	17.4	17.3	17.1	16.9	16.7	16.5	16.3	16.0	15.8	15.5	15.2	14.9	14.5	14.2
67	17.1	16.9	16.8	16.7	16.5	16.3	16.2	16.0	15.8	15.5	15.3	15.0	14.7	14.5	14.1	13.8
68	16.4	16.3	16.2	16.1	15.9	15.8	15.6	15.4	15.2	15.0	14.8	14.6	14.3	14.0	13.7	13.4
69	15.8	15.7	15.6	15.4	15.3	15.2	15.0	14.9	14.7	14.5	14.3	14.1	13.9	13.6	13.3	13.1
70	15.1	15.0	14.9	14.8	14.7	14.6	14.5	14.3	14.2	14.0	13.8	13.6	13.4	13.2	12.9	12.6
71	14.5	14.4	14.3	14.2	14.1	14.0	13.9	13.8	13.6	13.5	13.3	13.1	12.9	12.7	12.5	12.2
72	13.8	13.8	13.7	13.6	13.5	13.4	13.3	13.2	13.1	12.9	12.8	12.6	12.4	12.3	12.0	11.8
73	13.2	13.2	13.1	13.0	13.0	12.9	12.8	12.7	12.5	12.4	12.3	12.1	12.0	11.8	11.6	11.4
74	12.6	12.6	12.5	12.4	12.4	12.3	12.2	12.1	12.0	11.9	11.8	11.6	11.5	11.3	11.2	11.0
75	12.0	12.0	11.9	11.9	11.8	11.7	11.7	11.6	11.5	11.4	11.3	11.1	11.0	10.9	10.7	10.5
76	11.4	11.4	11.3	11.3	11.2	11.2	11.1	11.0	10.9	10.9	10.8	10.6	10.5	10.4	10.3	10.1
77	10.8	10.8	10.8	10.7	10.7	10.6	10.6	10.5	10.4	10.3	10.3	10.2	10.0	9.9	9.8	9.7
78	10.3	10.2	10.2	10.2	10.1	10.1	10.0	10.0	9.9	9.8	9.8	9.7	9.6	9.5	9.4	9.2
79	9.7	9.7	9.7	9.6	9.6	9.6	9.5	9.5	9.4	9.3	9.3	9.2	9.1	9.0	8.9	8.8
80	9.2	9.2	9.1	9.1	9.1	9.0	9.0	9.0	8.9	8.9	8.8	8.7	8.7	8.6	8.5	8.4
81	8.7	8.7	8.6	8.6	8.6	8.5	8.5	8.5	8.4	8.4	8.3	8.3	8.2	8.1	8.0	8.0
82	8.2	8.2	8.1	8.1	8.1	8.1	8.0	8.0	8.0	7.9	7.9	7.8	7.8	7.7	7.6	7.5
83	7.7	7.7	7.7	7.6	7.6	7.6	7.6	7.5	7.5	7.5	7.4	7.4	7.3	7.3	7.2	7.1
84	7.2	7.2	7.2	7.2	7.2	7.1	7.1	7.1	7.1	7.0	7.0	7.0	6.9	6.9	6.8	6.7
85	6.8	6.8	6.8	6.7	6.7	6.7	6.7	6.7	6.6	6.6	6.6	6.5	6.5	6.5	6.4	6.4
86	6.4	6.4	6.3	6.3	6.3	6.3	6.3	6.3	6.2	6.2	6.2	6.2	6.1	6.1	6.0	6.0
87	6.0	6.0	6.0	5.9	5.9	5.9	5.9	5.9	5.9	5.8	5.8	5.8	5.8	5.7	5.7	5.6
88	5.6	5.6	5.6	5.6	5.6	5.5	5.5	5.5	5.5	5.5	5.5	5.4	5.4	5.4	5.3	5.3
89	5.2	5.2	5.2	5.2	5.2	5.2	5.2	5.2	5.2	5.1	5.1	5.1	5.1	5.1	5.0	5.0
90	4.9	4.9	4.9	4.9	4.9	4.9	4.9	4.9	4.9	4.8	4.8	4.8	4.8	4.8	4.7	4.7

Table VIA — Annuities for Joint Life Only — Two Lives — Expected Return Multiples

AGES	67	68	69	70	71	72	73	74	75	76	77	78	79	80	81	82
67	13.5	...	...	...	...	...	...	...	...	...	...	...	...	...	...	...
68	13.1	12.8	...	...	...	...	...	...	...	...	...	...	...	...	...	...
69	12.8	12.5	12.1	...	...	...	...	...	...	...	...	...	...	...	...	...
70	12.4	12.1	11.8	11.5	...	...	...	...	...	...	...	...	...	...	...	...
71	12.0	11.7	11.4	11.2	10.9	...	...	...	...	...	...	...	...	...	...	...
72	11.6	11.4	11.1	10.8	10.5	10.2	...	...	...	...	...	...	...	...	...	...
73	11.2	11.0	10.7	10.5	10.2	9.9	9.7	...	...	...	...	...	...	...	...	...
74	10.8	10.6	10.4	10.1	9.9	9.6	9.4	9.1	...	...	...	...	...	...	...	...
75	10.4	10.2	10.0	9.8	9.5	9.3	9.1	8.8	8.6	...	...	...	...	...	...	...
76	9.9	9.8	9.6	9.4	9.2	9.0	8.8	8.5	8.3	8.0	...	...	...	...	...	...
77	9.5	9.4	9.2	9.0	8.8	8.6	8.4	8.2	8.0	7.8	7.5	...	...	...	...	...
78	9.1	9.0	8.8	8.7	8.5	8.3	8.1	7.9	7.7	7.5	7.3	7.0	...	...	...	...
79	8.7	8.6	8.4	8.3	8.1	8.0	7.8	7.6	7.4	7.2	7.0	6.8	6.6	...	...	...
80	8.3	8.2	8.0	7.9	7.8	7.6	7.5	7.3	7.1	6.9	6.8	6.6	6.3	6.1	...	...
81	7.9	7.9	7.7	7.5	7.4	7.3	7.1	7.0	6.8	6.7	6.5	6.3	6.1	5.9	5.7	...
82	7.5	7.4	7.3	7.2	7.1	6.9	6.8	6.7	6.5	6.4	6.2	6.0	5.9	5.7	5.5	5.3
83	7.1	7.0	6.9	6.8	6.7	6.6	6.5	6.4	6.2	6.1	5.9	5.8	5.6	5.5	5.3	5.1
84	6.7	6.6	6.5	6.4	6.4	6.3	6.2	6.0	5.9	5.8	5.7	5.5	5.4	5.2	5.1	4.9
85	6.3	6.2	6.2	6.1	6.0	5.9	5.8	5.7	5.6	5.5	5.4	5.3	5.2	5.0	4.9	4.7
86	5.9	5.9	5.8	5.8	5.7	5.6	5.5	5.4	5.4	5.3	5.1	5.0	4.9	4.8	4.7	4.5
87	5.6	5.6	5.5	5.4	5.4	5.3	5.2	5.2	5.1	5.0	4.9	4.8	4.7	4.6	4.4	4.3
88	5.3	5.2	5.2	5.1	5.1	5.0	5.0	4.9	4.8	4.7	4.6	4.5	4.4	4.3	4.2	4.1
89	5.0	4.9	4.9	4.8	4.8	4.7	4.7	4.6	4.5	4.5	4.4	4.3	4.2	4.1	4.0	3.9
90	4.7	4.6	4.6	4.6	4.5	4.5	4.4	4.4	4.3	4.2	4.2	4.1	4.0	3.9	3.8	3.8

AGES	83	84	85	86	87	88	89	90
83	4.9	...	...	...	...	...	...	...
84	4.7	4.6	...	...	...	...	...	...
85	4.6	4.4	4.2	...	...	...	...	...
86	4.4	4.2	4.1	3.9	...	...	...	...
87	4.2	4.1	3.9	3.8	3.6	...	...	...
88	4.0	3.9	3.8	3.6	3.5	3.4	...	...
89	3.8	3.7	3.6	3.5	3.4	3.2	3.1	...
90	3.7	3.5	3.4	3.3	3.2	3.1	3.0	2.9

Table VII — Percent Value of Refund Feature
Duration of Guaranteed Amount

Age	1 Yr.	2 Yrs.	3 Yrs.	4 Yrs.	5 Yrs.	6 Yrs.	7 Yrs.	8 Yrs.	9 Yrs.	10 Yrs.	11 Yrs.	12 Yrs.	13 Yrs.	14 Yrs.	15 Yrs.	16 Yrs.	17 Yrs.	18 Yrs.	19 Yrs.	20 Yrs.
19																				
20																				1
21																				1
22																				1
23																		1	1	1
24																		1	1	1
25																	1	1	1	1
26																	1	1	1	1
27																1	1	1	1	1
28															1	1	1	1	1	1
29															1	1	1	1	1	1
30														1	1	1	1	1	1	1
31														1	1	1	1	1	1	1
32													1	1	1	1	1	1	1	1
33												1	1	1	1	1	1	1	1	1
34											1	1	1	1	1	1	1	1	1	1
35											1	1	1	1	1	1	1	1	1	1
36										1	1	1	1	1	1	1	1	1	1	1
37									1	1	1	1	1	1	1	1	1	1	1	1
38									1	1	1	1	1	1	1	1	1	1	1	2
39								1	1	1	1	1	1	1	1	1	1	1	2	2
40							1	1	1	1	1	1	1	1	1	1	1	2	2	2
41						1	1	1	1	1	1	1	1	1	1	1	2	2	2	2
42					1	1	1	1	1	1	1	1	1	1	1	2	2	2	2	2
43					1	1	1	1	1	1	1	1	1	1	2	2	2	2	2	3
44				1	1	1	1	1	1	1	1	1	1	2	2	2	2	2	3	3
45				1	1	1	1	1	1	1	1	1	2	2	2	2	2	3	3	3
46				1	1	1	1	1	1	1	1	2	2	2	2	2	3	3	3	3
47				1	1	1	1	1	1	1	1	2	2	2	2	3	3	3	3	4
48				1	1	1	1	1	1	1	2	2	2	2	3	3	3	4	4	4
49				1	1	1	1	1	1	1	2	2	2	3	3	3	3	4	4	4
50				1	1	1	1	1	1	2	2	2	2	3	3	3	4	4	4	5
51				1	1	1	1	1	2	2	2	2	3	3	3	4	4	4	5	5
52				1	1	1	1	1	2	2	2	2	3	3	3	4	4	5	5	5
53			1	1	1	1	1	2	2	2	2	3	3	3	4	4	5	5	5	6
54			1	1	1	1	2	2	2	3	3	3	4	4	4	5	5	6	6	7
55			1	1	1	1	2	2	2	3	3	4	4	4	5	5	6	6	7	7
56			1	1	1	2	2	2	3	3	3	4	4	5	5	6	6	7	7	8
57			1	1	1	2	2	2	3	3	3	4	4	5	5	6	6	7	8	9
58		1	1	1	1	2	2	2	3	3	4	4	5	5	6	6	7	8	9	9
59		1	1	1	2	2	2	3	3	4	4	5	5	6	6	7	8	9	9	10
60		1	1	1	2	2	2	3	3	4	4	5	6	6	7	8	9	10	10	11
61		1	1	1	2	2	3	3	4	4	5	6	6	7	8	9	10	10	11	13
62		1	1	2	2	3	3	4	4	5	5	6	7	8	9	10	11	12	13	14
63		1	1	2	2	3	3	4	5	5	6	7	8	9	10	11	12	13	14	15
64		1	1	1	2	2	3	3	4	5	6	7	8	9	10	12	13	14	15	17
65		1	2	2	3	3	4	5	6	6	7	8	9	10	12	13	14	15	17	18
66	1	1	2	2	3	4	5	5	6	7	8	9	10	12	13	14	15	17	18	20
67	1	1	2	3	4	5	6	7	8	9	10	11	12	13	14	15	17	18	20	22
68	1	1	2	3	4	5	6	7	8	9	10	11	13	14	15	17	19	20	22	24
69	1	1	2	3	4	5	6	7	8	10	11	12	14	15	17	19	20	22	24	26
70	1	2	3	4	5	6	7	8	9	11	12	14	15	17	19	20	22	24	26	28
71	1	2	3	4	5	6	8	9	10	12	13	15	17	18	20	22	24	26	28	30
72	1	2	3	4	6	7	8	10	11	13	15	17	18	20	22	24	26	28	30	32
73	1	2	4	5	6	8	9	11	13	14	16	18	20	22	24	26	28	31	33	35
74	1	3	4	5	7	9	10	12	14	16	18	20	22	24	26	28	31	33	35	37
75	1	3	4	6	8	9	11	13	15	17	19	22	24	26	28	31	33	35	38	40
76	2	3	5	7	9	10	12	15	17	19	21	24	26	28	31	33	36	38	40	43
77	2	4	5	7	9	12	14	16	18	21	23	26	28	31	33	36	38	41	43	45
78	2	4	6	8	10	13	15	18	20	23	25	28	31	33	36	38	41	43	46	48
79	2	4	7	9	11	14	17	19	22	25	28	30	33	36	38	41	44	46	48	51
80	2	5	7	10	13	15	18	21	24	27	30	33	36	38	41	44	46	49	51	53
81	3	5	8	11	14	17	20	23	26	29	32	35	38	41	44	47	48	51	54	56
82	3	6	9	12	15	19	22	25	28	32	35	38	41	44	47	49	52	54	56	58
83	3	7	10	13	17	20	24	27	31	34	38	41	44	47	49	52	54	57	59	61
84	4	7	11	15	19	22	26	30	33	37	40	44	47	49	52	55	57	59	61	63
85	4	8	12	16	20	24	28	32	36	40	43	46	49	52	55	57	59	62	63	65
86	4	9	13	18	22	27	31	35	39	42	46	49	52	55	57	60	62	64	66	67
87	5	10	15	20	24	29	33	37	41	45	48	52	55	57	60	62	64	66	68	69
88	5	11	16	21	26	31	36	40	44	48	51	54	57	60	62	64	66	68	70	71
89	6	12	18	23	28	33	38	43	47	50	54	57	60	62	65	67	68	70	72	73
90	7	13	19	25	31	36	41	45	49	53	56	59	62	64	67	69	70	72	74	75

Table VII — Percent Value of Refund Feature
Duration of Guaranteed Amount

Age	21 Yrs.	22 Yrs.	23 Yrs.	24 Yrs.	25 Yrs.	26 Yrs.	27 Yrs.	28 Yrs.	29 Yrs.	30 Yrs.	31 Yrs.	32 Yrs.	33 Yrs.	34 Yrs.	35 Yrs.	36 Yrs.	37 Yrs.	38 Yrs.	39 Yrs.	40 Yrs.
5	…	…	…	…	…	…	…	…	…	…	…	1	1	1	1	1	1	1	1	1
6	…	…	…	…	…	…	…	…	…	…	…	1	1	1	1	1	1	1	1	1
7	…	…	…	…	…	…	…	…	…	…	1	1	1	1	1	1	1	1	1	1
8	…	…	…	…	…	…	…	…	…	1	1	1	1	1	1	1	1	1	1	1
9	…	…	…	…	…	…	…	…	1	1	1	1	1	1	1	1	1	1	1	1
10	…	…	…	…	…	…	…	1	1	1	1	1	1	1	1	1	1	1	1	1
11	…	…	…	…	…	…	1	1	1	1	1	1	1	1	1	1	1	1	1	1
12	…	…	…	…	…	1	1	1	1	1	1	1	1	1	1	1	1	1	1	1
13	…	…	…	…	1	1	1	1	1	1	1	1	1	1	1	1	1	1	1	1
14	…	…	…	1	1	1	1	1	1	1	1	1	1	1	1	1	1	1	1	1
15	…	…	1	1	1	1	1	1	1	1	1	1	1	1	1	1	1	1	1	1
16	…	1	1	1	1	1	1	1	1	1	1	1	1	1	1	1	1	1	1	1
17	…	1	1	1	1	1	1	1	1	1	1	1	1	1	1	1	1	1	1	1
18	1	1	1	1	1	1	1	1	1	1	1	1	1	1	1	1	1	1	1	2
19	1	1	1	1	1	1	1	1	1	1	1	1	1	1	1	1	1	1	2	2
20	1	1	1	1	1	1	1	1	1	1	1	1	1	1	1	1	1	2	2	2
21	1	1	1	1	1	1	1	1	1	1	1	1	1	1	1	1	2	2	2	2
22	1	1	1	1	1	1	1	1	1	1	1	1	1	1	1	2	2	2	2	2
23	1	1	1	1	1	1	1	1	1	1	1	1	1	1	2	2	2	2	2	2
24	1	1	1	1	1	1	1	1	1	1	1	1	1	2	2	2	2	2	2	2
25	1	1	1	1	1	1	1	1	1	1	1	1	2	2	2	2	2	2	2	3
26	1	1	1	1	1	1	1	1	1	1	1	2	2	2	2	2	2	2	3	3
27	1	1	1	1	1	1	1	1	1	1	2	2	2	2	2	2	2	3	3	3
28	1	1	1	1	1	1	1	1	1	2	2	2	2	2	2	2	3	3	3	3
29	1	1	1	1	1	1	1	1	2	2	2	2	2	2	2	3	3	3	3	4
30	1	1	1	1	1	1	1	2	2	2	2	2	2	2	3	3	3	3	4	4
31	1	1	1	1	1	1	2	2	2	2	2	2	2	3	3	3	3	4	4	4
32	1	1	1	1	1	2	2	2	2	2	2	2	3	3	3	3	4	4	4	5
33	1	1	1	1	2	2	2	2	2	2	2	3	3	3	3	4	4	4	5	5
34	1	1	1	2	2	2	2	2	2	3	3	3	3	3	4	4	4	5	5	5
35	1	2	2	2	2	2	2	2	3	3	3	3	4	4	4	4	5	5	5	6
36	2	2	2	2	2	2	2	3	3	3	3	4	4	4	4	5	5	5	6	6
37	2	2	2	2	2	2	3	3	3	3	4	4	4	4	5	5	6	6	6	7
38	2	2	2	2	2	3	3	3	3	4	4	4	5	5	5	6	6	7	7	8
39	2	2	2	2	3	3	3	3	4	4	4	5	5	5	6	6	7	7	7	8
40	2	2	3	3	3	3	3	4	4	4	5	5	5	6	6	7	7	8	8	9
41	2	3	3	3	3	3	4	4	4	5	5	5	6	6	7	7	8	8	9	10
42	3	3	3	3	3	4	4	4	5	5	6	6	6	7	7	8	9	9	10	11
43	3	3	3	4	4	4	4	5	5	6	6	7	7	8	8	9	9	10	11	12
44	3	3	4	4	4	4	5	5	6	6	7	7	8	8	9	10	10	11	12	13
45	3	4	4	4	4	5	5	6	6	7	7	8	8	9	10	10	11	12	13	14
46	4	4	4	5	5	5	6	6	7	7	8	9	9	10	11	11	12	13	14	15
47	4	4	5	5	5	6	6	7	7	8	9	9	10	11	12	12	13	14	15	16
48	4	5	5	5	6	6	7	7	8	9	9	10	11	12	13	14	15	16	17	18
49	5	5	5	6	6	7	8	8	9	10	10	11	12	13	14	15	16	17	18	19
50	5	5	6	6	7	7	8	9	9	10	11	12	13	14	15	16	17	18	20	21
51	5	6	6	7	8	8	9	10	11	11	12	13	14	15	16	17	19	20	21	22
52	6	6	7	7	8	9	10	11	11	12	13	14	15	17	18	19	20	21	23	24
53	7	7	8	8	9	10	11	12	13	14	15	16	17	18	19	20	22	23	24	26
54	7	8	8	9	10	11	12	13	14	15	16	17	18	19	21	22	23	25	26	28
55	8	9	9	10	11	12	13	14	15	16	17	18	20	21	22	24	25	27	28	30
56	9	9	10	11	12	13	14	15	16	18	19	20	21	23	24	26	27	29	30	32
57	9	10	11	12	13	14	15	17	18	19	20	22	23	25	26	28	29	31	32	34
58	10	11	12	13	14	16	17	18	19	21	22	24	25	27	28	30	31	33	34	36
59	11	12	13	15	16	17	18	20	21	22	24	25	27	28	30	32	33	35	36	38
60	12	14	15	16	17	19	20	21	23	24	26	27	29	31	32	34	35	37	38	40
61	14	15	16	17	19	20	22	23	25	26	28	29	31	33	34	36	37	39	40	42
62	15	16	18	19	20	22	23	25	27	28	30	32	33	35	36	38	40	41	42	44
63	16	18	19	21	22	24	25	27	29	30	32	34	35	37	39	40	42	43	45	46
64	18	19	21	23	24	26	28	29	31	33	34	36	38	39	41	42	44	45	47	48
65	20	21	23	25	26	28	30	31	33	35	37	38	40	42	43	45	46	47	49	50
66	21	23	25	27	28	30	32	34	35	37	39	41	42	44	45	47	48	50	51	52
67	23	25	27	29	31	32	34	36	38	40	41	43	45	46	48	49	50	52	53	54
68	25	27	29	31	33	35	37	39	40	42	44	45	47	48	50	51	52	54	55	56
69	28	29	31	33	35	37	39	41	43	44	46	48	49	51	52	53	54	56	57	58
70	30	32	34	36	38	40	42	43	45	47	48	50	51	53	54	55	57	58	59	60
71	32	34	36	38	40	42	44	46	47	49	51	52	54	55	56	57	59	60	61	62
72	35	37	39	41	43	45	46	48	50	51	53	54	56	57	58	59	60	62	62	63
73	37	39	41	43	45	47	49	51	52	54	55	57	58	59	60	61	62	63	64	65
74	40	42	44	46	48	50	51	53	54	56	57	59	60	61	62	63	64	65	66	67
75	42	44	46	48	50	52	54	55	57	58	59	61	62	63	64	65	66	67	69	69
76	45	47	49	51	53	54	56	58	59	60	62	63	64	65	66	67	68	69	69	70
77	47	50	51	53	55	57	58	60	61	62	64	65	66	67	68	69	70	70	71	72
78	50	52	54	56	57	59	61	62	63	64	66	67	68	69	70	70	71	72	73	73
79	53	55	56	58	60	61	63	64	65	66	67	68	69	70	71	72	73	73	74	75
80	55	57	59	60	62	63	65	66	67	68	69	70	71	72	73	74	74	75	76	76
81	58	59	61	63	64	66	67	68	69	71	72	73	74	74	75	76	76	77	77	78
82	60	62	63	65	66	68	69	70	71	72	73	74	74	75	76	77	77	78	78	79
83	62	64	66	67	68	70	71	72	73	74	75	76	77	77	78	79	79	80	80	80
84	65	66	68	69	70	71	72	73	74	75	76	77	77	78	79	79	80	80	81	81
85	68	70	71	72	73	74	75	76	77	78	79	79	80	81	81	82	82	83	83	83
86	69	70	72	73	74	75	76	77	77	78	79	80	80	81	81	82	82	83	83	84
87	72	73	73	75	76	77	77	78	79	80	80	81	81	82	82	83	83	84	84	85
88	73	74	75	76	77	78	79	80	80	81	82	82	82	83	83	84	84	85	85	86
89	74	76	77	78	79	79	80	81	81	82	83	83	84	84	85	85	85	86	86	87
90	76	77	78	79	80	81	81	82	83	83	84	84	85	85	86	86	86	87	87	87

Appendix B

EXAMPLES OF EXCLUSION
RATIO CALCULATIONS

Single Life Annuity

Example 1. On October 1, 2002, Mr. Smith purchased an immediate nonrefund annuity which will pay him $125 a month ($1,500 a year) for life, beginning November 1, 2002. He paid $16,000 for the contract. Mr. Smith's age on his birthday nearest the annuity starting date (October 1st) was 68. According to Table V (which he uses because his investment in the contract is post-June 1986), his life expectancy is 17.6 years. Consequently, the expected return under the contract is $26,400 (12 x $125 x 17.6). And the exclusion percentage for the annuity payments is 60.6% ($16,000 ÷ $26,400). Since Mr. Smith received 2 monthly payments in 2002 (a total of $250), he will exclude $151.50 (60.6% of $250) from his gross income for 2002, and he must include $98.50 ($250 - $151.50). Mr. Smith will exclude the amounts so determined for 17.6 years. In 2002, he could exclude $151.50; each year thereafter through 2019, he could exclude $909, for a total exclusion of $15,604.50 ($151.50 excluded in 1998 and $15,453 excluded over the next 17 years). In 2020, he could exclude only $395.50 ($16,000 - $15,604.50). In 2020, he would include in his income $1,104.50 ($1,500 - $395.50) and $1,500 in 2021 and in each year thereafter.

Example 2. If Mr. Smith purchased the contract illustrated above on October 1, 1986 (so that it had an annuity starting date before January 1, 1987), he would exclude $151.50 (60.6% of $250) from his 1986 gross income and would include $98.50 ($250 - $151.50). For each succeeding tax year in which he receives 12 monthly payments (even if he outlives his life expectancy of 17.6 years), he will exclude $909 (60.6% of $1,500), and he will include $591 ($1,500 - $909).

Refund or Period Certain Guarantee

Example 1. On January 1, 2002, a husband, age 65, purchased for $21,053 an immediate installment refund annuity which pays $100 a month for life. The contract provides that in the event the husband does not live long enough to recover the full purchase price, payments will be made to his wife until the total payments under the contract equal the purchase price. The investment in the contract is adjusted for the purpose of determining the exclusion ratio as follows:

Unadjusted investment in the contract .... $ 21,053
Amount to be received annually .... $ 1,200
Duration of guaranteed amount ($21,053 ÷ $1,200) .... 17.5 yrs.
Rounded to nearest whole number of years 18
Percentage value of guaranteed refund
  (Table VII for age 65 and 18 years) 15%
Value of refund feature rounded to nearest dollar
  (15% of $21,053) .... $ 3,158
Adjusted investment in the contract ($21,053 - $3,158) .... $ 17,895

Example 2. Assume the contract in Example 1 was purchased as a deferred annuity and the pre-July 1986 investment in the contract is $10,000 and the post-June 1986 investment in the contract is $11,053. If the annuitant elects, as explained earlier, to compute a separate exclusion percentage for the pre-July 1986 and the post-June 1986 amounts, separate computations must be performed to determine the adjusted investment in the contract. The pre-July 1986 investment in the contract and the post-June 1986 investment in the contract are adjusted for the purpose of determining the exclusion ratios in the following manner:

Pre-July 1986 adjustment:
  Unadjusted investment in the contract .... $ 10,000
  Allocable part of amount to be received annually
    (($10,000 ÷ $21,053) x $1,200) .... $ 570
  Duration of guaranteed amount ($10,000 ÷ $570) 17.5
  Rounded to nearest whole number of years 18
  Percentage in Table III for age 65 and 18 years 30%
  Present value of refund feature rounded to nearest dollar
    (30% of $10,000) .... $ 3,000
  Adjusted pre-July 1986 investment in the contract
    ($10,000 - $3,000) .... $ 7,000

Post-June 1986 adjustment:
  Unadjusted investment in the contract .... $ 11,053
  Allocable part of amount to be received annually
    (($11,053 ÷ $21,053) x $1,200 .... $ 630
  Duration of guaranteed amount ($11,053 ÷ $630) 17.54
  Rounded to nearest whole number of years 18
  Percentage in Table VII for age 65 and 18 years 15%
  Present value of refund feature rounded to nearest dollar
    (15% of $11,054) .... $ 1,658
  Adjusted post-June 1986 investment in the contract
    ($11,053 - $1,658) .... $ 9,395

Once the investment in the contract has been adjusted by subtract-ing the value of the refund or period certain guarantee, an exclusion ratio is determined in the same way as for a straight life annuity. Expected return is computed; then the *adjusted* investment in the contract is divided by expected return. Taking the two examples above, the exclu-sion ratio for each contract is determined as follows.

Example (1) above.

Investment in the contract (adjusted for refund guarantee) .... $ 17,895
One year's guaranteed annuity payments (12 x $100) .... $ 1,200
Life expectancy for Table V, age 65 .... 20 yrs.
Expected return (20 x $1,200) .... $ 24,000
Exclusion ratio ($17,895 ÷ $24,000) 74.6%
Amount excludabe from gross income each year in which 12
   payments are received (74.6% of $1,200)* .... $ 895.20
Amount includable in gross income ($1,200 - $895.20)* .... $ 304.80

* Since the annuity starting date is after December 31, 1986, the total amount excludable is limited to the investment in the contract; after that has been recovered, the remaining amounts received are includable in income. However, the Small Business Job Protection Act of 1996 (P.L. 104-188) changed the manner in which the "unrecovered investment" in the contract is calculated when the annuity has a refund or guarantee feature. Generally, the portion of any amount received as an annuity that can be excluded using the exclusion ratio is not to exceed the unrecovered investment in the contract. In calculating this figure, the value of the refund or guarantee feature was subtracted prior to the 1996 Act. After the 1996 Act, for this purpose, the value of the refund or guarantee feature is not subtracted. Although this change was made in 1996 legislation, it is effective for individuals with annuity starting dates after December 31, 1986. IRC Sec. 72(b)(4). Please note, this change does not affect the calculation of the refund or guarantee feature for purposes of calculating the exclusion ratio; it only affects the unrecov-ered investment in the contract and, thus, the date on which the investment in the contract is recovered.

Example (2) above.

Pre-July 1986 investment in the contract
   (adjusted for period certain guarantee) .... $ 7,000
One year's guaranteed annuity payments (12 x $100) .... $ 1,200
Life expectancy from Table I, male age 65 .... 15 yrs.
Expected return (15 x $1,200) .... $ 18,000
Exclusion ratio ($7,000 ÷ $18,000) 38.9%

Post-June 1986 investment in the contract
(adjusted for period certain guarantee) .... $ 9,395
One year's guaranteed annuity payments (12 x $100) .... $ 1,200
Life expectancy from Table V, age 65 .... 20 yrs.
Expected return (20 x $1,200) .... $ 24,000
Exclusion ratio ($9,395 ÷ $24,000) 39.1%
Sum of pre-July and post-June 1986 ratios 78%
Amount excludable from gross income each year in which
twelve payments are received (78% of $1,200)* .... $ 936.00
Amount includable in gross income ($1,200 - 936.00)* .... $ 264.00

* Since the annuity starting date is after December 31, 1986, the total amount excludable is limited to the investment in the contract; after that has been recovered, the remaining amounts received are includable in income. (Note that 1996 legislation changed the manner in which the unrecovered investment in the contract is calculated for this purpose as explained above in Example 1.)

Joint and Survivor Annuity (Same Income to Survivor as to Both Annuitants Before Any Death)

Example 1. After June 30, 1986, Mr. and Mrs. Jones purchase an immediate joint and survivor annuity. The annuity will provide payments of $100 a month while both are alive and until the death of the survivor. Mr. Jones' age on his birthday nearest the annuity starting date is 65; Mrs. Jones', 63. The single premium is $22,000.

Investment in the contract .... $ 22,000
One year's annuity payments (12 x $100) 1,200
Joint and survivor multiple from Table VI
(age 65, 63) 26
Expected return (26 x $1,200) .... $ 31,200
Exclusion ratio ($22,000 ÷ $31,200) 70.5%
Amount excludable from gross income each year in which 12
payments are received (70.5% of $1,200)* .... $ 846.00
Amount includable in gross income
($1,200 - $846.00)* 354.00

* If the annuity starting date is after December 31, 1986, the total amount excludable is limited to the investment in the contract; after that has been recovered, the remaining amounts received are includable in income.

Joint and Survivor Annuity (Income To Survivor Differs From Income Before First Death)

Example 1. After July 30, 1986, Mr. and Mrs. Smith buy an immediate joint and survivor annuity which will provide monthly payments of $117 ($1,404 a year) for as long as both live, and monthly payments of $78 ($936 a year) to the survivor. As of the annuity starting date he is 65 years old; she is 63. The expected return is computed as follows.

Joint and survivor multiple from Table VI (ages 65, 63) 26
Portion of expected return (26 x $936) $24,366.00
Joint life multiple from Table VIA (ages 65, 63) 15.6
Difference between annual annuity payment before the first death
    and annual annuity payment to the survivor ($1,404 - $936) $468
Portion of expected return (15.6 x $468) .... $ 7,300.80

Expected return $31,636.80

Assuming that Mr. Smith paid $22,000 for the contract, the exclusion ratio is 69.5% ($22,000 ÷ $31,636.80). During their joint lives the portion of each monthly payment to be excluded from gross income is $81.31 (69.5% of $117), or $975.72 a year. The portion to be included is $35.69 ($117 - $81.31), or $428.28 a year. After the first death, the portion of each monthly payment to be excluded from gross income will be $54.21 (69.5% of $78), or $650.52 a year. And $23.79 of each payment ($78 - $54.21), or $285.48 a year, will be included. If the annuity starting date is after December 31, 1986, the total amount excludable is limited to the investment in the contract. Thus, if Mr. Smith lives for 23 years, he may exclude $81.31 from each payment for 22 years ((12 x 22) x $81.31 = $21,465.84). In the 23rd year he may exclude $534.16 ($22,000 - $21,465.84) or $81.31 from each of the first six payments, but only $46.30 from the seventh. The balance is entirely includable in his income, and on his death, his widow must include the full amount of each payment in income.

Example 2. Assume that in the example above, there is a pre-July 1986 investment in the contract of $12,000 and a post-June 1986 investment in the contract of $10,000. Mr. Smith elects to calculate the exclusion percentage for each portion. The pre-July exclusion ratio would be 44.6% ($12,000 ÷ $26,910—the expected return on the contract determined by using Tables II and IIA and the age and sex of both annuitants). The post-June 1986 exclusion ratio is $10,000 ÷ $31,636.80 or 31.6%. The amount excludable from each monthly payment while both are alive would be $89.15 (44.6% of $117 plus 31.6% of $117) and the remaining $27.85 would be included in gross income. If the annuity starting date is after December 31, 1986, the total amount excludable is limited to the investment in the contract.

Appendix C

INTERNAL REVENUE CODE SECTIONS

INTERNAL REVENUE CODE SECTION 72

72. ANNUITIES; CERTAIN PROCEEDS OF ENDOWMENT AND LIFE INSURANCE CONTRACTS

(a) GENERAL RULE FOR ANNUITIES

Except as otherwise provided in this chapter, gross income includes any amount received as an annuity (whether for a period certain or during one or more lives) under an annuity, endowment, or life insurance contract.

(b) EXCLUSION RATIO

(1) IN GENERAL

Gross income does not include that part of any amount received as an annuity under an annuity, endowment, or life insurance contract which bears the same ratio to such amount as the investment in the contract (as of the annuity starting date) bears to the expected return under the contract (as of such date).

(2) EXCLUSION LIMITED TO INVESTMENT

The portion of any amount received as an annuity which is excluded from gross income under paragraph (1) shall not exceed the unrecovered investment in the contract immediately before the receipt of such amount.

THE ANNUITY HANDBOOK

(3) DEDUCTION WHERE ANNUITY PAYMENTS CEASE BE-
FORE ENTIRE INVESTMENT RECOVERED

(A) IN GENERAL

If—

(i) after the annuity starting date, payments as an
annuity under the contract cease by reason of the death of
an annuitant, and

(ii) as of the date of such cessation, there is unrecovered investment in the contract, the amount of such unrecovered investment (in excess of any amount specified in
subsection (e)(5) which was not included in gross income)
shall be allowed as a deduction to the annuitant for his last
taxable year.

(B) PAYMENTS TO OTHER PERSONS

In the case of any contract which provides for payments meeting the requirements of subparagraphs (B) and
(C) of subsection (c)(2), the deduction under subparagraph
(A) shall be allowed to the person entitled to such payments
for the taxable year in which such payments are received.

(C) NET OPERATING LOSS DEDUCTIONS PROVIDED

For purposes of section 172, a deduction allowed under
this paragraph shall be treated as if it were attributable to
a trade or business of the taxpayer.

(4) UNRECOVERED INVESTMENT

For purposes of this subsection, the unrecovered investment in
the contract as of any date is—

(A) the investment in the contract (determined without regard to
subsection (c)(2)) as of the annuity starting date, reduced by

(B) the aggregate amount received under the contract on or after
such annuity starting date and before the date as of which the
determination is being made, to the extent such amount was excludable from gross income under this subtitle.

(c) DEFINITIONS

(1) INVESTMENT IN THE CONTRACT

For purposes of subsection (b), the investment in the contract as of the annuity starting date is—

(A) the aggregate amount of premiums or other consideration paid for the contract, minus

(B) the aggregate amount received under the contract before such date, to the extent that such amount was excludable from gross income under this subtitle or prior income tax laws.

(2) ADJUSTMENT IN INVESTMENT WHERE THERE IS RE-FUND FEATURE

If—

(A) the expected return under the contract depends in whole or in part on the life expectancy of one or more individuals;

(B) the contract provides for payments to be made to a beneficiary (or to the estate of an annuitant) on or after the death of the annuitant or annuitants; and

(C) such payments are in the nature of a refund of the consideration paid, then the value (computed without discount for interest) of such payments on the annuity starting date shall be subtracted from the amount determined under paragraph (1). Such value shall be computed in accordance with actuarial tables prescribed by the Secretary. For purposes of this paragraph and of subsection (e)(2)(A), the term "refund of the consideration paid" includes amounts payable after the death of an annuitant by reason of a provision in the contract for a life annuity with minimum period of payments certain, but (if part of the consideration was contributed by an employer) does not include that part of any payment to a beneficiary (or to the estate of the annuitant) which is not attributable to the consideration paid by the employee for the contract as determined under paragraph (1)(A).

(3) EXPECTED RETURN

For purposes of subsection (b), the expected return under the contract shall be determined as follows:

(A) LIFE EXPECTANCY

    If the expected return under the contract, for the period on and after the annuity starting date, depends in whole or in part on the life expectancy of one or more individuals, the expected return shall be computed with reference to actuarial tables prescribed by the Secretary.

(B) INSTALLMENT PAYMENTS

    If subparagraph (A) does not apply, the expected return is the aggregate of the amounts receivable under the contract as an annuity.

(4) ANNUITY STARTING DATE

    For purposes of this section, the annuity starting date in the case of any contract is the first day of the first period for which an amount is received as an annuity under the contract; except that if such date was before January 1, 1954, then the annuity starting date is January 1, 1954.

* * *

(e) AMOUNTS NOT RECEIVED AS ANNUITIES

(1) APPLICATION OF SUBSECTION

(A) IN GENERAL

    This subsection shall apply to any amount which—

    (i) is received under an annuity, endowment, or life insurance contract, and

    (ii) is not received as an annuity, if no provision of this subtitle (other than this subsection) applies with respect to such amount.

(B) DIVIDENDS

    For purposes of this section, any amount received which is in the nature of a dividend or similar distribution shall be treated as an amount not received as an annuity.

(2) GENERAL RULE

Any amount to which this subsection applies—

(A) if received on or after the annuity starting date, shall be included in gross income, or

(B) if received before the annuity starting date—

(i) shall be included in gross income to the extent allocable to income on the contract, and

(ii) shall not be included in gross income to the extent allocable to the investment in the contract.

(3) ALLOCATION OF AMOUNTS TO INCOME AND INVESTMENT

For purposes of paragraph (2)(B)—

(A) ALLOCATION TO INCOME

Any amount to which this subsection applies shall be treated as allocable to income on the contract to the extent that such amount does not exceed the excess (if any) of—

(i) the cash value of the contract (determined without regard to any surrender charge) immediately before the amount is received, over

(ii) the investment in the contract at such time.

(B) ALLOCATION TO INVESTMENT

Any amount to which this subsection applies shall be treated as allocable to investment in the contract to the extent that such amount is not allocated to income under subparagraph (A).

(4) SPECIAL RULES FOR APPLICATION OF PARAGRAPH (2)(B)

For purposes of paragraph (2)(B)—

(A) LOANS TREATED AS DISTRIBUTIONS

If, during any taxable year, an individual—

(i) receives (directly or indirectly) any amount as a loan under any contract to which this subsection applies, or

(ii) assigns or pledges (or agrees to assign or pledge) any portion of the value of any such contract, such amount or portion shall be treated as received under the contract as an amount not received as an annuity. The preceding sentence shall not apply for purposes of determining investment in the contract, except that the investment in the contract shall be increased by any amount included in gross income by reason of the amount treated as received under the preceding sentence.

(B) TREATMENT OF POLICYHOLDER DIVIDENDS

Any amount described in paragraph (1)(B) shall not be included in gross income under paragraph (2)(B)(i) to the extent such amount is retained by the insurer as a premium or other consideration paid for the contract.

(C) TREATMENT OF TRANSFERS WITHOUT ADEQUATE CONSIDERATION

(i) IN GENERAL

If an individual who holds an annuity contract transfers it without full and adequate consideration, such individual shall be treated as receiving an amount equal to the excess of—

(I) the cash surrender value of such contract at the time of transfer, over

(II) the investment in such contract at such time, under the contract as an amount not received as an annuity.

(ii) EXCEPTION FOR CERTAIN TRANSFERS BETWEEN SPOUSES OR FORMER SPOUSES

Clause (i) shall not apply to any transfer to which section 1041(a) (relating to transfers of property between spouses or incident to divorce) applies.

(iii) ADJUSTMENT TO INVESTMENT IN CONTRACT OF TRANSFEREE

If under clause (i) an amount is included in the gross income of the transferor of an annuity contract, the investment in the contract of the transferee in such contract shall be increased by the amount so included.

(5) RETENTION OF EXISTING RULES IN CERTAIN CASES

(A) IN GENERAL

In any case to which this paragraph applies—

(i) paragraphs (2)(B) and (4)(A) shall not apply, and

(ii) if paragraph (2)(A) does not apply, the amount shall be included in gross income, but only to the extent it exceeds the investment in the contract.

(B) EXISTING CONTRACTS

This paragraph shall apply to contracts entered into before August 14, 1982. Any amount allocable to investment in the contract after August 13, 1982, shall be treated as from a contract entered into after such date.

(C) CERTAIN LIFE INSURANCE AND ENDOWMENT CONTRACTS

Except as provided in paragraph (10) and except to the extent prescribed by the Secretary by regulations, this paragraph shall apply to any amount not received as an annuity which is received under a life insurance or endowment contract.

(D) CONTRACTS UNDER QUALIFIED PLANS

Except as provided in paragraph (8), this paragraph shall apply to any amount received—

(i) from a trust described in section 401(a) which is exempt from tax under section 501(a),

(ii) from a contract—

(I) purchased by a trust described in clause (i),

(II) purchased as part of a plan described in section 403(a),

(III) described in section 403(b), or

(IV) provided for employees of a life insurance company under a plan described in section 818(a)(3), or

(iii) from an individual retirement account or an individual retirement annuity. Any dividend described in section 404(k) which is received by a participant or beneficiary shall, for purposes of this subparagraph, be treated as paid under a separate contract to which clause (ii)(I) applies.

(E) FULL REFUNDS, SURRENDERS, REDEMPTIONS, AND MATURITIES

This paragraph shall apply to—

(i) any amount received, whether in a single sum or otherwise, under a contract in full discharge of the obligation under the contract which is in the nature of a refund of the consideration paid for the contract, and

(ii) any amount received under a contract on its complete surrender, redemption, or maturity. In the case of any amount to which the preceding sentence applies, the rule of paragraph (2)(A) shall not apply.

(6) INVESTMENT IN THE CONTRACT

For purposes of this subsection, the investment in the contract as of any date is—

(A) the aggregate amount of premiums or other consideration paid for the contract before such date, minus

(B) the aggregate amount received under the contract before such date, to the extent that such amount was excludable from gross income under this subtitle or prior income tax laws.

(7) [Repealed. Pub. L. 100-647, title I, 1011A(b)(9)(A), Nov. 10, 1988, 102 Stat. 3474]

(8) EXTENSION OF PARAGRAPH (2)(B) TO QUALIFIED PLANS

(A) IN GENERAL

Notwithstanding any other provision of this subsection, in the case of any amount received before the annuity starting date from a trust or contract described in paragraph (5)(D), paragraph (2)(B) shall apply to such amounts.

(B) ALLOCATION OF AMOUNT RECEIVED

For purposes of paragraph (2)(B), the amount allocated to the investment in the contract shall be the portion of the amount described in subparagraph (A) which bears the same ratio to such amount as the investment in the contract bears to the account balance. The determination under the preceding sentence shall be made as of the time of the distribution or at such other time as the Secretary may prescribe.

(C) TREATMENT OF FORFEITABLE RIGHTS

If an employee does not have a nonforfeitable right to any amount under any trust or contract to which subparagraph (A) applies, such amount shall not be treated as part of the account balance.

(D) INVESTMENT IN THE CONTRACT BEFORE 1987

In the case of a plan which on May 5, 1986, permitted withdrawal of any employee contributions before separation from service, subparagraph (A) shall apply only to the extent that amounts received before the annuity starting date (when increased by amounts previously received under the contract after December 31, 1986) exceed the investment in the contract as of December 31, 1986.

(9) EXTENSION OF PARAGRAPH (2)(B) TO QUALIFIED STATE TUITION PROGRAMS AND EDUCATION INDIVIDUAL RETIREMENT ACCOUNTS

Notwithstanding any other provision of this subsection, paragraph (2)(B) shall apply to amounts received under a qualified tuition program (as defined in section 529(b)) or under a Coverdell education savings account (as defined in section 530(b)). The rule of paragraph (8)(B) shall apply for purposes of this paragraph.

(10) TREATMENT OF MODIFIED ENDOWMENT CONTRACTS

(A) IN GENERAL

Notwithstanding paragraph (5)(C), in the case of any modified endowment contract (as defined in section 7702A)—

(i) paragraphs (2)(B) and (4)(A) shall apply, and

(ii) in applying paragraph (4)(A), "any person" shall be substituted for "an individual".

(B) TREATMENT OF CERTAIN BURIAL CONTRACTS

Notwithstanding subparagraph (A), paragraph (4)(A) shall not apply to any assignment (or pledge) of a modified endowment contract if such assignment (or pledge) is solely to cover the payment of expenses referred to in section 7702(e)(2)(C)(iii) and if the maximum death benefit under such contract does not exceed $25,000.

(11) ANTI-ABUSE RULES

(A) IN GENERAL

For purposes of determining the amount includible in gross income under this subsection—

(i) all modified endowment contracts issued by the same company to the same policyholder during any calendar year shall be treated as 1 modified endowment contract, and

(ii) all annuity contracts issued by the same company to the same policyholder during any calendar year shall be treated as 1 annuity contract. The preceding sentence shall not apply to any contract described in paragraph (5)(D).

(B) REGULATORY AUTHORITY

The Secretary may by regulations prescribe such additional rules as may be necessary or appropriate to prevent avoidance of the purposes of this subsection through serial purchases of contracts or otherwise.

* * *

(g) RULES FOR TRANSFEREE WHERE TRANSFER WAS FOR VALUE

Where any contract (or any interest therein) is transferred (by assignment or otherwise) for a valuable consideration, to the extent that the contract (or interest therein) does not, in the hands of the transferee, have a basis which is determined by reference to the basis in the hands of the transferor, then—

(1) for purposes of this section, only the actual value of such consideration, plus the amount of the premiums and other consideration paid by the transferee after the transfer, shall be taken into account in computing the aggregate amount of the premiums or other consideration paid for the contract;

(2) for purposes of subsection (c)(1)(B), there shall be taken into account only the aggregate amount received under the contract by the transferee before the annuity starting date, to the extent that such amount was excludable from gross income under this subtitle or prior income tax laws; and

(3) the annuity starting date is January 1, 1954, or the first day of the first period for which the transferee received an amount under the contract as an annuity, whichever is the later. For purposes of this subsection, the term "transferee" includes a beneficiary of, or the estate of, the transferee.

(h) OPTION TO RECEIVE ANNUITY IN LIEU OF LUMP SUM

If—

(1) a contract provides for payment of a lump sum in full discharge of an obligation under the contract, subject to an option to receive an annuity in lieu of such lump sum;

(2) the option is exercised within 60 days after the day on which such lump sum first became payable; and

(3) part or all of such lump sum would (but for this subsection) be includible in gross income by reason of subsection (e)(1), then, for purposes of this subtitle, no part of such lump sum shall be considered as includible in gross income at the time such lump sum first became payable.

* * *

(j) INTEREST

Notwithstanding any other provision of this section, if any amount is held under an agreement to pay interest thereon, the interest payments shall be included in gross income.

* * *

(n) ANNUITIES UNDER RETIRED SERVICEMAN'S FAMILY PROTECTION PLAN OR SURVIVOR BENEFIT PLAN

Subsection (b) shall not apply in the case of amounts received after December 31, 1965, as an annuity under chapter 73 of title 10 of the United States Code, but all such amounts shall be excluded from gross income until there has been so excluded (under section 122(b)(1) or this section, including amounts excluded before January 1, 1966) an amount equal to the consideration for the contract (as defined by section 122(b)(2)), plus any amount treated pursuant to section 101(b)(2)(D) (as in effect on the day before the enactment of the Small Business Job Protection Act of 1996) as additional consideration paid by the employee. Thereafter all amounts so received shall be included in gross income.

* * *

(q) 10-PERCENT PENALTY FOR PREMATURE DISTRIBUTIONS FROM ANNUITY CONTRACTS

(1) IMPOSITION OF PENALTY

If any taxpayer receives any amount under an annuity contract, the taxpayer's tax under this chapter for the taxable year in which such amount is received shall be increased by an amount equal to 10 percent of the portion of such amount which is includible in gross income.

(2) SUBSECTION NOT TO APPLY TO CERTAIN DISTRIBUTIONS

Paragraph 1 shall not apply to any distribution—

(A) made on or after the date on which the taxpayer attains age 59½,

(B) made on or after the death of the holder (or, where the holder is not an individual, the death of the primary annuitant (as defined in subsection (s)(6)(B))),

(C) attributable to the taxpayer's becoming disabled within the meaning of subsection (m)(7),

(D) which is a part of a series of substantially equal periodic payments (not less frequently than annually) made for the life (or life expectancy) of the taxpayer or the joint lives (or joint life expectancies) of such taxpayer and his designated beneficiary,

(E) from a plan, contract, account, trust, or annuity described in subsection (e)(5)(D),

(F) allocable to investment in the contract before August 14, 1982, or

(G) under a qualified funding asset (within the meaning of section 130(d), but without regard to whether there is a qualified assignment),

(H) to which subsection (t) applies (without regard to paragraph (2) thereof),

(I) under an immediate annuity contract (within the meaning of section 72(u)(4)), or

(J) which is purchased by an employer upon the termination of a plan described in section 401(a) or 403(a) and which is held by the employer until such time as the employee separates from service.

(3) CHANGE IN SUBSTANTIALLY EQUAL PAYMENTS

If—

(A) paragraph (1) does not apply to a distribution by reason of paragraph (2)(D), and

(B) the series of payments under such paragraph are subsequently modified (other than by reason of death or disability)—

(i) before the close of the 5-year period beginning on the date of the first payment and after the taxpayer attains age 59½, or

(ii) before the taxpayer attains age 59½, the taxpayer's tax for the 1st taxable year in which such modification occurs shall be increased by an amount, determined under regulations, equal to the tax which (but for paragraph

(2)(D)) would have been imposed, plus interest for the deferral period (within the meaning of subsection (t)(4)(B)).

* * *

(s) REQUIRED DISTRIBUTIONS WHERE HOLDER DIES BEFORE ENTIRE INTEREST IS DISTRIBUTED

(1) IN GENERAL

A contract shall not be treated as an annuity contract for purposes of this title unless it provides that—

(A) if any holder of such contract dies on or after the annuity starting date and before the entire interest in such contract has been distributed, the remaining portion of such interest will be distributed at least as rapidly as under the method of distributions being used as of the date of his death, and

(B) if any holder of such contract dies before the annuity starting date, the entire interest in such contract will be distributed within 5 years after the death of such holder.

(2) EXCEPTION FOR CERTAIN AMOUNTS PAYABLE OVER LIFE OF BENEFICIARY

If—

(A) any portion of the holder's interest is payable to (or for the benefit of) a designated beneficiary,

(B) such portion will be distributed (in accordance with regulations) over the life of such designated beneficiary (or over a period not extending beyond the life expectancy of such beneficiary), and

(C) such distributions begin not later than 1 year after the date of the holder's death or such later date as the Secretary may by regulations prescribe, then for purposes of paragraph (1), the portion referred to in subparagraph (A) shall be treated as distributed on the day on which such distributions begin.

(3) SPECIAL RULE WHERE SURVIVING SPOUSE BENEFICIARY

If the designated beneficiary referred to in paragraph (2)(A) is the surviving spouse of the holder of the contract, paragraphs (1) and

(2) shall be applied by treating such spouse as the holder of such contract.

(4) DESIGNATED BENEFICIARY

For purposes of this subsection, the term "designated beneficiary" means any individual designated a beneficiary by the holder of the contract.

(5) EXCEPTION FOR CERTAIN ANNUITY CONTRACTS

This subsection shall not apply to any annuity contract—

(A) which is provided—

(i) under a plan described in section 401(a) which includes a trust exempt from tax under section 501, or

(ii) under a plan described in section 403(a),

(B) which is described in section 403(b),

(C) which is an individual retirement annuity or provided under an individual retirement account or annuity, or

(D) which is a qualified funding asset (as defined in section 130(d), but without regard to whether there is a qualified assignment).

(6) SPECIAL RULE WHERE HOLDER IS CORPORATION OR OTHER NON-INDIVIDUAL

(A) IN GENERAL

For purposes of this subsection, if the holder of the contract is not an individual, the primary annuitant shall be treated as the holder of the contract.

(B) PRIMARY ANNUITANT

For purposes of subparagraph (A), the term "primary annuitant" means the individual, the events in the life of whom are of primary importance in affecting the timing or amount of the payout under the contract.

(7) TREATMENT OF CHANGES IN PRIMARY ANNUITANT WHERE HOLDER OF CONTRACT IS NOT AN INDIVIDUAL

For purposes of this subsection, in the case of a holder of an annuity contract which is not an individual, if there is a change in a primary annuitant (as defined in paragraph (6)(B)), such change shall be treated as the death of the holder.

* * *

(u) TREATMENT OF ANNUITY CONTRACTS NOT HELD BY NATURAL PERSONS

(1) IN GENERAL

If any annuity contract is held by a person who is not a natural person—

(A) such contract shall not be treated as an annuity contract for purposes of this subtitle (other than subchapter L), and

(B) the income on the contract for any taxable year of the policyholder shall be treated as ordinary income received or accrued by the owner during such taxable year. For purposes of this paragraph, holding by a trust or other entity as an agent for a natural person shall not be taken into account.

(2) INCOME ON THE CONTRACT

(A) IN GENERAL

For purposes of paragraph (1), the term "income on the contract" means, with respect to any taxable year of the policyholder, the excess of—

(i) the sum of the net surrender value of the contract as of the close of the taxable year plus all distributions under the contract received during the taxable year or any prior taxable year, reduced by

(ii) the sum of the amount of net premiums under the contract for the taxable year and prior taxable years and amounts includible in gross income for prior taxable years with respect to such contract under this subsection. Where necessary to prevent the avoidance of this subsection, the Secretary may substitute "fair market value of the contract" for "net surrender value of the contract" each place it appears in the preceding sentence.

(B) NET PREMIUMS

For purposes of this paragraph, the term "net premiums" means the amount of premiums paid under the contract reduced by any policyholder dividends.

(3) EXCEPTIONS

This subsection shall not apply to any annuity contract which—

(A) is acquired by the estate of a decedent by reason of the death of the decedent,

(B) is held under a plan described in section 401(a) or 403(a), under a program described in section 403(b), or under an individual retirement plan,

(C) is a qualified funding asset (as defined in section 130(d), but without regard to whether there is a qualified assignment),

(D) is purchased by an employer upon the termination of a plan described in section 401(a) or 403(a) and is held by the employer until all amounts under such contract are distributed to the employee for whom such contract was purchased or the employee's beneficiary, or

(E) is an immediate annuity.

(4) IMMEDIATE ANNUITY

For purposes of this subsection, the term "immediate annuity" means an annuity—

(A) which is purchased with a single premium or annuity consideration,

(B) the annuity starting date (as defined in subsection (c)(4)) of which commences no later than 1 year from the date of the purchase of the annuity, and

(C) which provides for a series of substantially equal periodic payments (to be made not less frequently than annually) during the annuity period.

$$* \quad * \quad *$$

(w) CROSS REFERENCE

For limitation on adjustments to basis of annuity contracts sold, see section 1021.

INTERNAL REVENUE CODE SECTION 1035

1035. CERTAIN EXCHANGES OF INSURANCE POLICIES.

(a) GENERAL RULES

No gain or loss shall be recognized on the exchange of—

(1) a contract of life insurance for another contract of life insurance or for an endowment or annuity contract; or

(2) a contract of endowment insurance (A) for another contract of endowment insurance which provides for regular payments beginning at a date not later than the date payments would have begun under the contract exchanged, or (B) for an annuity contract; or

(3) an annuity contract for an annuity contract.

(b) DEFINITIONS

For the purpose of this section—

(1) ENDOWMENT CONTRACT

A contract of endowment insurance is a contract with an insurance company which depends in part on the life expectancy of the insured, but which may be payable in full in a single payment during his life.

(2) ANNUITY CONTRACT

An annuity contract is a contract to which paragraph (1) applies but which may be payable during the life of the annuitant only in installments.

(3) LIFE INSURANCE CONTRACT

A contract of life insurance is a contract to which paragraph (1) applies but which is not ordinarily payable in full during the life of the insured.

(c) EXCHANGES INVOLVING FOREIGN PERSONS

To the extent provided in regulations, subsection (a) shall not apply to any exchange having the effect of transferring property to any person other than a United States person.

(d) CROSS REFERENCES

(1) For rules relating to recognition of gain or loss where an exchange is not solely in kind, see subsections (b) and (c) of section 1031.

(2) For rules relating to the basis of property acquired in an exchange described in subsection (a), see subsection (d) of section 1031.

INTERNAL REVENUE CODE SECTION 2033

2033. PROPERTY IN WHICH THE DECEDENT HAD AN INTEREST.

The value of the gross estate shall include the value of all property to the extent of the interest therein of the decedent at the time of his death.

INTERNAL REVENUE CODE SECTION 2039

2039. ANNUITIES.

(a) GENERAL

The gross estate shall include the value of an annuity or other payment receivable by any beneficiary by reason of surviving the decedent under any form of contract or agreement entered into after March 3, 1931 (other than as insurance under policies on the life of the decedent), if, under such contract or agreement, an annuity or other payment was payable to the decedent, or the decedent possessed the right to receive such annuity or payment, either alone or in conjunction with another for his life or for any period not ascertainable without reference to his death or for any period which does not in fact end before his death.

(b) AMOUNT INCLUDIBLE

Subsection (a) shall apply to only such part of the value of the annuity or other payment receivable under such contract or agreement as is proportionate to that part of the purchase price therefor contributed by the decedent. For purposes of this section, any contribution by the decedent's employer or former employer to the purchase price of such contract or agreement (whether or not to an employee's trust or fund forming part of a pension, annuity, retirement, bonus or profit sharing plan) shall be considered to be contributed by the decedent if made by reason of his employment.

Appendix D

SAMPLE ANNUITY APPLICATIONS

SAMPLE FIXED ANNUITY APPLICATION

	FIXED INDIVIDUAL ANNUITY APPLICATION	
Type of Product	☐ Immediate Annuity ☐ Flexible Premium Annuity	
Ownership	The Contract Owner is ☐ Annuitant ☐ Plan Trustee (qualified) ☐ Individual Other Than Annuitant ☐ Other	
Annuitant	Name	Social Security Number
	Street Address	Date of Birth / /
	City State Zip	Sex ☐ M ☐ F
Contract Owner	Name	Social Security Number
	Street Address	Date of Birth / /
If different from Annuitant	City State Zip	Sex ☐ M ☐ F
Beneficiary	Primary	Relationship to Annuitant
Must be Trustee for qualified plan.	Contingent	Relationship to Annuitant
Type of Contract	☐ IRA ☐ SEP ☐ Non-Qualified ☐ Tax-Sheltered Annuity (403(b)) ☐ Non-corporate qualified retirement plan (Keogh) ☐ Other _____	
	☐ New Contract ☐ Rollover ☐ Transfer ☐ 1035 Exchange	
Plan Name Complete for qualified pension plans only.	Legal Name of Plan (as specified in Plan Document). _____	
Initial Payment	Initial Payment included with Application $_____	

Subsequent Payments	☐ Annual ☐ Semiannual ☐ Quarterly ☐ Monthly ☐ Other____ Check here to make subsequent payments by pre-authorized check. Payments made on ☐ 5th ☐ 15th ☐ 20th ☐ 25th
Replacement	Will the proposed contract replace any existing annuity or insurance contract? ☐ Yes ☐ No
Signatures	All statements made in this application are true to the best of my knowledge and belief, and I agree to all terms and conditions as shown on the front and back. I certify that the Social Security (or taxpayer identification) number is correct as it appears in this application. _____ _____ Signed at (State) Location of Plan Trust (State) X_____ _____ Signature of Contract Owner or Plan Trustee Date Signed X_____ _____ Signature of Annuitant (if different from Contract Owner) Date Signed

The following sections must be completed by the AGENT.

Insurance in Force	Does this contract replace or change any existing life insurance or annuity? ☐ Yes ☐ No
Additional Remarks	_____ _____
Agent's Signature	The representative hereby certifies he/she witnessed the signature(s) and that all information contained in this application is true to the best of his/her knowledge and belief. X_____ Agent(s) Signature

SAMPLE VARIABLE ANNUITY APPLICATION

VARIABLE DEFERRED ANNUITY APPLICATION	
ANNUITANT INFORMATION	
Name (First, MI, Last)	Social Security Number
Address (No., Street, City, State, Zip)	Birth Date (Mo/Day/Yr)
Sex ☐ M ☐ F Occupation	Telephone Number ( )

CONTINGENT ANNUITANT INFORMATION

Name (First, MI, Last)	Social Security Number
Address (No., Street, City, State, Zip)	Birth Date (Mo/Day/Yr)
Sex ☐ M ☐ F Occupation	Telephone Number ( )

PARTICIPANT INFORMATION

Same as Annuitant: ☐ Name (First, MI, Last)	Tax I.D./Soc. Sec. Number	
Address (No., Street, City, State, Zip)	Birth Date (Mo/Day/Yr)	Telephone Number ( )

BENEFICIARY INFORMATION

Primary Beneficiary: Name (First, MI, Last)	Relationship	Social Security Number
Address (No., Street, City, State, Zip)	Birth Date (M/D/Y)	Telephone Number ( )
Secondary Beneficiary(ies): Name (First, MI, Last)	Relationship	Social Security Number
Address (No., Street, City, State, Zip)	Birth Date (M/D/Y)	Telephone Number ( )
Name (First, MI, Last)	Relationship	Social Security Number
Address (No., Street, City, State, Zip)	Birth Date (M/D/Y)	Telephone Number ( )

PLAN INFORMATION

<u>Non-Qualified</u>   <u>Qualified</u>

☐ Individual Plan   ☐ IRA (check one): Regular____Rollover____Transfer____ Self Employed, Plan Type _____
              Deduction Tax Year_____
        ☐ Simplified Employee Pension Plan
        ☐ Corporate, Plan Type_____

INVESTMENT   **Initial Investment $**

ACCOUNT ALLOCATION

Account Description	Initial Allocation %	Future Allocation %
General Account	_____	_____
Growth Sub-Account	_____	_____
Money Market Sub-Account	_____	_____
Income Sub-Account	_____	_____
Total Return Sub-Account	_____	_____
TOTAL	100%	100%

ANNUITY INCOME DATE | (Mo/Day/Yr):

HEALTH INFORMATION	**ANNUITY ACTIVITY**

Do you have any reason to believe that the death benefit will become payable to the beneficiary in the first certificate year? Yes ☐ No ☐

Have you purchased another annuity in the past 12 months? Yes ☐ No ☐

ANNUITY OPTIONS

☐ **Option 1** Life Income

☐ **Option 2** Life Income with Period Certain: 5 Yr. 10 Yr. 20 Yr.

☐ **Option 3** Joint and Last Survivor

☐ **Option 4** Joint and 2/3 Survivor

☐ **Option 5** Period Certain: # of Years _____

ANNUITANT AND PARTICIPANT SIGNATURE

I hereby represent that the above information is correct and true to the best of my knowledge and belief and agree that this application shall be a part of the Certificate issued by the Company. ALL PAYMENTS AND VALUES PROVIDED BY THE CERTIFICATE BEING APPLIED FOR WHEN BASED ON INVESTMENT EXPERIENCE OF A VARIABLE ACCOUNT ARE VARIABLE AND ARE NOT GUARANTEED AS TO DOLLAR AMOUNT. I acknowledge receipt of a current Prospectus.

Signed at: _____ _____   On: __/__/__
                City   State   Date

Annuitant's Signature _____   Contingent Annuitant's Signature _____
                                              (If applicable)

Participant's Signature _____
(If other than the Annuitant)

AGENT REPLACEMENT INFORMATION

Will the annuity applied for replace or change any existing individual or group life insurance or annuity? If yes, I have complied with all state replacement requirements. Yes ☐ No ☐

Is this replacement meant to be a tax-free exchange under Section 1035? Yes ☐ No ☐

	WITNESS	
	Signature of Licensed Agent(s)	**Printed Name of Agent**
(1)	_____	_____
(2)	_____	_____
(3)	_____	_____

GA Name   Agency Address   City   State   Zip

_____   (   ) _____
Agency Number   Agency Telephone Number

THE ANNUITY HANDBOOK

INDEX

A

Accumulation phase 9
Accumulation value 9
Administrative fees 25-27
Annual exclusion 173-175
Annual fee 25-27
Annual reset indexing method 82
Annuitant
  death of 152-153
  defined 16
  rights of................................ 16-18
Annuitization phase 10
Annuity
  alternatives to 119-122
  basis in...................................... 145
  charitable gift 71-73, 108, 179
  deferred...................................... 69
  definition of 1-3
  equity-indexed 77-98
  estate taxation of............. 157-168
  gift of 106-107, 139, 141
  gift taxation of 169-184
  fixed 52-53
  flexible premium 51-52
  immediate 68-69
  income taxation of 125-155
  loans from 128-129
  multiple contracts 135
  nonqualified.............................. 1-3
  private.................... 73-75, 167-168
  sale of.................................. 141-142
  single premium 47-51
  standard provisions of........... 23-46
  time line of.............................. 9-11
  unique feature of........................ 5
  variable 54-68
Annuity starting date 144
Annuity Tables 147-148, 185-199
Annuity term 90
Assignment of annuity
  interest....................... 128-129, 181
Assumption of risk 55-56
Automatic rebalancing 63-64

B

Bailout provision....................... 24-25
Bank savings account 119-121
Basis, in annuity.......................... 145
Beneficiary
  designated 19, 151
  of annuity contract 18-20
  of death benefit...................... 18-20
Benefit payments
  election of.............................. 34-40
  taxation of......................... 142-150
Bonus plan 119
Business planning 114-119

C

Cap rate 85-86
Cash value build-up taxation
  natural persons 126
  nonnatural persons 126-128
CD 121
Certificate of deposit............. 94, 121
Charges
  administrative 25-27
  annual fee 25-27
  equity-indexed annuities 87
  fixed annuities 25-26
  mortality and expense risk 27
  variable annuities 26-27
Charitable deduction
  estate tax 161-162
  gift tax.................................... 177
Charitable gift
  annuity 71-73, 108, 179
Charitable lead trust 110
Charitable planning 106-111
Charitable remainder
  trust 108-110
Charitable trusts 108-111
  lead trust 110
  remainder trust 108-110
College funding 111-114
Contract term............................... 90

Cost recovery rule 132-135
Credit, unified 157, 174, 176
CRT 108-110

D

Death
  of annuitant 152-153
  of owner 150-152
Death Benefit
  estate tax 162
  income tax 152
  variable annuity, under 67-68
Deferred annuity 69-71
Definition, of annuity 1-3
Designated beneficiary 19, 151
Distribution
  requirements at death of
    owner 150
Dollar cost averaging.................... 28

E

EIA 54, 77-98
Equity-indexed annuity
  advantages of............................. 78
  annuity term 90
  cap rate 85-86
  contract term 90
  death benefit............................. 86
  definition 78
  disadvantages of........................ 78
  expenses.................................... 87
  fees 87
  free withdrawal
    provision 81, 88
  guaranteed interest rate 87
  indexing methods 81-85, 87
  insurance company,
    investment of premiums 82
  issue ages, maximum 87
  loans from 90
  maximum issue ages 87
  minimum guaranteed
    interest rate 87
  minimum premium 88
  partial withdrawal from 88

  participation rate 89
  policy term 91
  sales of 77
  settlement options 92
  surrender charges 92
  uses of 94-96
  vesting schedules 93
  withdrawal from.................. 88, 93
Estate tax
  annuity in accumulation
    phase 162-164
  annuity in annuitization
    phase 164-166
  annuity on life of
    another 166-167
  deductions
    charitable 161-162
    marital............................... 161
  generally 157-168
  gift, of annuity 167
  private annuity.................. 167-168
  rates 158-160
  survivor benefits 163
Exchanges, Section 1035
  effect on pre-82
    grandfathering..................... 135
  generally 136-139
Exclusion, annual 173-175
  split gifts 175
Exclusion ratio 143-144
  examples of calculation 201-205
Expected return 145-146
Expense risk and mortality
  charges 27

F

FDIC 120
Federal Deposit Insurance
  Corporation............................... 120
Fixed amount annuity
  settlement option 39
Fixed annuity 52-53
Fixed period annuity
  settlement option 39
Flexible premium annuity........ 51-52

G

Gift
gift tax 169-184
irrevocable beneficiary 182
joint and survivor annuity 180
of annuity 106-107,
139-141, 180
of funds to buy annuity 181
of funds to pay annuity
premium 181-182
valuation of 183
Gift tax
annuity 169-184
charitable deduction 177
future interest 176
marital deduction 177
present interest 176
rates 170-172
split gifts 173
unified credit 174, 176
Grandfathering
of pre-1982 annuity 135
Guaranteed account 59-61
Guaranteed interest rate 87

H

High water mark
indexing method 83-84

I

Immediate annuity 68-69
Index, market 81-82
Indexing methods, with
equity-indexed annuity 81-85
annual reset (or ratchet)
method 83
Asian method 83
Asian-end call method 82
capped cliquet method 83
cliquet method 83
daily average method 85
European method 82
high water mark
method 83-84
point-to-point
method 83, 84-85

Individual Retirement
Account (IRA) 102
Individual Retirement
Annuity (IRA) 102
Individual Retirement
Arrangement (IRA) 102-104
Insurance companies
issuing 20-22
ratings of 22
Interest first rule 132-135
Interest income option 40
Interest rate crediting methods
new money method 59-61
portfolio method 59-61
rate banded method 59-61
Interest rates
current 28-31
equity-indexed annuity 77-98
fixed annuity 28-30
guaranteed 28-30, 87-88
variable annuity 30-31
Internal Revenue Code
Section 72, text of 207-224
Section 1035, text of 224-225
Section 2033, text of 225
Section 2039, text of 225-226
Investment in the contract 145
Issue ages, maximum 31

J

Joint and one-half survivor
annuity settlement option 37-38
Joint and survivor life annuity
settlement option 37-38
Joint and two-thirds survivor
annuity settlement
option 37-38

L

License requirements 96-98
Life annuity settlement
option 35
Life expectancy
Annuity Tables 147-148,
185-199

Life refund annuity settlement
option 36-37
Life with period certain
guarantee settlement
option 35-36
Loans 45-46, 128-129

M

Marital deduction
estate tax 161
gift tax...................................... 177
Market index...................... 54, 81-82
Maximum age for benefits
to begin 32
Maximum issue age 31
Medically-related surrender 33
Minimum guaranteed interest
rate, with equity-indexed
annuity 87-88
Mortality and expense risk
charge 27
Multiple annuity contracts.......... 135
Mutual funds 121-122

N

Nonnatural person
rule 116, 126-128
Nonqualified annuity
definition of 1-3
Nonqualified deferred
compensation plan 116-117
Nursing home waiver 33

O

Owner
corporation as 126-128
death of 150-152
of annuity 14-16

P

Participation rate 89
Parties
to annuity contract................ 13-22
Penalty tax, 10% 130-132

Point-to-point indexing
method 83-85
Policy term 90-91
Pooled income funds 110-111
Premature distribution
penalty tax 130-132
Premiums
allocation of 55
deductibility of......................... 125
minimum amount 33-34
payment of............................ 33-34
Private annuity
defined 73-75
estate tax 167-168
income tax 74
Profile prospectus 55
Prospectus 55
Provisions, of annuity
contract 23-46
Purchasers of annuities 8, 142

Q

Qualified annuity,
definition of 5
Qualified retirement
plans 104-105

R

Retirement planning 99-106,
115-116

S

S&P 500.................................... 81-82
Sale of an annuity 141-142
Sale of a business................. 117-118
Savings account 119-120
Section 72, text of 207-224
Section 162 Bonus Plan.............. 119
Section 1035 exchange 136-139
Section 1035, text of 224-225
Section 2033, text of 225
Section 2039, text of 225-226
Self-employed, retirement
planning for 115
Seller, of an annuity 141-142

Settlement options 34-40
  fixed amount annuity 39
  fixed period annuity 39
  joint and survivor life
    annuity 37-38
  life annuity 35
  life refund annuity 36-37
  life with period certain
    guarantee 35-36
Single premium annuity 47-51
Standard annuity
  provisions............................. 23-46
Standard & Poor's 500 81-82
Suitability 55
Surrender Charges 40-42,
                        129-130
Surrenders
  complete 44, 136
  equity-indexed
    annuities 92-93
  full 44, 136
  medically-related 33
  partial 43, 129
Surviving spouse, as designated
  beneficiary 18, 151
Survivors benefits,
  estate taxation 163
Systematic withdrawal
  option 45

T

Tax Sheltered Annuity
  (TSA) 105-106
Ten percent penalty
  tax 130-132
Ten percent withdrawal
  feature................................... 44-45
1035 exchange 136-139
Time line of annuity 9-11
Transfer features
  between investment
    accounts............................... 61
  dollar cost averaging 28

Transfer tax
  estate tax 157-168
  gift tax 169-184
Trusts, charitable 108-111
Trust, charitable lead 110
Trust, charitable
  remainder 108-110
Types of annuities 48

U

Unified Credit
  estate tax 157
  gift tax 174, 176

V

Valuation
  gift of annuity 183
Variable accounts 56-59
Variable annuity
  assumption of risk 55-56
  benefit payments from 64-67,
                        148-150
  death benefit from 67-68
  interest rates 28-31
  investment options 56-61
  sales of 1-2
  security, considered as 54-55
  step up in basis 150
  transfers between
    accounts 61-62
Vesting schedules, with
  equity-indexed annuities 93-94

W

Withdrawals
  equity-indexed annuity,
    from 88, 93
  partial 43-46, 129
  systematic 45
  taxation of 132-135
  10% per year 44-45